PERSUASION
AND
HEALING

PERSUASION AND HEALING

A Comparative Study
of Psychotherapy

JEROME D. FRANK, M. D., PH. D.

SCHOCKEN BOOKS · NEW YORK

**To the memory of
Lester H. Gliedman
friend and colleague**

First SCHOCKEN PAPERBACK *edition 1963*

Seventh Printing, 1971

Library of Congress Catalog Card Number 60–53243

Manufactured in the United States of America

Contents

"What is it you want to buy?" the Sheep said at last . . . .
"I don't *quite* know yet," Alice said very gently. "I should
like to look all round me first, if I might." (Lewis Carroll,
Through the Looking Glass, 1872, Chapter 5)

1 | Psychotherapy in America Today

Throughout his life every person is influenced by
the behavior of others towards him. His relationships with
his fellows shape his own behavior, attitudes, values, self-image,
and world view and also affect his sense of well-being. It is
customary to classify different forms of personal influence in
accordance with their settings and the role of the influencing
figure. Thus we say that a person is brought up by his parents
in the family, educated by his teachers in school, and led by
his officers in battle, for example.

Attempts to enhance a person's feeling of well-being are
usually labeled treatment, and every society trains some of
its members to apply this form of influence. Treatment always involves a personal relationship between healer and sufferer. Certain types of therapy rely primarily on the healer's
ability to mobilize healing forces in the sufferer by psychological means. These forms of treatment may be generically termed
psychotherapy.

Although psychotherapeutic methods have existed since time immemorial and a vast amount of accumulated experience supports a belief in their value, some of the most elementary questions about them remain unanswered. Research has not yet yielded sufficient information to permit description of the different methods in generally acceptable terms, specification of the conditions for which different methods are most suitable, or comparison of their results. These difficulties spring largely from persisting lack of precise knowledge concerning the nature of psychotherapeutic principles.

The purpose of this book is to review data from various sources that may help to identify and clarify the active ingredients of various forms of psychotherapy in our own and other cultures by searching for their common features. If these features can be found, they will presumably include the active components since they would otherwise be unlikely to reappear under so many guises and circumstances. In embarking on this review, it seems appropriate to begin with a definition of psychotherapy, followed by a brief consideration of its historical roots and its place in America today, and a brief consideration of the problems involved in the evaluation of the relative efficacy of its different forms.

WHAT IS PSYCHOTHERAPY?

Since practically all forms of personal influence may affect a person's sense of well-being, the definition of psychotherapy must of necessity be somewhat arbitrary. We shall consider as psychotherapy only those types of influence characterized by the following features:

1. A trained, socially sanctioned healer, whose healing powers are accepted by the sufferer and by his social group or an important segment of it.

2. A sufferer who seeks relief from the healer.

3. A circumscribed, more or less structured series of contacts between the healer and the sufferer, through which the

healer, often with the aid of a group, tries to produce certain changes in the sufferer's emotional state, attitudes, and behavior. All concerned believe these changes will help him. Although physical and chemical adjuncts may be used, the healing influence is primarily exercised by words, acts, and rituals in which sufferer, healer, and—if there is one—group, participate jointly.

These three features are common not only to all forms of psychotherapy as the term is generally used, but also to methods of primitive healing, religious conversion, and even so-called brain-washing, all of which involve systematic, time-limited contacts between a person in distress and someone who tries to reduce the distress by producing changes in the sufferer's feelings, attitudes, and behavior. By this definition, the administration of an inert medicine by a doctor to a patient is also a form of psychotherapy, since its effectiveness depends on its symbolization of the physician's healing function, which produces favorable changes in the patient's feelings and attitudes. Our search for the active ingredients of psychotherapy, then, will require exploration of these activities, as well as a consideration of experimental studies of the transmission of influence.

HISTORICAL ROOTS OF PSYCHOTHERAPY

Since at least part of the efficacy of psychotherapeutic methods lies in the shared belief of the participants that these methods will work, the predominant method would be expected to differ in different societies and in different historical epochs. This is, in fact, the case. Modern psychotherapies are rooted in two historical traditions of healing— the religio-magical and the naturalistic, or scientific. The former, originating before recorded history, regards certain forms of suffering or of alienation from one's fellows as caused by some sort of supernatural or magical intervention, such as loss of one's soul, possession by an evil spirit, or a sorcerer's curse. Treatment consists in suitable rites conducted by a healer who combines the roles of priest and physician. These rites typically require the active participation of the sufferer and members of his family or social group and are highly charged emotionally. If successful, they undo the supernaturally or magically caused damage, thereby restoring the victim's health and re-establishing or strengthening his ties with his group. As we shall see, the religio-magical tradition is still influential, even in secularized Western society, and many of its principles have been incorporated into naturalistic forms of psychotherapy.

The earliest surviving account of these principles is in the writings attributed to the Greek physician Hippocrates in the fifth century B.C. He viewed mental illness, like all other forms of illness, as a phenomenon that could be studied and treated scientifically. Though largely eclipsed in the Middle Ages, this view has come into increasing prominence since the early nineteenth century and is the dominant one today in the Western world.

Like the religio-magical view, the naturalistic view originally did not clearly distinguish mental illness from other forms of illness, and treatment for both was essentially similar. The emergence of psychotherapy as a distinctive form of healing probably began with the dramatic demonstration by Anton Mesmer, in the late eighteenth century, that he could cause the symptons of certain patients to disappear by putting them into a trance. Though his particular theories and methods were soon discredited, mesmerism was the precursor of hypnotism, which rapidly became recognized as a method of psychotherapy. Through the use of hypnosis, Sigmund Freud and Joseph Breuer discovered, towards the end of the nineteenth century, that many symptoms of their patients seemed to be symbolic attempts to express and resolve chronic conflicts that had their roots in upsetting experiences of early life. This led Freud to develop a form of treatment based on minute exploration of patients' personal histories, with emotional reliving of childhood experiences in the treatment setting. From the information thus gained he formed a theory of human nature and mental illness known as psychoanalysis, which supplied a rationale for his psychotherapy. During the same period the Russian physiologist I. P. Pavlov demonstrated by experiments with conditioned reflexes that dogs could be made "neurotic" by exposing them to insoluble conflicts, and this led to a "conditioned reflex" theory of mental illness and treatment.

In recent years American experimental psychologists have developed various theories of learning based on experiments with animals and humans. Some of these concepts seem applicable to mental illnesses conceived as disorders of the learning process. Thus most current naturalistic theories of mental illness and its treatment represent various combinations and modifications of ideas derived from Freud, Pavlov, and experimental studies of learning.[1] Fortunately these three conceptual schemes are not incompatible, despite differences in terminology. They supply a scientifically respectable rationale for contemporary naturalistic methods of psychotherapy. In America, which accords high prestige to science, this probably contributes to their efficacy.

CULTURAL ASPECTS OF MENTAL ILLNESS AND PSYCHOTHERAPY

As the preceding discussion implies, the definition of mental illness depends heavily on the attitudes and values of the society or group in which it occurs.[2] For example, the same symptoms that in the Middle Ages were viewed as evidence of demoniacal possession to be treated by exorcism are now regarded as signs of mental illness to be treated by a psychiatrist. In World War II Russian soldiers were never classified as having psychoneuroses, which can only mean that the Russian army did not recognize this condition. Presumably soldiers with complaints that we would term psychoneurotic were regarded either as malingerers subject to disciplinary

action or medically ill and therefore treated by regular physicians. In the American army, by contrast, many commonplace
reactions to the stresses of military life were initially regarded
as signs of psychoneurotic illness, warranting discharge·from
the service. Today many of these same soldiers would be
promptly returned to duty.

Similarly, whether or not a person is sent to a mental hospital for treatment depends at least as much on the attitudes of
those around him as on his symptoms. Many actively hallu-
cinating persons function in the community because their
families, neighbors, and employers are willing to put up with
their eccentricities, while other persons, especially among the
elderly, wind up in the hospital largely because the family
want to rid themselves of responsibility for their care.[3]

Contemporary America has gone far in the direction of regarding socially deviant behavior as illness, which requires
treatment rather than punishment. This is probably partially
attributable to the strong humanitarian trend in American
society and the high value it places on the welfare of the
individual.

Probably more significant, however, is the recognition that
certain criminals, alcoholics, and sex deviates, for example, appear to be attempting to cope with the same types of conflicts and other stresses as other persons who are regarded as
mentally ill, but their efforts take the form of deviant behavior rather than symptom formation.

An interesting, if somewhat unfortunate, consequence of
the fact that social attitudes play such a big role in the definition of mental illness is that mental health education may
be a two-edged sword. By teaching people to regard certain
types of distress or behavioral oddities as illnesses rather than
as normal reactions to life's stresses, harmless eccentricities, or
moral weaknesses, it may cause alarm and increase the demand for psychotherapy. This may explain the curious fact
that the use of psychotherapy tends to keep pace with its
availability. The greater the number of treatment facilities

and the more widely they are known, the larger the number of persons seeking their services. Psychotherapy is the only form of treatment which, at least to some extent, appears to create the illness it treats. It can never suffer the unfortunate fate of Victor Borge's physician uncle who became despondent on realizing that he had discovered a cure for which there was no disease.

Cultural values influence not only the definition of mental illness but also the nature of its treatment. Psychotherapies in societies or groups with a primarily religious world view are based on religio-magical theories and healing rituals merge with religious rites. The scientific world view of Western societies is reflected in the tendency to regard psychotherapy as a form of medical treatment, based on scientific understanding of human nature. Furthermore, naturalistic psychotherapies tend to express the dominant values of their cultures. Thus, methods of psychotherapy in Germany and the U.S.S.R.[4] tend to reflect the authoritarian values of these societies. In the United States, permissive, democratic therapies have a higher prestige, consistent with the high value placed on individual freedom and responsibility.[5]

Within a given society, the dominant type of treatment depends in part on the class position and group affiliation of the recipient. In America, religio-magical forms of healing are practiced by certain religious groups. Lower-class patients, who view treatment as something the doctor does to one, are more likely to receive directive treatment, often accompanied by physical measures of medication. Middle- and upper-class patients, who put a high value on self-knowledge and self-direction, are more likely to receive permissive forms of treatment stressing insight.[6]

In mid-twentieth-century America, mental illness has not fully shaken off its demonological aura, as evidenced by the stigma still attached to it. In the minds of many it implies moral weakness. The insane still tend to elicit a kind of fascinated horror, reflected in their being shunted off to isolated hospitals on the one hand and being objects of morbid curiosity on the other, as shown by the popularity of novels, plays, and films about them. Nevertheless, all forms of suffering or troublesome behavior that involve emotional or psychological factors are viewed as treatable by psychotherapy. This is reflected in the great variety of recipients and purveyors of psychotherapy and its settings. To reduce this chaotic scene to some sort of order, we shall describe it first from the standpoint of those receiving psychotherapy and then from the standpoint of those offering it.

WHO RECEIVES PSYCHOTHERAPY?

The many thousands of Americans who undergo some form of psychotherapy cover an extraordinarily broad range. At one extreme are some who are best characterized as mental hypochondriacs, searching for someone to lift the normal burdens of living from their shoulders. At the other are persons who are severely ill with disturbances of thinking, feeling, and behavior. They constitute the populations of our mental hospitals. In between is a vast group of persons suffering from chronic emotional stress produced by faulty patterns of living.

The most clearly definable recipients of psychotherapy are persons who are regarded by themselves or others as patients. Candidates for psychotherapy are distinguished from those who do not receive this type of treatment by the presence of a recognizable emotional or psychological component in their illnesses. The difficulty here is the word "recognizable." As the contributions of unhealthy emotional states to all forms of illness and disability are becoming increasingly recognized, psychotherapeutic principles are being incorporated into all forms of medical healing. It is possible, however, to distinguish four classes of patients for whom psychotherapy constitutes the entire treatment or a major part of it.

The first class comprises the hospitalized insane, patients who are so disturbed that they cannot carry out the ordinary tasks of life and need to be protected. The bulk of these are senile and schizophrenic patients. Both can be helped by psychotherapy, but it can do more for the latter, because their adaptive capacity has not been irreversibly reduced by brain damage. The second class of psychiatric patients consists of neurotics, whose distress seems clearly related to chronic emotional strain and often involves some disturbance of bodily functioning. Akin to these is the third group, patients with so-called "psychosomatic" illnesses such as asthma, peptic ulcer, and certain skin diseases, in whom definite and chronic disorders of bodily organs seem related to emotional tension. The fourth group of patients in whose treatment psychotherapy should play a prominent part are the chronically ill. This category cuts across the other three and also includes those with chronic disease or disability that was initially unrelated to psychological causes, such as loss of a limb, epilepsy, rheumatic heart disease, and so on. Since the emotional stresses created by chronic disease probably contribute more to the distress and disability of these patients than their bodily damage, increasing use of psychotherapeutic principles is being made in rehabilitation methods.

No one questions that psychotics, psychoneurotics, the psychosomatically ill, and the chronically ill are suitable candidates for psychotherapy, but from this point on confusion reigns. The difficulty is that many emotional stresses result in misbehavior, which comes into conflict with the standards and values of society, so that its moral and medical aspects are inseparable. Alcoholics, drug addicts, and sexual deviates are clearly sick in the sense that they are caught up in behavior patterns they cannot control, but they also offend against social standards, which brings them to the attention of the legal authorities. Their deviant behavior often seems attributable to emotional difficulties related to disturbing childhood experiences, such as parental mistreatment or neglect, broken homes, and lack of adequate socialization, suggesting that they might respond to psychotherapy. Modern criminology is increasingly emphasizing the use of psychotherapeutic principles in the rehabilitation of offenders, but much work remains to be done to determine which approach is most suitable for different types of criminals.[7] Current views distinguish the socialized criminal, who represents the values of his own deviant group and is a well-integrated member of it, from the so-called sociopath or psychopath, who cannot get along with anyone and is always in trouble. The proper handling of offenders is a knotty problem requiring co-operation of the healing, legal, and corrective professions.

A large and heterogeneous group of people who may receive psychotherapy may be termed "misfits." Their distress results from failure to cope satisfactorily with their environments, yet they are not severely enough out of step to be considered either ill or criminal. The failure to adjust may be temporary or permanent, and sometimes the chief fault lies in the environment, sometimes in the patient. Misfits include those who seek help or are brought to it because of difficulties on the job, at home, or, in the younger age groups, at school. They include tired business executives, married couples on the verge of divorce, unruly or emotionally disturbed children and their parents, and the like. In this category may also be included members of the intelligentsia or middle and upper classes who have leisure to worry about themselves and who look to psychotherapy to solve their general state of dissatisfaction, malaise, spiritual unrest, or feeling that they are not living life to the full.

Finally, mention must be made of psychotherapists in training who are required to undergo psychotherapy as part of their training program. Although these are in no sense patients and represent a very small proportion of persons receiving psychotherapy, they are of some importance in the total scene because their psychotherapy occupies a large proportion of the time of some of the most able and experienced psychotherapists, at the expense of the patients who might receive their services.

WHO CONDUCTS PSYCHOTHERAPY?

The variety of practitioners of psychotherapy in one form or another is almost as great as the range of persons they seek to help. Psychotherapists in the naturalistic tradition include a relatively small group specifically trained for this art, and a much larger number of professionals who practice psychotherapy without labeling it as such in connection with their healing or advisory activities. The largest group of professionals trained to conduct psychotherapy are psychiatrists, numbering about ten thousand. Their ranks are supplemented by well over four thousand clinical psychologists and five thousand social workers.[8]

Psychologists enter the field of psychotherapy through the scientific study of human thinking and behavior, and they supply most of the sophisticated researchers in this field. In clinical settings such as hospitals and psychiatric clinics they carry out diagnostic tests and do therapy under the more or less nominal supervision of psychiatrists. The major institutional settings in which they work independently are schools and universities. Increasing numbers, especially in the larger cities, are going into independent private practice as both diagnosticians and therapists.

Psychiatric social workers are specialists within the helping profession of social work. Like clinical psychologists, they are members of treatment teams in hospitals and clinics under psychiatric supervision, but they also operate independently in social agencies, family agencies, marriage counseling centers, and so on, and as private practitioners.

Psychotherapy in one guise or another forms part of the practice of many other professional groups. An indeterminate number of America's approximately 215,000 nonpsychiatric physicians[9] use psychotherapy with many of their patients, often without recognizing it as such. To them must be added osteopaths and healers on the fringes of medicine such as chiropractors, naturopaths, and others. The effectiveness of these latter, especially with emotionally disturbed persons, probably rests primarily on their intuitive use of psychotherapeutic principles.[10]

In addition to the healers more or less linked to medicine, a wide variety of counselors and guides may use psychotherapeutic principles with their clientele. These include marriage counselors, rehabilitation and vocational counselors, parole officers, group workers, clergymen, and others.

Members of different disciplines tend to describe their activities in different terms. For example, medical and quasi-medical healers treat patients, psychiatric social workers do case work with clients, clergymen offer pastoral counseling, and group workers do group work. For obvious reasons, each discipline tends to emphasize the special features of its approach, leading to a greater appearance of difference than may actually exist. In all likelihood their similarities far outweigh their differences.

The distinction between different healers and advisers lies less in what they do than in the persons with whom they do it, and this, in turn, depends largely on the settings in which they work. Certain settings sharply limit the kinds of persons who seek or receive psychotherapeutic help. Thus the bulk of the population of mental hospitals consists of the insane; those using the services of social agencies tend to be persons struggling with economic, social, marital, or parental problems. The school psychologist inevitably deals with children with school problems, the prison psychologist or psychiatrist with offenders, and so on.

The private office of the independent practitioner, however, sets no such limits on the kind of person who comes to him. A person may wind up in different hands depending on the referral channel he happens to pick, or the way in which he defines his problems. The very same patient might be treated by a psychiatrist, a psychologist, a psychiatric social worker, or even a clergyman, depending on where his feet carry him. As a result, the relationships among the different professions that conduct psychotherapy are in a state of flux. Clergymen and psychiatrists have formally recognized their field of common concern by forming the Academy of Religion and Mental Health. Jurisdictional problems are most acute in the larger cities where, in response to the increasing demand for psychotherapy, psychologists and psychiatric social workers have gone into independent private practice in direct competition with psychiatrists, resulting in attempts by the various groups involved to settle the issue by legislation.

This review of psychotherapeutic practitioners would be seriously incomplete without mention of the thousands of religious healers who are members of established sects such as Christian Science and New Thought, and, on their fringes, cultists of all sorts whose claim to healing powers rests solely on their own assertions. Though there is no way of counting these last, they must treat vast numbers of troubled people indistinguishable from those receiving more recognized forms of psychotherapy.[11]

WHAT ARE THE EFFECTS OF PSYCHOTHERAPY?

The ever-increasing investment of time, effort, and money in psychotherapy and its steadily increasing popularity imply that both its recipients and its practitioners are convinced that it does some good. Patients must believe it to be helpful or they would not seek it in increasing numbers, and every psychotherapist has seen permanent and striking improvement in a patient following some occurrence in psychotherapy. To date, however, although proponents of every method present persuasive accounts of their successes and vast amounts have been spent on research in psychotherapy,[12] convincing objective demonstration that one form of psychotherapy produces better results than another is lacking.

Statistical studies of psychotherapy consistently report that about two-thirds of neurotic patients and 40 per cent of schizophrenic patients are improved immediately after treatment, regardless of the type of psychotherapy they have received, and

the same improvement rate has been found for patients who
have not received any treatment that was deliberately psychotherapeutic. Thus about 70 per cent of neurotic patients
who received only custodial care in state hospitals are released,
and the same percentage of patients with neurotically based
disabilities treated by insurance doctors have returned to work
at the end of two years.[13] Similarly, the few follow-up studies
that exist fail to show differences in long-term improvement
from different types of treatment.[14] Indeed, with hospitalized
psychotics, although certain procedures such as electroconvulsive therapy seem able to accelerate improvement of certain
illnesses, no procedure has been shown to produce five-year
improvement rates better than those occurring under routine
hospital care.[15]

The question of the relative effectiveness of different forms
of psychotherapy is also puzzling when viewed from the standpoint of the amount or duration of therapeutic contact. Within wide limits, these seem to depend largely on the therapist's
notion of how much treatment is necessary, rather than on
the patient's condition. With respect to amount of contact, an
eminent psychiatrist has pointed out that when psychoanalysis
was transplanted from Europe to America, the frequency of
sessions soon dropped from six times a week to five, then to
three times a week or even less. There is no reason to think
that this reduction depended on differences in the severity of
illness between European and American patients, and the
writer suggests that it was probably a reflection of the increasing demands on the therapists' time created by the growing
number of patients seeking help. Yet "in actual duration of
treatment, in terms of months or years, the patient going five
times a week takes about as long to be cured as the patient
going three times."[16]

Duration of treatment also may be more closely related to
the therapist's conception of how long treatment should take
than to the patient's condition. Practitioners of long-term
therapy find that their patients take a long time to respond;
those who believe that they can produce good results in a few

weeks report that their patients respond promptly.[17] There is no evidence that a larger proportion of patients in long-term treatment improve or that improvement resulting from long-term treatment is more enduring than that produced by briefer treatment.

However, psychotherapy has tended to become increasingly prolonged in settings where there are no external obstacles to its continuance. Psychoanalysis that originally lasted a year or two at most now often lasts five to six years. At one university counseling center the average number of sessions increased from six in 1949 to thirty-one in 1954.[18] It is hard to believe that the lengthening of treatment reflects changes in the severity of patients' or clients' illnesses. More probably it reflects certain changes in the therapist's attitudes produced by increasing experience.[19]

At this point it must be emphasized that the failure to find differences in improvement rate from different forms or amounts of psychotherapy is a sign of ignorance, not knowledge. These negative results may well be due to lack of criteria of improvement that would permit comparison of different forms of treatment.[20] In many reports improvement is left undefined, so that there is no way of knowing precisely what the therapist had in mind, or whether or not he shifted his criterion from one patient to another.

When improvement is defined, the relationship between criteria used in different studies is usually unclear. Criteria determining the discharge of patients from state hospitals, the resumption of work by patients receiving disability payments, and the diagnosis of "recovered" by a psychoanalyst obviously may have little in common.

The problem of lack of comparability of measures of improvement is most acute in studies that define improvement in terms of a particular theory of psychotherapy. Criteria based on such definitions often can be precisely measured, but their relevance to clinical improvement may be problematical. Moreover, in order to get precise quantitative results, the research must confine itself to special types of patients. One such study, for example, compared changes on certain psychological test scores in a group of outpatients who received eight months of psychotherapy with a matched group who received no treatment over seven months, and found no differences between them.[21] But the experiment had to be confined to persons who were able to do the test, and also were willing to forego treatment for seven months, so one can draw no general conclusion from the negative findings.

In short, the inability to prove that a phenomenon exists is quite different from proving that it does *not* exist. The difficulty in demonstrating by statistical or experimental methods that therapy works or that one form is superior to another may lie in our inability to define adequately any of the variables involved. We cannot yet describe patients, therapies, or improvement in terms that permit valid comparison of the effects of different therapies on the same class of patient.

In the present state of ignorance, the most reasonable assumption is that all forms of psychotherapy that persist must do some good, otherwise they would disappear. Furthermore, it is likely that the similarity of improvement rate reported from different forms of psychotherapy results from features common to them all. The improvement rate for each form, then, would be composed of patients who responded to the features it shares with other forms and therefore would have improved with any type of psychotherapy, plus, perhaps, some patients who would have responded favorably only to the particular type of psychotherapy under consideration. If this were so, it would be hard to tease out the unique contributions of different forms of treatment until the features they share—and the attributes of patients that cause them to respond favorably to these features—were better understood.

The purpose of the book is to try to define these shared active ingredients, looking for features common to many different forms of interpersonal healing, and then seeing if these features also are present in psychotherapy. This exploration will lead quite far afield, and into some largely uncharted areas. Therefore, before setting out, it seems desirable to identify home base more clearly. To this end, the next chapter outlines a theoretical framework for psychotherapy.

SUMMARY

This chapter has attempted a general definition of psychotherapy, briefly reviewed its historical roots, and described the types of patients, therapists, and settings characteristic of psychotherapy in America today. It appears that many thousands of troubled people of all sorts seek psychotherapy or have it thrust upon them, and its practitioners are almost as varied as its recipients. Despite this feverish activity, there is little established knowledge about the relative efficacy of various forms, and the therapist's expectations seem to influence the length and amount of treatment required to produce improvement. These observations lead to the tentative conclusion that the features common to all types of psychotherapy probably contribute more to their efficacy than the characteristics that differentiate them.

Alice knew it was the Rabbit coming to look for her, and she trembled till she shook the house, quite forgetting that she was now about a thousand times as large as the Rabbit and had no reason to be afraid of it. (Lewis Carroll, *Alice's Adventures in Wonderland*, 1865, Chapter 4)

2 | A Conceptual Framework for Psychotherapy

The attempt to describe features common to all forms of psychotherapy requires consideration of a wide variety of patterned personal and social interactions. To keep our bearings in this exploration, a general conceptual framework is needed. Such a scheme should be able to relate a person's inner life to his interactions with other persons and to his group allegiances. It should suggest how certain kinds of distress might arise from and contribute to disturbed relationships with others, and how particular types of interpersonal experience might help to ameliorate both. This is obviously a very big order, and to handle it adequately would require a complete theory of personality development and structure as related to social and cultural influences, which is beyond the scope of this book.[1] The following presentation attempts only to sketch a few useful concepts in sufficient detail for orientation purposes. It makes no pretense at completeness. Although the exposition is primarily in terms of psychiatric patients and psychotherapy as they exist in America, with slight modifications it also applies to the other forms of influence and healing to be considered.

PSYCHOTHERAPY AND ADAPTATION TO STRESS

Although the conditions for which psychotherapy may be used are protean, they can all be viewed as temporary or persistent unsuccessful adaptations to stress. Everyone repeatedly must deal with experiences that temporarily disturb his equanimity and bring him into conflict with others. The healthy person is able to handle most of them promptly and effectively, without excessive expenditure of energy. Thus he can push ever forward and may often seek stress to enjoy the triumph of mastering it, like Sir Edmund Hillary, who was impelled to climb Mt. Everest simply because it was there.

The psychiatric patient, the ill savage, the person on the verge of religious conversion, and the prisoner of the Communists all are in distress because of their inability to master certain stresses, which arise in large part from their interactions with other persons or groups, present or past. Failures of adaptation are determined by an imbalance between the stress and the person's susceptibility to it. Sometimes the stress is so great that it exceeds the adaptive capacity of almost everyone. Examples are the prisoner who finally yields to the prolonged tortures and deprivations of thought reform, the soldier who collapses after overwhelming battle stress,[2] or the housewife with no income, six young children, and an alcoholic husband who mistreats her. That persons show emotional strain under such circumstances is hardly surprising, but their treatment obviously must focus on alleviating the environmental stress.

Failures of adaptation caused by personal inadequacies arising from personally meaningful life experiences are our primary concern. For completeness, however, brief mention may be made of impersonal or organic handicaps limiting adaptive capacity. One of these is aging, which is characterized by generalized reduction of ability to adjust to stress. There may also be constitutional differences in adaptive capacity. Some persons seem unduly inflexible, others perhaps too flexible so that they are at the mercy of every new experience.

The ability to cope with stress may be limited by inborn bodily defects or by damage occurring any time after conception. Many disabilities formerly thought to be genetic in origin apparently may be produced by prenatal mishaps.[3] After birth, a host of illnesses may limit adjustive capacity through nonprogressive handicaps such as a residual paralysis from poliomyelitis or, more seriously, through progressive chronic disease. Psychotherapy may have something to offer such patients by enabling them to modify their concepts of the implications of these handicaps for future happiness and ability to function. Since they account for only a small portion of the distress for which people come to psychotherapists, however, and their relevance to psychotherapy is largely indirect, they may be passed over with this brief mention.

Let us now turn to the task of characterizing defects in adaptive mechanisms that arise from interpersonal experiences and result in more or less persistent maladaptations, reflected in both a person's relationships with others and his inner life.

THE ASSUMPTIVE WORLD

In order to be able to function at all, everyone must impose an order and regularity on the welter of experiences impinging upon him. To do this, he develops out of his personal experiences a set of more or less implicit assumptions about the nature of the world in which he lives, which enables him to predict the behavior of others and the outcome of his own actions. The totality of each person's assumptions may be conveniently termed his "assumptive world."[4]

This is a short-hand expression for a highly structured, complex, interacting set of values, expectations, and images of one-self and others, which guide and in turn are guided by a person's perceptions and behavior and which are closely related to his emotional states and his feelings of well-being. Assumptions range widely in scope. An example of one extreme would be assumptions connected with the importance of brushing one's teeth; of the other, those concerning the nature of God. They also vary in their time reference, some being primarily concerned with the past, some with the present, and some with the future.

Assumptive systems may be enduring or transient. Assumptions about the attractiveness of a hat can usually be changed as easily as the hat itself; not so assumptions about the nature of God. Some assumptions are held only tentatively, others with firm conviction. The degree of subjective conviction accompanying them need not parallel their persistence—a lady may be absolutely convinced that a hat becomes her one day and that it is hideous the next—but conviction and tenacity do tend to vary together.

Different parts of the assumptive world exist at different levels of consciousness. Only a minute part of it is in awareness at any one time, and the relative accessibility to awareness of different aspects of it may differ greatly. A person may be clearly aware of his assumptions about the nuclear arms race, let us say, but be oblivious of his assumption that he must be perfect in order to gain his mother's love. Yet the latter conviction may have considerably more effect on his behavior than the former. Unconscious assumptive systems are especially pertinent to psychotherapy, not only because they are of profound importance to personal functioning but because, for reasons to be considered shortly, they resist change.

Assumptive systems may vary in their degree of mutual harmony or conflict. Internal conflicts are major sources of distress and disability, and much of psychotherapy can be viewed as an effort to help the patient resolve them.

A person's assumptive systems powerfully affect and are affected by his emotional states. Those systems that lead to a sense of uncertainty or confusion or to the prediction of an unfavorable outcome of a course of action tend to generate unpleasant emotions such as anxiety, panic, and despair. Those that give the person a sense of security and promise a better future are related to feelings of hope, faith, and the like. As will be seen, these emotional states not only have direct bearing on a person's ability to modify his perceptions and behavior, but also largely determine his state of well-being.

Anything that casts doubt on an established assumptive system seems to arouse an emotional reaction. An experience that does not meet expectations arouses a feeling of surprise. This may be tinged with fear or other unpleasant feeling if the person doubts his ability to make the necessary adjustment, or exhilaration if he is confident he can cope with the situation. That is, the emotional impact of an experience seems related to the extent to which it implies the necessity of a change in the assumptive world. It' seems as if the more extensive, and possibly the more abrupt, the change required, the greater is the concomitant emotional upheaval. Contrast the emotions accompanying the discovery that what one took to be a robin is really a bluebird with those accompanying a religious conversion involving far-reaching changes in the convert's values.

Although it seems likely that no change in a person's assumptive world takes place without a concomitant emotional reaction, an emotional upheaval in itself is not sufficient to produce major change. Even when a person is much upset by being compelled to reorganize an error in his assumptive world, no correction occurs automatically. He may, however, be strongly motivated by the experience to re-examine his assumptions and seek more reliable guides to expectation.

In order to function successfully and enjoy life, a person must possess an integrated set of assumptions that correspond to conditions as they actually are. For it is only to the extent that a person can successfully predict the results of his acts that he can behave in such a way as to maximize chances for success and minimize those for failure. Thus everyone is strongly motivated constantly to check the validity of his assumptions, and every act is both a consequence of a more or less explicit expectation and a test of its validity. If the consequences of the act fail to confirm the prediction, the person is in trouble. He must either modify his expectations and the corresponding behavior or resort to maneuvers to conceal their incorrectness and evade their unfortunate consequences. This process for the most part goes on automatically and outside of awareness.

The validity of some aspects of the assumptive world can be checked against experiences unmediated by other persons. For example, the test of the assumption that a glowing poker is hot is to touch it. But since man is a social creature, his most significant experiences are with other persons, and those aspects of his assumptive world most essential to his functioning—his attitudes and values—can only be validated through his interactions with others, individually or in groups. An example of an interaction chain between two persons, which is guided by, and helps to form, the attitudes of each, is the following:

A man comes home late for supper after a hard day at the office and greets his wife with a warm kiss. She responds in kind and makes a sympathetic remark about his work load as they go in to supper. This encourages him to tell her about the events of the day. She shows interest, so he continues until he has gotten everything off his chest. Then he is prepared to listen to his wife's account of her doings, which he encourages with appropriate signs of interest, and so they have a pleasant chatty meal. Such an interactional chain is based on mutual expectations of affection and understanding and, in turn, strengthens these expectations, increasing the likelihood of similar mutually gratifying behavior on subsequent occasions. Thus the favorable behavior and assumptive systems of each member of the couple with respect to their relationship continually reinforce each other.

Starting the same way, the interaction might run quite a different course. The wife does not return her husband's kiss, but says coldly that he is late for supper again. As they go in to dinner he makes an angry rejoinder to which she responds in kind. He picks up the paper and buries himself in it while he eats. She does the same with a book. Here the husband's initial favorable expectations, which he expressed by a warm kiss, are disappointed by his wife's coolness. This leads him to alter his assumption about his wife's attitude and to change his behavior correspondingly. The subsequent interactions lead to a progressive breakdown of communication, confirming the unfavorable mutual expectancies of each spouse and increasing the likelihood that future interactional chains will run the same unsatisfactory course. This example illustrates how interactions between two persons form a mutually regulative system in which the behavior of each influences the other and simultaneously helps each to form his own psychic life.

Interactions with the members of a person's family, especially during his early years, are important formative influences of his assumptive world. If the family group provides a rich variety of experiences enabling the person to develop a wide repertory of adaptive skills, and if his parents make him feel loved and wanted and treat him as if he is capable and good, then he comes to see himself as a well-equipped, competent, lovable person in a friendly, secure universe. The world is his oyster. He welcomes new experiences, tackles them with confidence, and easily modifies his behavior and assumptive world according to the outcome. Thus he readily learns and develops.

The family environment may fall short of this ideal in many ways. It may be lacking in opportunities for certain experience. For example, there may be no adequate father figure or inadequate opportunity to play with other children. Thus the child may grow up lacking certain important assumptive systems simply for want of a chance to develop them. More serious difficulties occur if the child is unfortunate enough to have unloving or inconsistent parents. If they are profoundly inconsistent, he may become so confused that he loses all confidence in his ability to interpret experience. This may be a major source of schizophrenia.[5] Parental rejection may lead him to see himself as unlovable, in a hostile world: "I a stranger and afraid. In a world I never made."[6] If he has been constantly belittled, he may grow up feeling inadequate to deal with many situations. Assumptive systems like these obviously tend to cause a person to avoid new experiences since he fears the worst from them.

Persons often try to resolve stresses initially created by their families by means that bring temporary relief but lay the ground for future trouble. The following example of a miniature neurosis illustrates how a person resorted to such a solution in childhood and was able to correct it years later through a lucky combination of circumstances. A scientist walking with some professional colleagues on the boardwalk at Atlantic City suddenly launched into an angry diatribe against the worthlessness of the merchandise in the curio shops. Although his remarks had some justification, the intensity of his feelings was so disproportionate as to arouse quizzical looks. Noting this, he became uncomfortable and began to wonder about it himself. He then suddenly remembered a long-forgotten childhood experience. At the age of seven he spent a few days at Atlantic City with his mother and grandmother. To give his grandmother a birthday present he emptied his piggy bank and bought her a cuckoo clock. Instead of being pleased, the grandmother angrily criticized his mother for letting him be so extravagant. As he told of this, he laughed and seemed relieved.

Let us describe this little episode in theoretical terms. In giving a birthday present to his grandmother the boy was acting on the assumption that she would be pleased. The unexpected failure of his prediction must have been most unpleasant for him. He probably felt resentment and anger at his grandmother as well as guilt for upsetting her and especially for the pain that he had inadvertently caused his mother. He might even have been angry at his mother for letting him get into such a fix.

A young child obviously cannot resolve such feelings by "having it out" with the adults who caused them, but must resort to more oblique solutions. Our patient, if he may be so termed for the moment, resorted to two common neurotic "mechanisms of defense"[7]—repression and displacement. He blotted the unpleasant episode from awareness, and displaced the object of his angry feelings from his grandmother to the curio shops. This solution had two advantages. It afforded a less dangerous object for his anger than his grandmother, and it allowed him to relieve his guilt by blaming the shops instead of himself. Like all neurotic solutions, however, it also had drawbacks. It left him with an error in his assumptive world and prevented him from correcting it through subsequent experience, because its source was unconscious. It also left him with a definite, if trivial, psychic scar, in that curio shops aroused an unduly unpleasant feeling in him. When circumstances again brought him in contact with these shops, he experienced this unpleasant feeling. By sharing it with his peers, he was implicitly validating it, and they failed to confirm it. Their quizzical looks communicated that they did not share this aspect of his assumptive world. This led him to examine himself for the source of his inappropriate feeling, and he discovered a past situation for which the feeling had been appropriate. By the same act he realized that this situation no longer existed. That is, he gained insight and with it was able to bring his assumptive systems into line with those of his colleagues.

Emotions were involved when his grandmother initially failed to confirm his assumptive world, leading him to modify it, and again when he modified it years later on the basis of his insight based on a different interaction, as shown by his discomfiture and his laugh. It is worth noting that the supportive, relaxed attitude of his colleagues made it relatively easy for him first to express his feelings, then to search himself for their source, and finally to offer a bit of self-revelation that explained and resolved them.

The family is only one source of experiences from which

a person develops his assumptive world. He also interacts with many other groups, who transmit not only their own cultures, but also aspects of the larger culture of which they are a part. The relative power of the cultural assumptions depends on how well knit the culture is and on the extent to which its world view permeates the lives of its members. The assumptive worlds of, let us say, the members of an isolated tribe on a small Pacific atoll probably have more in common than those of twentieth-century Americans.

How the assumptive world of a culture affects the percep-tions of its members can be demonstrated by a stereopticon. This device permits the presentation of two different pictures simultaneously, one to each eye. It has been found that if a picture of a baseball player is shown to one eye and a bull-fighter to the other, Americans tend to see the baseball player, Mexicans the bullfighter. Thus members of each culture select from the stimuli reaching them those that best accord with their assumptive worlds.[8]

Societies often contain built-in conflicts, or sources of stress, which create disharmonies in the assumptive worlds of their members. Often a society also contains institutionalized ways of resolving the stresses it creates. As we shall see, societies that believe in witchcraft, for example, also have ways of counteracting witches' spells. However, too often there is no readily available institutionalized way of handling a conflict engendered by discrepancies in the assumptive world of a society. Americans, for example, often have considerable diffi-culty in reconciling within themselves the disapproval of violence conveyed by the "official" American Christian ideology and its glorification in the media of mass communication. This conflict at a social level may be reflected in confused individual attitudes towards violence, often accompanied by feelings of anxiety or guilt.

How the assumptive world of a group can pose virtually in-soluble conflicts for its members, and how these conflicts can predispose to solutions that aggravate them, is illustrated by an "experiment of nature"—an outbreak of a fluke infestation known as schistosomiasis among American troops in the Phillipines in World War II.[9] Many patients hospitalized with this disease seemed to stay sick after obvious signs of infestation had disappeared, suggesting that emotional reactions might be contributing importantly to their persistent invalidism. Accordingly, fifty patients who had been hospitalized for two to four months were selected at random and interviewed about their attitudes. Only two seemed completely well. Of the remaining forty-eight, only seven had objective signs of schistosomiasis and most of these were questionable, so forty-one, or four fifths, of these patients had complaints with nothing physical to show for them. The complaints were mainly weakness, shakiness, headaches, and upper abdominal cramps. Review of the attitudes of all fifty patients showed that all but seven were anxious, resentful, or confused, or showed some combination of these feelings.

The assumptive world of the little society in which these men lived confronted them with a vague menace against which there was no clearly indicated course of action. It should be emphasized that this threat arose solely from the meaning of the situation to them. They were well fed and housed, did not feel very ill, and most had never been very uncomfortable at any time. Nor, as their subsequent recovery showed, were they in any actual danger from the disease. Yet they were badly demoralized. At least three aspects of their assumptive world contributed to this. First they believed the disease to be a threat to their survival since prognosis was considered uncertain and the efficacy of treatment questionable. Only two of the fifty were convinced that they had been cured, while thirty-two expected either to die of the disease or to become invalids. Second, the situation was highly ambiguous. Doctors could not avoid conveying their own uncertainties to the patients. They might say different things at different times, or different doctors might contradict each other. As one man put it, " (The doctors) tell you one thing one day and kind of contradict themselves. Like they say the sickness is all in your head and then they want to give you more shots."

Moreover, at the same moment that the doctors were trying to be reassuring, the radio on the wards carried alarmist reports of the disastrous nature of the disease to discourage bathing in infected streams. The soldiers did not know whom to believe: "Either the radio or the doctors are screwed up about something. I suppose the doctors are right, but then I suppose the doctors write the radio programs."

Finally, the soldiers felt that nobody really cared about them. This feeling seemed to have been created by fluctuations in disposition policies, reflecting the lack of knowledge about the disease, so that the decisions to return some soldiers to duty, hold others in the hospital, and promptly send others home appeared to the men to be purely capricious. The feeling of abandonment was accentuated by the attitudes of the harassed doctors, who, burdened with huge caseloads and not knowing what to make of the patients' endless complaints, inevitably tended to become somewhat aloof: "I tell them something and they pass it off as though it didn't exist. I feel I might as well be talking to myself."

The healthy way of coping with an ambiguous, threatening assumptive world is to clear up the uncertainty by getting more information, and the soldiers went at this with a vengeance. They read every scrap of literature on schistosomiasis they could find, wrote friends to look up the disease in medical texts, pestered the treatment staff for information, and compared notes with each other. Of course, this only made matters worse. The lack of authoritative information, the inability to comprehend the information that was available, and the general level of anxiety conspired to create a mass of rumors that enhanced the general confusion and intensified the morbid atmosphere.

Concomitantly with unsuccessful efforts to deal with the threat in appropriate fashion, the patients inevitably fell back on patterns of behavior that they had developed in early life to cope with similar predicaments. They "regressed" in that, like children, their complaints became a way of trying to elicit signs of interest and caring from the doctors, who were, in

a sense, parent surrogates. Their symptoms, furthermore, afforded an indirect and acceptable way of expressing their resentment towards the treatment staff. A patient can legiti-
mately complain that his headache has not been relieved,
but it is considerably more difficult to complain of the doctor's
incompetence.

This regressive way of dealing with the stressful assumptive
world tended to confirm and heighten its threatening quality.
By constantly dwelling on their symptoms, patients heightened
their fears and forebodings. The variety and vagueness of
their complaints added to the doctors' confusion and increased
their uneasiness. They reacted by becoming impatient, intensifying the patients' anxiety and resentment.

It must be emphasized, however, that despite the self-aggra-
vating nature of the threat and its apparent insolubility, individual reactions to it varied greatly. At one extreme, as already mentioned, two soldiers in the sample interviewed were
apparently completely unscathed, while at the other, two were
so disturbed emotionally as to require hospitalization on this
basis alone. Even when an assumptive world is widely shared,
people show widely differing abilities to cope with it successfully.

THE ASSUMPTIVE WORLD OF THE PSYCHIATRIC
PATIENT IN RELATION TO PSYCHOTHERAPY

According to the formulation offered here, the aim
of psychotherapy is to help a person to feel and function better
by enabling him to make appropriate modifications in his assumptive world. What helps or hinders such changes? In
general, assumptive systems, once established, tend to resist
change. Facts and experiences contradictory to assumptions do
not universally, immediately, and automatically lead to their
revision, but are more apt to be ignored or rationalized away.
There are several reasons for the stability of assumptive systems. A major one is that they are anchored to internalized
reference points.

The examples illustrate how the assumptive systems of persons or groups present at the moment can influence the assumptive systems of individuals exposed to them. Most groups against which a person tests his assumptions, however, are not actually present at the time, but exist as the residues of past experiences that he has internalized. These "reference groups" range from single concrete individuals such as "my father" to groups that exist only as concepts—such as "the scientific community" or "patriotic Americans." These internalized standards of reference are necessary for a stable personality organization, and they help a person withstand the temporary pressures of the groups he may be in at different times. At the same time, they may impair his ability to profit from new experiences that might lead to beneficial change.

Another reason why assumptive systems tend to perpetuate and reinforce themselves lies in the reciprocal nature of many interactions. Each participant tends to elicit from another responses in kind. Friendliness tends to beget friendly responses, and anger, angry ones, thus strengthening the assumptions on which the initial act was based. Furthermore, a person's own behavior, guided by his expectations, influences his interpretation of the other person's response. Thus in the example cited earlier, the husband would interpret the same response of the wife quite differently, depending on how he perceived his own initial greeting. If he saw it as friendly, this would predispose him to interpret her response as such; if he meant it to be cool, he would be inclined to interpret her response as being similar. In either case, he would guide his next action accordingly, predisposing the wife to respond in accord with his expectations. Thus a continuing relationship tends to lead each participant to develop an enduring, structured set of expectations about himself and the other person, with corresponding behaviors, which become ever harder to modify by new experience.

Unhealthy assumptive worlds of mental patients present certain special obstacles to change. It would lead too far afield to consider in detail how various neurotic resolutions of stress tend to impede new learning. Repression, as used by the man who hated curio shops, may serve as an illustration. Blotting an experience from awareness prevents the erroneous conclusion that has been drawn from it from being modified by subsequent experiences, in part because the patient cannot link them to the original one. Moreover, repressed emotions or thoughts reduce both a person's adaptive capacity and his sense of security. He must expend some effort to keep them out of awareness, thus decreasing energy available for meeting current stresses. Since repression is seldom perfect, repressed emotions or thoughts are apt to erupt into consciousness attached to obviously inappropriate objects or at inappropriate times, so that they are mysterious to the patient. In the example, the scientist was startled at the inappropriate intensity of his dislike of the shops. The sense of not being able to account for one's feelings or thoughts may be partly responsible for the common fear of psychiatric patients that they are going crazy.

In addition to presenting specific blocks to new learning, such as repression, the faulty assumptive systems of mental patients impede their ability to benefit from new experiences in more general ways. To the extent that the assumptive world of a person is erroneous, his predictions as to the behavior of others will be wrong, leading him to suffer repeated shocks, failures, and frustrations. Chronic frustration arouses anger and other unacceptable feelings, which increase his feelings of unworthiness. He may be further demoralized by the knowledge that he is not living up to his capacities. Finally, the contempt or impatience of those about him, reflecting cultural attitudes towards mental illness, contributes to his loss of self-esteem, and he may view his need for psychotherapy as conclusive evidence of his inferiority.

Emotions like anxiety, depression, and feelings of inadequacy tend to reduce a person's willingness and capacity to experiment. Since nothing is more anxiety-producing than uncertainty, a chronically anxious patient clings fearfully to his old solutions, however inadequate, because they are familiar, whereas experimentation would require venturing into unknown territory. The depressed patient cannot muster the necessary energy or interest to attempt a change. Although moderate anxiety and depression cause some persons to seek help and so facilitate psychotherapy, they tend to cause others to withdraw. Isolation from others, besides being distressing in itself, reduces opportunities to correct errors in one's assumptive world by checking them against the assumptions of others.

But probably the greatest block to new learning in psychiatric patients is that they are saddled with ways of dealing with stress that aggravate rather than alleviate it. The major problem here arises from the reciprocal nature of human transactions, mentioned earlier. A person's behavior tends to "train" others to respond in such a way as to confirm his expectations. This training is especially effective if the patient's behavior is already restricted to a narrow range so that he does the same thing repeatedly.[10] A paranoid patient, who is convinced that everyone hates him, may by his surly, suspicious manner antagonize a person who initially bore him no ill will. The reaction he receives confirms the patient's belief that everyone dislikes him, intensifying his dislike-creating behavior. In the schistosomiasis example, patients came to expect the doctors to confuse them and show a lack of interest in them. By their vague but constant complaining they tended to elicit from the doctors precisely such behavior. This, in turn, aggravated their complaints. Thus patients tend to get caught in "self-fulfilling prophecies,"[11] and their behavior is both self-perpetuating and self-defeating. Breaking these vicious circles is the main goal of psychotherapy.

In view of the resistance of assumptive systems, especially unhealthy ones, to change, the psychotherapist's task would appear to be well-nigh hopeless, and the extent of the personality changes he can help patients to achieve is indeed limited. However, these changes need not be negligible, for the psychotherapist may be able to mobilize powerful influencing forces.

To oversimplify vastly, the two major sources of interpersonal influence are individuals on whom a person feels dependent and those whom he perceives to be like himself. The former, first represented by his parents, later by teachers, bosses, and so on, gain their power through their direct control of his well-being. The sources of influence of the latter—his friends and colleagues—are not so apparent, but probably spring in part from the fact that their attitudes of acceptance or rejection determine his sense of group belonging.[12]

A person's feelings of dependency on others may spring from his perception of them as possessing information that would be useful to him, or as being able to harm or help him in a variety of ways. Perceived power to harm readily induces outward conformity to escape reprisal, but at the same time generates feelings such as resentment, which may impede genuine acceptance of the powerful figure's goals or ideas. Perceived power to help seems to be a particularly potent source of influence. Through engendering hope, it directly improves the perceiver's sense of well-being, and heightens his self-confidence, increasing his willingness to modify his attitudes and behavior. At the same time it strengthens his sense of dependence without directly stirring up conflicting emotions.

The psychotherapist gains his potential power to influence the patient's assumptive world from all these sources. Patients who have similar educational and social backgrounds perceive him as like themselves. In many settings he is a representative of the larger culture, so that his acceptance of the patient implies acceptance by the larger group. He may use specific group methods to take full advantage of the patient's hunger for group acceptance. His cultural role and special training predispose the patient to perceive him both as an expert in problems of living and as a healer. These favorable, socially determined perceptions are complicated, especially in long-term therapy, by idiosyncratic ones encompassed by the term "transference." That is, patients tend to transfer to the therapist emotions that are really appropriate to other persons in their lives. Transference reactions may both help and impede the therapist's power depending on whom he represents to the patient.

Consideration of the sources and nature of the psychotherapist's influence is a major object of this book. For the present, it suffices to indicate that although patients may present formidable resistance to change, the psychotherapist often has forces at his disposal that can overcome this, at least to some extent.

SUMMARY

Psychotherapy tries to relieve a person's distress and improve his functioning by helping him to correct errors and resolve conflicts in his assumptions concerning himself and others. These assumptions are organized into systems existing at varying levels of consciousness and in harmonious or conflicting relationships with one another. They affect and are affected by emotional states, and changes in them are regularly accompanied by emotion. Healthy assumptive systems are characterized by internal consistency and close correspondence with actual conditions. They thus lead to reliable, satisfactory interactions with other persons, accompanied by a sense of competence, inner security, and well-being, which enables them to be readily modified when necessary. Unhealthy assumptive systems are internally full of conflict and do not accurately correspond to circumstances, leading to experiences of frustration and failure. Efforts to cope with or evade these feelings tend to intensify distortions and conflicts and to become both self-perpetuating and self-defeating, resulting in cumulative adaptational difficulties.

Despite the stubborness of maladaptive assumptive systems, the psychotherapist, as a socially sanctioned expert and healer and a representative of the larger society, may be able to mobilize forces sufficiently powerful to produce beneficial changes in them.

"I can't believe *that*," said Alice. "Can't you?" the Queen said in a pitying tone. "Try again; draw a long breath, and shut your eyes." (*Through the Looking Glass,* Chapter 5)

3 | Religious Healing

Examination of religious healing in so-called primitive societies and in Western society illuminates certain aspects of human functioning that are relevant to psychotherapy. Methods of supernatural healing highlight the close interplay of assumptive systems and emotional states and the intimate relation of both to health and illness. They also bring out the parallel between inner disorganization and disturbed relations with one's group, and indicate how patterned interaction of patient, healer, and group within the framework of a self-consistent assumptive world can promote healing. Certain properties of healing rituals in primitive societies, finally, show interesting resemblances to naturalistic psychotherapeutic methods that may serve to increase understanding of both.

The view that illness can be caused and cured by the intervention of supernatural forces stretches back to furthest antiquity and continues to be important, though often in attenuated form, in most modern cultures. It is possible to make all kinds of distinctions in regard to the type of supernatural theories invoked, as to whether they dominate a society or are believed only by deviant groups, and in regard to the social acceptance and status of the healers. We shall consider primarily those theories that are integral parts of the religion of the total society or of a respectable and numerous portion of it, and in which the healing rituals are public and socially sanctioned. Thus the term "religious" seems applicable to them, even though few readers of this book would accept the validity of the religious beliefs on which most of these forms of healing are based.

Religious healing in primitive societies, as in the Western world, tends to exist side by side with naturalistic treatment by medicines, manipulations, and surgical operations. Its sphere of influence tends to shrink in the face of secularization and the introduction of scientific medicine. In all cultures its chief realm of operation is in the treatment of illnesses that have important emotional components; that is, the conditions for which naturalistically based psychotherapies are also used. It therefore is not surprising that, although their theoretical foundations differ profoundly, religious and naturalistic healing methods have much in common. Furthermore, both types of healing have persisted through the ages, suggesting that their efficacy may lie partly in their common features. In this chapter we shall search for these features in religious healing methods of primitive societies and note to what extent they are also found in a great contemporary shrine of miraculous healing.

To avoid the necessity of qualifying every statement, let it be said at the start that although the characteristics to be discussed are widespread, they are not universal. The diversity of healing methods in primitive societies is very great so that exceptions can be found to any generalization. Moreover, the examples are not offered to prove a line of argument (which would require consideration of negative instances) but simply to support and illustrate it.

ILLNESSES IN PRIMITIVE SOCIETIES

The world views of primitive societies regard illness as a misfortune involving the entire person, with direct consequences on his relationships with the spirit world and with other members of his group. Although they recognize different kinds of illness, their classifications often bear no relation to those of Western medicine. In particular, they may not distinguish sharply between mental and bodily illness, or between that due to natural and that due to supernatural causes.

Illnesses tend to be viewed as symbolic expressions of internal conflicts or of disturbed relationships to others, or both. Thus they may be attributed to soul loss, possession by an evil spirit, the magical insertion of a harmful body by a sorcerer, or the machinations of offended or malicious ancestral ghosts. It is usually assumed that the patient laid himself open to these calamities through some witting or unwitting transgression against the supernatural world, or through incurring the enmity of a sorcerer or someone who has employed a sorcerer to wreak revenge. The transgression need not have been committed by the patient himself. He may fall ill through the sin of a kinsman.

Although many societies recognize that certain illnesses have natural causes, this does not preclude the simultaneous role of supernatural ones. A broken leg may be recognized as caused by a fall from a tree, but the cause of the fall may have been an evil thought or a witch's curse.

Because of the high mortality rates among primitive peoples, diseases in primitive tribes represent a greater threat to the patient than they do in countries with highly developed means of treatment. The longer the illness lasts, the greater the threat becomes. In societies subsisting on a marginal level, illness is a threat to the group as well as to the invalid. It prevents the invalid's making his full contribution to the group's support and diverts the energies of those who must

look after him from group purposes. Therefore, it seems likely
that every illness has overtones of anxiety, despair, and similar
emotions, mounting as cure is delayed. That is, persons for
whom healing rituals are performed probably are experiencing
emotions that aggravate their distress and disability, whatever
their underlying pathological condition may be. The invalid,
then, is in conflict within himself and out of harmony with
his group. The group is faced with the choice of abandoning
him to his fate by completing the process of extrusion, or of
making strenuous efforts to heal him, thereby restoring him
to useful membership in his community.

Before considering the healing of illness in primitive societies, it seems appropriate to examine a type of personal disaster
that can befall members of certain groups and that may have
a counterpart in civilized societies. This is the so-called taboo
death, which apparently results from noxious emotional states
related to certain individual and group assumptive systems
about supernatural forces and which also involve the victim's
relationships with his group.

Anthropological literature contains anecdotes of savages who,
on learning that they have inadvertently broken a taboo, go
into a state of panic and excitement that eventuates in death
in a few hours.[1] Unfortunately in none of these cases can
more mundane causes of rapid death, such as overwhelming
infection, be entirely excluded. The evidence that members
of certain tribes may pine away and die within a brief period
after learning that they have been cursed is more fully documented and more convincing. The *post hoc* nature of the
explanations cannot be overlooked, especially since in groups
where this type of death occurs, practically all illness and
death is attributed to having been cursed. Nevertheless, the
process has been observed in sufficient detail in different tribes
to make the explanation highly plausible.

The most convincing examples are those in which a native
at the point of death from a curse rapidly recovers when the
spell is broken by a more powerful one, as in the following
anecdote, which can be multiplied many times:

Some years ago my father, who lived in Kenya, employed a Kikuyu garden "boy," of whom we were all fond. Njombo was gay, cheerful and in the prime of life. He was paying goats to purchase a wife and looking forward to marriage and a bit of land of his own. One day we noticed he was beginning to lose weight and looked pinched and miserable. We dosed him with all the usual medicines to no avail. Then we persuaded him, much against his will, to go into a hospital. Three weeks later he was back with a note from the doctor: "There is nothing wrong with this man except that he has made up his mind to die."

After that Njombo took to his bed, a heap of skins, and refused all food and drink. He shrank to nothing and at last went into a coma. Nothing we could do or say would strike a spark, and all seemed to be up with him.

As a last resort, my father went to the local chief and threatened him with all sorts of dreadful penalties if he did not take action to save Njombo's life. This was largely bluff, but the chief fell for it. That evening we saw a man with a bag of stoppered gourds entering Njombo's hut. We did not interfere, and no doubt a goat was slaughtered. Next morning, Njombo allowed us to feed him a little beef tea. From that moment he started to rally—the will to live was restored. We asked no questions, but learned some time later that Njombo had had a serious quarrel over the girl and that his rival had cursed him. Only when the curse was removed could he hope to survive.[2]

In certain societies, the victim's expectation of death may be powerfully reinforced by the attitudes of his group. For example, in the Murngin, a North Australian tribe, when the theft of a man's soul becomes general knowledge, he and his tribe collaborate in hastening his demise.[3] Having lost his soul, he is already "half dead." Since his soul is in neither this world nor the next, he is a danger to himself as a spiritual entity and also to his tribe because his soul, not having been properly laid away, is likely to cause illness and death among his kin. All normal social activity with him therefore ceases and he is left alone. Then, shortly before he dies, the group returns to him under the guidance of a ceremonial leader to perform mourning rites, the purpose of which is "to cut him off entirely from the ordinary world and ultimately place him . . . in . . . the . . . world . . . of the dead." The victim, concomitantly, recognizes his change of status: ". . . the wounded feudist killed by magic dances his totem dance to . . . insure his immediate passage to the totem well . . . . His effort is not to live but to die." The writer concludes: "If all a man's near kin . . . business associates, friends, and all other members of the society, should suddenly withdraw themselves because of some dramatic circumstance . . . looking at the man as one already dead, and then after some little time perform over him a sacred ceremony believed with certainty to guide him out of the land of the living . . . the enormous suggestive power of this twofold movement of the community . . . can be somewhat understood by ourselves."

Although this account stresses the role of group influences, the major source of the victim's decline is probably the emotional state induced by his conviction—grounded in his belief system—that he has lost his soul. In this example the group's withdrawal reinforces this conviction. It is conceivable, however, that the victim would have died even if surrounded by their loving care if his conviction that the situation was hopeless were sufficiently strong. Calling attention to the interpersonal forces involved in the process should not be taken as minimizing the importance of intrapersonal ones.

Plausible speculations based on work with animals have been offered to explain the physiological mechanism of death in these cases. One hypothesis is that it might be due to prolonged adrenal overexcitation caused by terror, leading to a state analogous to surgical shock.[4] Another, based on studies of physiological changes in wild rats who give up and die when placed in a stressful situation after their whiskers have been clipped, suggests that the emotional state is more one of despair than terror, and that the mechanism of death is stoppage of the heart resulting from overactivity of the vagus nerve.[5] This view is supported by fascinating and suggestive parallels between this phenomenon in wild rats and taboo deaths in primitive peoples—for example, prompt recovery even at the point of death if the stress is suddenly removed. Both hypotheses are plausible, and each may account for a particular variety of emotionally caused death—the first for the rapid form, if it occurs and the second for the slower variety.

In civilized as well as primitive societies a person's conviction that his predicament is hopeless may cause or hasten his disintegration and death. For example, the death rate of the aged shortly after admission to state mental hospitals is unduly high, and with these and other age groups often no adequate cause of death is found at autopsy, raising the possibility that some of these deaths are caused by hopelessness, aggravated by abandonment by the patient's group. Similarly, some young schizophrenics may go into overactive panic states in which they exhaust themselves and die. This fortunately rare reaction usually occurs in conjunction with the patient's admission to the hospital; that is, at the moment when his family withdraws and he feels most alone. Sometimes it can be successfully interrupted if a member of the treatment staff succeeds in making contact with the patient and getting across to him, by one means or another, that someone still cares about him.[6]

Descriptions of the "give-up-itis" reaction of American prisoners of war of the Japanese and Koreans suggest a similar interaction of hopelessness and group isolation to produce death. A former prisoner of war well describes this reaction.[7] He lists the major factors that had to be dealt with in order to survive as: "the initial shock and subsequent depression induced by being taken prisoner by Oriental people; the feeling of being deserted and abandoned by one's own people; the severe deprivation of food, warmth, clothes, living comforts, and sense of respectability; the constant intimidation and physical beatings from the captors; loss of self-respect and the respect of others; the day-to-day uncertainty of livelihood and the vague indeterminable unknown future date of deliverance." It will be noted that physical and psychological threats are placed on the same footing. Under these circumstances: "Occasionally an individual would . . . lose interest in himself and his future, which was reflected in quiet or sullen with-drawal from the group, filth of body and clothes, trading of food for cigarettes, slowing of work rate . . . and an expressed attitude of not giving a damn . . . . If this attitude were not met with firm resistance . . . death inevitably resulted."

This is clearly a description of hopelessness. It could be successfully combatted by "forced hot soap-and-water bathing, shaving and delousing, special appetizing food, obtaining a few days rest in camp . . . a mixture of kindly sympathetic interest and anger-inducing attitudes. Victory was assured with the first sign of a smile or evidence of pique." It is of interest that successful measures may include anger-arousing as well as nurturant behavior. As another observer reports: "One of the best ways to get a man on his feet initially was to make him so mad, by goading, prodding, or blows, that he tried to get up and beat you. If you could manage this, the man invariably got well."[8] Thus it may be that any kind of emotional stimulus, whether pleasant or not, may successfully counteract lethal despair if it succeeds in breaking through the victim's isola-tion, demonstrates that his comrades care about him, and implies that there are things he can do to help himself.

HEALING IN PRIMITIVE SOCIETIES: THE ROLE OF THE SHAMAN[9]

Having considered how certain emotional states activated by personal assumptive systems interacting with group forces may contribute to disintegration and death, let us turn now to the role of these factors in healing, as illustrated by religious healing rituals in primitive societies. These rituals, which grow directly out of the tribe's world view, are usually conducted by a shaman[10] and involve participation of the patient and usually members of his family and tribe.

The powers of the shaman are explained in terms of the society's assumptive world and are unquestioningly accepted as genuine by it. The routes for acquiring shamanistic powers vary greatly. In some groups the shaman acquires them, some-times against his will, through personal and private mystical experiences, and he is regarded as a deviant person with little status except when his powers are invoked. In other groups shamans are drawn from the ranks of cured patients.[11] In others, as in the Kwakiutl, they undergo an elaborate course of training, analogous to medical training in our culture, and enjoy a high prestige.

Shamans usually are adept at distinguishing illnesses they can treat successfully from those that are beyond their powers, and they manage by one means or another to reject patients with whom they are likely to fail. This enables them to main-tain a reputation for success which, by arousing favorable expectancies in the patient and the group, undoubtedly en-hances their healing power.

The importance of the group's attitudes in determining not only the shaman's effectiveness but also his self-evaluation is well illustrated by the remarkable autobiography of Quesalid, a Kwakiutl shaman.[12] He entered training motivated by skepticism concerning the shamans' powers and by the desire to expose them. The training included learning to master various arts of deception, and especially how to spit out of one's mouth at the right moment a bit of down covered with blood, representing the foreign body that had made the patient ill and had been magically extracted from him.

Knowing that he was in training, a family called him in to treat a patient, and he was brilliantly successful. He at-tributed the cure to psychological factors: ". . . because the patient believed strongly in the dream he had had of me." What shook his skepticism was a visit to a neighboring Koskimo tribe, in which the shamans simply spit a little saliva into their hands and dared to pretend that this was the illness. In order to find out "what is the power of these shamans, if it is real or if they only pretend to be shamans," he asked and received permission to try his method since theirs had failed. Again the patient said she was cured. Apparently some forms of healing were more fraudulent than others. This presented Quesalid with a problem "not without parallel in the development of modern science: two systems, both known to be inadequate, nevertheless, compared with each other appear to differ in value both logically and experimentally. In what frame of reference should they be judged?"

The Koskimo shamans, "covered with shame" because they had been discredited in the eyes of their countrymen, and thrown into self-doubts, tried very hard to ferret out his secrets, but to no avail. Finally one of the most eminent challenged him to a healing duel, and Quesalid again succeeded where the other failed. Two interesting consequences followed. The old shaman, fearing to die of shame and unable to get Quesalid to reveal his secret, vanished the same night with all his relatives "sick at heart," returned a year later, insane, and died three years later. Quesalid, although he continues to expose imposters and is full of scorn for the profession, remains uncertain as to whether there are real shamans or not: "Only once have I seen a shaman who treated patients by suction and I was never able to find out if he was a real shaman or a faker. For this reason only, I believe that he was a shaman. He did not allow those he had cured to pay him. And truly I never once saw him laugh." At the end it is unclear whether he considers himself to be a real shaman: ". . . he pursues his calling with conscience . . . is proud of his successes and . . . defends heatedly against all rival schools the technique of the blood-stained down whose deceptive nature he seems completely to have lost sight of, and which he had scoffed at so much in the beginning." Quesalid's skepticism is not able to withstand his own successes and the belief of his group in his powers.

HEALING IN PRIMITIVE SOCIETIES: THE HEALING CEREMONY

Healing in primitive societies utilizes both individual and group methods. It may be conducted by the shaman with the patient alone, analogous to the pattern of

Western medicine. The shaman makes a diagnosis by performing certain acts and then offers a remedy, which may
be a medication or the performance of suitable incantations
as in the example cited above.[13] The healing power of these
procedures probably lies in the patient's expectation of help,
based on his perception of the shaman as possessing special
healing powers, derived from his ability to communicate with
the spirit world.

Other forms of primitive healing involve a long-term two-
person relationship between shaman and patient, which seems
to show certain analogies to long-term psychotherapy.[14] The
only available descriptions, however, are too sketchy to warrant
consideration here.

This section considers a third type of primitive healing,
which has been adequately described by anthropologists and
which bears on psychotherapy—the group healing ceremonial.
These rituals may involve ancestral or other spirits, for example, and are intensive, time-limited efforts aimed at curing
specific illness and involving members of the patient's family.
As a result, they cast little, if any, light on certain features
that may be of central importance in long-term individual
psychotherapy, such as the development and examination of
transference reactions between patient and therapist. On the
other hand, they throw certain aspects of long-term therapy
into relief, as it were, by compressing them into a brief time
span, and highlight the healing role of group and cultural
forces, the effect of which may be underestimated in individual
therapy because they are present only implicitly. With these
considerations in mind, it may be instructive to consider a
healing ceremony in some detail—the treatment of "espanto"
in a sixty-three-year-old Guatemalan Indian woman.[15] This
was her eighth attack. Her symptoms seem similar to those
that would lead an American psychiatrist to diagnose an agi-
tated depression. The Indians attribute it to soul loss.

The treatment began with a diagnostic session attended not
only by the patient but by her husband, a male friend, and
two anthropologists. The healer felt her pulse for a while,

while looking her in the eye, then confirmed that she was suffering from "espanto." He then told her in a calm, authoritative manner that it had happened near the river when she
saw her husband foolishly lose her money to a loose woman,
and he urged her to tell the whole story. After a brief period
of reluctance, the patient "loosed a flood of words telling of
her life frustrations and anxieties . . . . During the recital
. . . the curer . . . nodded noncommittally, but permissively,
keeping his eyes fixed on her face. Then he said that it was
good that she should tell him of her life." Finally they went
over the precipitating incident of the present attack in detail. In essence, she and her husband were passing near the
spot where he had been deceived by the loose woman. She
upbraided him, and he struck her with a rock.

The curer then told her he was confident she could be cured
and outlined in detail the preparations that she would have to
make for the curing session four days later. She was responsible for these preparations, which involved procuring and preparing certain medications, preparing a feast, persuading a
woman friend or kinsman to be her "servant" during the
preparatory period and healing session, and persuading one of
the six chiefs of the village to participate with the medicine
man in the ceremony.

The ceremony itself began at four in the afternoon and
lasted until five the next morning. Before the healer arrived,
the house and the house altar[16] had been decorated with pine
boughs, and numerous invited guests and participants had assembled. After they were all present, the healer made his en-
trance, shook hands all around, and checked the preparations
carefully. Then there was a period of light refreshment and
social chitchat, which apparently helped to organize a social
group around the patient and to relax tension.

After dusk the healer, chief, and others of the group went
off to church, apparently to appease the Christian deities in
advance, since "recovery of a soul involves dealing with rene-
gade saints and familiar spirits certainly not approved of by
God Almighty." When they returned, a large meal was served.

The patient did not eat, but was complimented by all present on her food. Then the healer carried out a long series of rituals involving such activities as making wax dolls of the chief of evil spirits and his wife, to whom the healer appealed for return of the patient's soul, and elaborate massage of the patient with whole eggs, which were believed to absorb some of the sickness from the patient's body. The curer, the chief, two male helpers, and the ever-present anthropologists next took the eggs and a variety of paraphernalia, including gifts for the evil spirits, to the place where the patient had lost her soul, and the healer pleaded with various spirits to restore her soul to her.

On their return they were met at the door by the patient, who showed an intense desire to know whether the mission had been successful. The curer spoke noncommittal but comforting words. This was followed by much praying by the healer and the chief before the house altar and a special ground altar set up outside, and by rites to purify and sanctify the house. Some of these activities were devoted to explaining to the household patron saint why it was necessary to deal with evil spirits. All this took until about 2 A.M., at which time the ceremony came to a climax. The patient, naked except for a small loin cloth, went outside. Before the audience, the healer sprayed her entire body with a magic fluid that had been prepared during the ritual and that had a high alcoholic content. Then she had to sit, naked and shivering, in the cold air for about ten minutes. Finally she drank about a pint of the fluid. Then they returned indoors, the patient lay down in front of the altar, and the healer massaged her vigorously and systematically with the eggs, then with one of his sandals. She then arose, put on her clothes, lay down on the rustic platform bed, and was covered with blankets. By this time she was thoroughly relaxed.

Finally, the healer broke the six eggs used in the massage into a bowl of water one by one, and as he watched their swirling whites he reviewed the history of the patient's eight "espantos," pointing out the "proofs" in the eggs. The sink-ing of the eggs to the bottom of the bowl showed that all the previous "espantos" had been cured and that the present symptoms would shortly disappear. The healer "pronounced the cure finished. The patient roused herself briefly on the bed and shouted hoarsely, 'That is right.' Then she sank back into a deep snoring sleep." This ended the ceremony and everyone left but the patient's immediate family.

The patient had a high fever for the following few days. This did not concern the healer, whose position was that everyone died sooner or later anyway, and if the patient died, it was better for her to die with her soul than without it. He refused to see her again, as his work was done. The anthropologist treated her with antibiotics, and she made a good recovery from the fever and the depression. The author notes that for the four weeks he was able to observe her "she seemed to have developed a new personality . . . . The hypochondriacal complaints, nagging of her husband and relatives, withdrawal from her social contacts, and anxiety symptoms all disappeared."

This example illustrates certain generalizations about religious healing which, if not universal, are at least widely applicable. It should be noted that healing rituals are not undertaken lightly. Usually they are resorted to only after simpler healing methods have failed. The analogy springs to mind that in America patients are often referred for psychiatric treatment only after all other forms of treatment have failed to relieve their suffering. In any case, this suggests that the state of mind of a patient receiving a healing ritual and that of one receiving psychotherapy may often resemble each other in some respects. Both types of patient are apt to be discouraged and apprehensive about their condition, while at the same time hopeful for relief from the treatment.

The theory of illness and healing, and the healing method itself, are integral parts of the culture's assumptive world. This makes comprehensible and orderly, events that otherwise would be mysterious. As has been said about another magical cure:

That the mythology of the shaman does not correspond to objective reality does not matter. The patient believes in it and belongs to a society that believes in it. The protecting spirits, the evil spirits, the supernatural monsters and magical monsters are elements of a coherent system which are the basis of the natives' concept of the universe. The patient accepts them, or rather she has never doubted them. What she does not accept are the incomprehensible and arbitrary pains which represent an element foreign to her system but which the shaman, by invoking the myth, will replace in a whole in which everything has its proper place.[17]

The conceptual scheme is validated and reinforced by the rituals that it prescribes. In the above example this occurred especially when the healer examined the eggs swirling in the water and pointed out to the assembled group the "proofs" of the patient's previous illnesses. The scheme, moreover, cannot be shaken by failure of the ritual to cure the patient. If this one had died, the ceremony would still have been regarded as successful in restoring her soul.[18]

The shaman's activities validate his supernatural powers. In this example his manner in the diagnostic interview and especially his revelation to the patient of an event that she did not know he knew, and that he therefore presumably learned about through magic, must have had this effect. In other rituals the shaman may start by reciting how he got his "call" or citing examples of the previous cures, to which others present may add confirmation. He may resort to legerdemain. as in the Kwakiutl, but most authorities agree that this is not regarded as trickery, even when the audience knows how it is done. They seem to give emotional assent to the proposition that the bloody bit of cotton is the patient's illness and has been extracted from his body, while at another level they know perfectly well that it is only a piece of cotton. Perhaps their state of mind is analogous to that of partakers of communion, for whom in one sense the bread and wine are the body and blood of Christ while in another they are just bread and wine. In any case, the healing ritual reinforces the image of the shaman as a powerful ally in the patient's struggle with the malign forces that have made him ill.

Rituals often involve a preparatory period, which represents a dramatic break in the usual routine of daily activities. In the case of "espanto" it served to jolt the patient out of her usual routines, heighten her sense of personal importance by letting her have a "servant," and start the process of rallying family and group forces to her aid. Also, like the rest of the ritual, it gave her something to do to combat her illness, in itself a powerful allayer of anxiety and strengthener of the expectancy of cure.

That patient's family, as well as respected representatives of the tribe, convey their concern for him by participating in the ritual. As they represent a healthy group, they are not likely to reinforce the patient's pathological trends, as may occur, for example, in a mental hospital.

Many rituals have an altruistic quality. All the participants try to help the patient by performing parts of the ritual, interceding for him with the powers he has presumably offended, or defending the patient to them. Sometimes the patient also performs services for the group. In our example, the patient was responsible for preparing the feast. The performance of services to others may help to counteract the patient's morbid self-absorption and enhance his sense of self-worth by demonstrating that he can still be of use to them. It also contributes to the meritorious quality of the ritual.

In those ceremonies that involve confession, atonement, and forgiveness, the gaining of merit is especially apparent. The fact that confession is required for cure implies a close link between illness and transgression, as discussed earlier. Impersonalized forms of confession and repentance, as in some Christian liturgies, serve the purpose of general purification.

Some healing rituals elicit confessions of specific personal transgressions based on detailed review of the patient's past history with special emphasis on the events surrounding his illness. These events are expressed or interpreted in terms of the tribe's assumptive world. In addition to its confessional aspect, this procedure brings the patient's vague, chaotic, conflicting, and mysterious feelings to the center of his attention and places them in a self-consistent conceptual system. Thus they are "realized in an order and on a level which permits them to unfold freely and leads to their resolution."[19]

It may be noted in passing that the shaman's technique of eliciting this type of confession may also be a way of demonstrating his powers as in the example cited. That is, he warns the patient that the spirits have already told him what the true facts are and that they cannot be hidden. As the patient confesses, the shaman confirms that this is what he already knew and urges the patient to confess further.[20] Often the other participants jog the patient's memory or bring up episodes with the patient in which they too transgressed, or even crimes ostensibly unrelated to the patient's illness. Thus the process further cements the group, and participants other than the patient may gain virtue from it. The confession may be followed by intercession with the spirit world on behalf of the patient by the whole group as well as by the shaman, heightening the patient's hope that forgiveness will be forthcoming.

Thus confession may have many implications.[21] It helps the patient to make sense of his condition, counteracts his consciousness of sin, brings him into closer relationship with his group, impresses him with the shaman's powers, and improves the relationship of all concerned with the spirit world. In these ways it counteracts his anxiety, strengthens his self-esteem, and helps him to resolve his conflicts.

Healing ceremonies tend to be highly charged emotionally.[22] The shaman may act out a life-and-death struggle between his spirit and the evil spirit that has possessed the patient. The patient may vividly re-enact past experiences or act out the struggles of spirit forces within himself. The emotional excitement may be intensified by rhythmic music, chanting, and dancing. It frequently mounts to the point of exhausting the patient and not infrequently is enhanced by some strong physical shock. In our example, it will be recalled, the patient was sprayed by an alcoholic liquid, which gave her a bad chill.

Finally, many rituals make a strong aesthetic appeal. The setting may be especially decorated for the occasion, and participants may be elaborately costumed, may perform stylized dances, and may draw sand paintings and the like. Since these trappings and activities have symbolic meanings, they not only are soothing and inspiring aesthetically but they represent tangible reinforcements of the conceptual organization that the ritual endeavors to impose on the patient's inchoate sufferings. Participation of the whole group either actively or as attentive spectators fosters group solidarity.

In short, methods of primitive healing involve an interplay between patient, healer, group, and the world of the supernatural, which serves to raise the patient's expectancy of cure, help him to harmonize his inner conflicts, reintegrate him with his group and the spirit world, supply a conceptual framework to aid this, and stir him emotionally. In the process they combat his anxiety and strengthen his sense of self-worth.

RELIGIOUS HEALING IN THE
WESTERN WORLD: LOURDES

From its inception, Christianity has included the notion of healing through divine intervention. Starting with the healing miracles of Christ, this form of curing has come down through the centuries to the present. Today healing sects like Christian Science and shrines of miraculous healing have millions of devotees. Since the rituals of these groups and places parallel religious healing in primitive societies in many ways, it may be of interest to take a look at one of them. The great modern shrine of Lourdes seems particularly suitable because it has been well described and because the cures of severe illness that have occurred there are exceptionally well documented and have received careful critical scrutiny.[23]

The history of Lourdes, starting with the visions of Bernadette Soubirous in 1858, is too well known to require retelling
here. It is perhaps odd, in view of subsequent developments,
that the apparition that appeared to Bernadette and told her
where to dig for the spring said nothing about its healing
powers. Be that as it may, miraculous cures following immersion in the spring were soon reported, and today over two
million pilgrims visit Lourdes every year, including over thirty
thousand sick.

The world view supporting Lourdes, like those on which
religious healing in primitive tribes is based, is all-inclusive
and is shared by almost all the pilgrims to the shrine. While
cures are regarded as validating it, failures cannot shake it.
Those who seek help at Lourdes have usually been sick a long
time and have failed to respond to medical remedies. Like
the primitives who undergo a healing ritual, most are close
to despair. Being chronic invalids, they have had to withdraw
from most or all of their community activities and have become
burdens to their families. Their activities have become routinized and constricted, their lives are bleak and monotonous, and
they have nothing to anticipate but further suffering and death.

The decision to make the pilgrimage to Lourdes changes
all this. The preparatory period is a dramatic break in routine.
Collecting funds for the journey, arranging for medical examinations, and making the travel plans requires the co-operative effort of members of the patient's family and the wider
community. Often the congregation contributes financial aid.
Prayers and masses are offered for the invalid. Members of
the family, and often the patient's physician or a priest, accompany him to Lourdes and serve as tangible evidence of the
interest of the family and larger group in his welfare. Often
pilgrims from many communities travel together, and there
are religious ceremonies while the train is en route and at
every stop. In short, the preparatory period is emotionally
stirring, brings the patient from the periphery of his group to
its center, and enhances his expectation of help. It is interesting in this connection that, except for the original cures,

Lourdes has failed to heal those who live in its vicinity. This suggests that the emotional excitement connected with the preparatory period and journey to the shrine may be essential for healing to occur.

On arrival at Lourdes after an exhausting, even life-endangering journey, the sufferer's expectation of help is further strengthened. He is plunged into "a city of pilgrims, and they are everywhere; people who have come from the four corners of the earth with but one purpose: prayer, and healing for themselves or for their loved ones . . . . One is surrounded by them, and steeped in their atmosphere every moment of existence in Lourdes." Everyone hopes to witness or experience a miraculous cure. Accounts of previous cures are on every tongue, and the pilgrim sees the votive offerings and the piles of discarded crutches of those who have been healed. Thus the ritual may be said to begin with a validation of the shrine's power, analogous to the medicine man's review of his cures in primitive healing rites.

The pilgrims' days are filled with religious services and trips to the Grotto, where they are immersed in the ice-cold spring. Every afternoon all the pilgrims and invalids who are at Lourdes at the time, and they number forty or fifty thousand, gather at the Esplanade in front of the shrine for the procession that is the climax of each day's activities. The bedridden are placed nearest the shrine, those who can sit up are behind them, the ambulatory invalids behind them, while the hordes of visitors fill the rest of the space. The enormous emotional and aesthetic impact of the procession is well conveyed by the following quotation:

> At four the bells begin to peal—the Procession begins to form. The priests in their varied robes assemble at the Grotto . . . . The bishop appears with the monstrance under the sacred canopy. The loud-speakers open up. A great hymn rolls out, the huge crowd joining in unison, magnificently. The Procession begins its long, impressive way down one side and up the other of the sunny Esplanade. First the Children of Mary, young girls in blue capes, white veils . . . then forty or fifty priests in black

cassocks . . . other priests in white surplices . . . then come the Bishops in purple . . . and finally the officiating Archbishop in his white and gold robes under the golden canopy. Bringing up the rear large numbers of men and women of the different pilgrimages, Sisters, Nurses, members of various religious organizations; last of all the doctors . . . . Hymns, prayers, fervent, unceasing. In the Square the sick line up in two rows . . . . Every few feet, in front of them, kneeling priests with arms outstretched praying earnestly, leading the responses. Nurses and orderlies on their knees, praying too . . . . Ardor mounts as the Blessed Sacrament approaches. Prayers gather intensity . . . . The Bishop leaves the shelter of the canopy, carrying the monstrance. The Sacred Host is raised above each sick one. The great crowd falls to its knees. All arms are outstretched in one vast cry to Heaven. As far as one can see in any direction, people are on their knees, praying . . . .

What are the results of the tremendous outpouring of emotion and faith? The great majority of the sick do not experience a cure. However, most of the pilgrims seem to derive some psychological benefit from the experience. The pilgrimage is regarded as meritorious in itself and the whole atmosphere of Lourdes is spiritually uplifting. In this connection, the altruism of all involved is especially worthy of note. Physicians, brancardiers (who serve the sick), and helpers of all sorts give their time and effort freely, and throughout the ceremonies the emphasis is on self-forgetfulness and devotion to the welfare of others. The pilgrims pray for the sick and the sick for each other, not themselves. Therefore, the words attributed to an old pilgrim may well be largely true: "Of the uncured none despair. All go away filled with hope and a new feeling of strength. The trip to Lourdes is never made in vain."

The evidence that an occasional cure of advanced organic disease does occur at Lourdes is as strong as that for any other phenomenon accepted as true. The reported frequency of such cures varies widely depending on the criteria used. The piles of crutches attest to the fact that many pilgrims achieve improved functioning, at least temporarily. In many of these cases, however, improvement is probably attributable to heightened morale, enabling them to function better in the face of an unchanged organic handicap. Fully documented cures of unquestionable and gross organic disease are extremely infrequent—probably no more frequent than similar ones occurring in secular settings.

In the century of the shrine's existence, less than a hundred cures have passed the stringent test leading the Church to declare them miraculous. This figure may well be much too low, as many convincing cases fail to qualify because they lack the extensive documentary support required. But even several thousand cures of organic disease would represent only a small fraction of one per cent of those who have made the pilgrimage. As a sympathetic student of spiritual healing writes: ". . . there is probably no stream in Britain which could not boast of as high a proportion of cures as the stream at Lourdes if patients came in the same numbers and in the same psychological state of expectant excitement."[24]

Inexplicable cures of serious organic disease occur in everyday medical practice. Every physician has either personally treated or heard about patients who mysteriously recovered from a seemingly fatal illness. One surgeon has recently assembled from the literature ninety cases of unquestionable cancer that disappeared without adequate treatment.[25] Had these cures occurred after a visit to Lourdes, many would have regarded them as miraculous. Since no physician sees enough of these phenomena to acquire a sufficient sample for scientific study, and since they cannot be explained by current medical theories, the fascinating questions they raise have tended to be pushed aside.

The processes by which cures at Lourdes occur do not seem to differ in kind from those involved in normal healing, although they are remarkably strengthened and accelerated. Careful reading of the reports reveals that healing is not instantaneous, as is often claimed, but that, like normal healing, it requires time. It is true that the consciousness of cure is often (not always) sudden and may be accompanied by immediate improvement in function—the paralyzed walk, the blind see, and those who had been unable to retain food suddenly regain their appetites. But actual tissue healing takes hours, days, or weeks, and persons who have lost much weight require the usual period of time to regain it, as would be expected if healing occurred by the usual processes. Moreover, gaps of specialized tissues such as skin are not restored but are filled by scar formation as in normal healing. No one has regrown an amputated limb at Lourdes.

It should be added that cures at Lourdes involve the person's total personality, not merely his body. The healed, whatever they were like before their recovery, all are said to be possessed of a remarkable serenity and a desire to be of service to others.

Rivers of ink have been spilled in controversy over whether or not the cures at Lourdes are genuine, based on the erroneous assumption that one's acceptance or rejection of them is necessarily linked to belief or disbelief in miracles or in the Catholic faith. Actually, it is perfectly possible to accept some Lourdes cures as genuine while maintaining skepticism as to their miraculous causation, or to be a devout Catholic while rejecting modern miracles. The world is full of phenomena that cannot be explained by the conceptual schemes current at a particular time. Today these include inexplicable cures of fatal illnesses, in secular as well as religious settings. Depending on one's theoretical predilections, one may choose to believe that all, none, or a certain class of these are miraculous. The mere fact of their occurrence leaves the question of their cause completely open.

A not implausible assumption, in the light of our review of primitive healing, is that Lourdes cures are in some way related to the sufferers' emotional state. This view is supported by the conditions under which the cures occur, and the type of person who seems most apt to experience them. Although they can occur en route to Lourdes, on the return journey, or even months later, most cures occur at the shrine and at the moments of greatest emotional intensity and spiritual fervor—while taking communion, or during immersion in the spring or when the host is raised over the sick at the passing of the sacrament during the procession. The persons who have been cured include the deserving and the sinful, believers and apparent skeptics, but they tend to have one. common characteristic: they are "almost invariably simple people—the poor and the humble; people who do not interpose a strong intellect between themselves and the Higher Power."[26] That is, they are not detached or critical. It is generally agreed that persons who remain entirely unmoved by the ceremonies do not experience cures.[27]

The skeptics who have been cured had a parent or spouse who was highly devout, suggesting either that their skepticism was a reaction-formation against an underlying desire to believe, or at least that the pilgrimage involved emotional conflict. In this connection, all cured skeptics have become ardent believers.

In short, the healing ceremonials at Lourdes, like those of primitive tribes, involve a climatic union of the patient, his family, the larger group, and the supernatural world by means of a dramatic, emotionally charged, aesthetically rich ritual that expresses and reinforces a shared ideology.

MAGICAL HEALING, CULTS, AND CHARLATANS

In most societies, in addition to institutionalized, public, "respectable" forms of religious healing, there are more-or-less clandestine, private forms of trafficking with supernatural forces, involving small, sometimes secret, groups, or a strictly private arrangement between patient and healer.[28] Despite the large following of cults and quacks, which suggests that they must help many persons, they do not repay extended attention because of their enormous variety and the lack of dispassionate, objective information about most of them.

The main interest of such cults for us is that their success seems to rest on their ability to evoke the patient's expectancy of help, a factor also involved in religious healing. Two sources of this expectancy are discernible. The first is the personal magnetism of the healer, often strengthened by his own faith in what he does. As an investigator who interviewed many such healers writes: "The vast majority of the sectarians sincerely believe in the efficacy of their practices . . . the writer has talked to (chiropractors) whose faith was . . . nothing short of evangelistic, whose sincerity could no more be questioned than that of Persia's 'whirling dervishes.' "[29] However, the success of peddlers of obviously worthless nostrums and gadgets attests to the fact that the healer need not necessarily believe in the efficacy of his methods to be able to convince his patients of their power.

Another source of the patient's faith is the ideology of the healer or sect, which offers him a rationale, however absurd, for making sense of his illness and the treatment procedure, and places the healer in the position of transmitter or controller of impressive healing forces. In this he is analogous to the shaman. Often these forces are supernatural, but the healer may pose as a scientist who has discovered new and potent scientific principles of healing, thus surrounding himself with the aura that anything labeled scientific inspires in members of modern Western societies. These healers characteristically back up their pretensions with an elaborate scientific-sounding patter and often add an imposing array of equipment complete with dials, flashing lights, and sound effects.

The apparent success of healing methods based on all sorts of ideologies and methods compels the conclusion that the healing power of faith resides in the patient's state of mind, not in the validity of its object. At the risk of laboring this point, an experimental demonstration of it with three severely ill, bedridden women may be reported.[30] One had chronic inflammation of the gall bladder with stones, the second had failed to recuperate from a major abdominal operation and was practically a skeleton, and the third was dying of widespread cancer. The physician first permitted a prominent local faith healer to try to cure them by absent treatment without the patients' knowledge. Nothing happened. Then he told the patients about the faith healer, built up their expectations over several days, and finally assured them that he would be treating them from a distance at a certain time the next day. This was a time in which he was sure that the healer did *not* work. At the suggested time all three patients improved quickly and dramatically. The second was permanently cured. The other two were not, but showed striking temporary responses. The cancer patient, who was severely anemic and whose tissues had become waterlogged, promptly excreted all the accumulated fluid, recovered from her anemia, and regained sufficient strength to go home and resume her household duties. She remained virtually symptom free until her death. The gall bladder patient lost her symptoms, went home, and had no recurrence for several years. These three patients were greatly helped by a belief that was false—that the faith healer was treating them from a distance—suggesting that "expectant trust"[31] in itself can be a powerful healing force.

SUMMARY

This review of religious healing, with a side glance at its questionable fringes, emphasizes the profound influence of emotions on health and suggests that anxiety and despair can be lethal, confidence and hope, life-giving. The modern assumptive world of Western society, which includes mind-body dualism, has had difficulty incorporating this obvious fact and has therefore tended to underemphasize it.

Part of the deleterious effect of all illness, especially if prolonged, results from the emotional states it fosters. Constant misery, forced relinquishment of the activities and roles that give significance to life, the threat of dissolution, all may intensify feelings of anxiety and despair, and these may be further enhanced by reactions of anxiety, impatience, and progressive withdrawal in those around the patient, especially when his illness threatens their security as well as his own. Thus illness may lead to a vicious circle by fostering emotional states that aggravate it.

Methods of religious healing may evoke emotions that are equally intense and perhaps as distressing as those produced by the illness itself, but they do it in a different context. The sufferings of a debilitated invalid caused by the rigors of the trip to Lourdes, and culminating in an icy bath, must often be very severe. This suggests that the effects of strong emotions on one's well-being depend on their meaning or context. If they imply hopelessness and lead to progressive isolation of the patient from his usual sources of support, they may kill him. If they are aroused in a setting of massive human and supernatural encouragement and can be discharged through organized activities in a context of hopefulness, they can be healing.

The core of the effectiveness of methods of religious and magical healing seems to lie in their ability to arouse hope by capitalizing on the patient's dependency on others. This dependency ordinarily focuses on one person, the healer, who may work privately with the patient or in a group setting. In either case, the patient's expectation of help is aroused partly by the healer's personal attributes, but more by his paraphernalia, which gains its power from its culturally determined symbolic meaning. Even in private forms of healing, group and cultural factors are implicit.

This becomes explicit in healing ceremonies, in which the healer acts as the mediator between the patient, his group, and the supernatural world, and the patient's faith in him rests largely on his institutionalized role and the powers attributed to him by the group.[32] The role of the healer may be diffused among many persons, as at Lourdes, where it resides in the participating priests.

The patient's hope is enhanced by a set of assumptions about illness and healing that he shares with his society and a ritual based on it. The theory cannot be shaken by failures, while every repetition of the ritual validates and reinforces it. Thus knowledge of previous failures need not diminish the patient's belief that he will be helped.

The ideology and ritual supply the patient with a conceptual framework for organizing his chaotic, mysterious, and vague distress and give him a plan of action, helping him to regain a sense of direction and mastery and to resolve his inner conflicts. To the extent that the ritual includes participation of the group and healer, it heightens the patient's hope by demonstrating to him that he has allies.

Methods of religious healing also have aspects that heighten the patient's sense of self-worth. Performance of the ritual is usually regarded as meritorious in itself—all involved gain virtue by participating. The patient becomes the focus of the group's attention and, by implication, worthy of the invocation of supernatural forces on his behalf. If he is cured, this may be taken as a mark of divine favor, permanently elevating his value in his own and the group's eyes. In fact, one factor in maintaining a cure may be the changed attitude of the group, which continually reinforces it. That is, if the patient relapsed, he would be letting the group down.

An aspect of the interplay of patient and group in religious cures that deserves special comment is the emphasis on mutual service. Often the patient does things for the group, and the group intercedes for the patient. At Lourdes, pilgrims pray for each other, not for themselves. This stress on service counteracts the patient's morbid self-preoccupation, strengthens his self-esteem by demonstrating that he can do something for others, and cements the tie between patient and group.

Many religious healing rituals include a detailed review of the patient's past life, with especial emphasis on the events surrounding his illness, usually coupled with some form of confession and forgiveness. These activities can be helpful in several ways. By bringing certain feelings and problems to the forefront of the patient's attention, they help him to conceptualize, clarify, and re-integrate them. They also strengthen the patient's bonds with his group and with the supernatural world, in that the members of the group, after hearing the worst, still stand by him and join their pleas for supernatural forgiveness with his. Finally, in religious healing, relief of suffering and production of attitude change are inseparable. Healing is accompanied not only by a profound change in the patient's feelings about himself and others, but by a strengthening of previous assumptive systems or, sometimes, conversion to new ones.

"I know *something* interesting is sure to happen," she said to herself, "whenever I eat or drink anything: so I'll just see what this bottle does." (*Alice's Adventures in Wonderland,* Chapter 4)

4 | The Placebo Effect in Medical and Psychological Treatment

Our review of religious healing has revealed considerable evidence that measures which combat anxiety and arouse hope can have curative power in themselves. Physicians have always known that their ability to inspire expectant trust in a patient has something to do with the success of treatment. Until recently this knowledge, like that obtained from anthropological studies, rested on uncontrolled observations and clinical impressions, so that it was impossible to define in any systematic way the sources and limits of the effects of hope on different kinds of patients and their illnesses. The problem has been to domesticate the question, as it were, to lure it away from the bedside into the laboratory where the factors involved could be systematically manipulated and their effects sorted out.

Fortunately, there is one form of medical treatment that makes this possible, since its effectiveness rests solely on its ability to mobilize the patient's expectancy of help. This is the use of a "placebo." A placebo is a pharmacologically inert substance that the doctor administers to a patient to relieve his distress when, for one reason or another, he does not wish to use an active medication. Thus he may use a placebo rather than a sedative in treating a patient's chronic insomnia to avoid the danger of addiction. Since a placebo is inert, its beneficial effects must lie in its symbolic power. The most likely supposition is that it gains its potency through being a tangible symbol of the physician's role as a healer. In our society, the physician validates his power by prescribing medication, just as a shaman in a primitive tribe may validate his by spitting out a bit of bloodstained down at the proper moment.

In this connection it may be worth while to recall that until the last few decades most medications prescribed by physicians were pharmacologically inert. That is, physicians were prescribing placebos without knowing it, so that, in a sense, the "history of medical treatment until relatively recently is the history of the placebo effect."[1] Despite their inadvertent reliance on placebos, physicians maintained an honored reputation as successful healers, implying that these remedies were generally effective. Yet, when a physician today knowingly prescribes a placebo, he may tend to feel a little guilty. For it seems to imply deception of the patient, which the physician finds hard to reconcile with his professional role. The dictionary definition of a placebo is illuminating in this regard: "a medicine, especially an inactive one, given merely to satisfy a patient."[2] The little word "merely" has been the stumbling block, since it implies that a placebo does nothing but satisfy the patient. Perhaps because of this implication, the conditions determining the effects of placebo administration and the nature of these effects have failed to receive the careful study they deserve.

In recent years the mounting flood of new pharmaceuticals requiring evaluation has given impetus to the study of placebo effects, for the pharmacological effects of any new drug must be disentangled from those due simply to the power of any new remedy to arouse hopes of physicians and patients. A common experimental approach to this problem has been the so-called "double-blind" method. In this technique neither physcian nor patient knows whether a particular dose contains the medicine or a placebo. The patient's responses to each dose or course of treatment are carefully recorded, and after the experiment is completed, responses to medication and placebo are compared. Any consistent differences can then be reliably attributed to the pharmacological action of the drug.

Study of the patients' reactions to pharmacologically inert medication is a means of investigating effects of their expectations, mediated by the doctor-patient relationship, on their physical and emotional states. A look at the present state of knowledge on this subject is therefore pertinent to the aims of this book.

In passing, it may be mentioned that a patient's expectations have been shown to affect his physiological responses so powerfully as even to reverse the pharmacological action of a drug. For example, the drug ipecac is an emetic, which normally causes cessation of normal stomach contractions shortly after ingestion. The patient experiences this as nausea. By having a patient swallow a balloon, which is inflated in the stomach and hooked to the proper equipment, these changes in stomach motility can be directly observed. A pregnant patient suffering from excessive vomiting showed the normal response of cessation of stomach contractions with nausea and vomiting after receiving a dose of ipecac. When the same medication was given to her through a tube, so that she did not know what it was, with strong assurance that it would cure her vomiting, gastric contractions started up at the same interval after its administration that they would normally have stopped, and simultaneously the patient's nausea ceased.[3]

Evidence that placebos can have marked physiological effects has been afforded by demonstrations of their ability to heal certain kinds of tissue damage. The placebo treatment of warts, for example, by painting them with a brightly colored but inert dye and telling the patient that the wart will be gone when the color wears off, is as effective as any other form of treatment, including surgical excision, and works just as well on patients who have been unsuccessfully treated by other means as on untreated ones.[4] Apparently the emotional reaction to a placebo can change the physiology of the skin so that the virus which causes warts can no longer thrive.

Placebo treatment can also activate healing of more severely damaged tissues, especially when the damage seems related to physiological changes connected with unfavorable emotional states. In one study of patients hospitalized with bleeding peptic ulcer, for example, 70 per cent showed "excellent results lasting over a period of one year," when the doctor gave them an injection of distilled water and assured them that it was a new medicine that would cure them. A control group who received the same injection from a nurse with the information that it was an experimental medication of undetermined effectiveness showed a remission rate of only 25 per cent.[5]

The symbolic meaning of medication may not always be favorable. Some patients fear drugs and distrust doctors. In these patients a placebo may produce severe untoward physiological reactions including nausea, diarrhea, and skin eruptions.[6]

Placebos can have powerful effects on hospitalized psychiatric patients. Using double-blind techniques, it has been found that some of the beneficial effects of tranquilizers, especially when they were first introduced into mental hospitals, were really due to the hope they inspired in both staff and patients. They increased the therapeutic zeal of the staff, and this in itself helped the patients. In this connection, the mere introduction of a research project into a ward in a veterans hospital was followed by considerable behavioral improvement in the patients, although no medications or other special treatments were involved at all. The most likely explanation seemed to be that participation in the project raised the general level of interest of the treatment staff, and the patients responded favorably to this.[7]

Psychiatric outpatients also often respond favorably to inert medications. In five separate studies involving a total of fifty-six patients, an average of 55 per cent showed significant symptomatic improvement from placebos.[8] This figure is about the same as that reported with medical patients whose disorders have an emotional component, suggesting that placebos produce their benefits through favorably affecting certain emotional states.

The duration of the placebo effect depends on many factors. When the source of the pain is independent of the patient's emotional condition, like a surgical wound, the relief afforded by a placebo tends to be transient, although it may last as long as that produced by analgesics. When the improvement in emotional state produced by the placebo also diminishes the physiological disorder producing the pain, then the effect may be enduring, as in the peptic ulcer patients reported above. The placebo, by combating anxiety, probably diminished stomach mobility and secretion, thereby facilitating healing of the ulcers. The maximum duration of the placebo effect in psychiatric patients is unknown because a placebo has seldom been given for more than two or three weeks. It remains undiminished for at least this length of time with many patients. In one study the effect was undiminished at the end of at least eight weeks.[9]

The kinds of symptoms that are particularly susceptible to relief by placebos confirm the hypothesis that they combat anxiety and similar feelings. Their ability to relieve the pain in patients following surgical operations—and they are temporarily effective in over a third of these patients—has been attributed to their success in combating the "processing" aspects of pain,[10] that is, the apprehensiveness and other emotions that aggravate painful sensations. In psychiatric outpatients psychic symptoms, especially anxiety and depression, respond more often and more markedly to placebos than do bodily ones, though these also are somewhat relieved.

If the effectiveness of the placebo lies in its ability to mobilize the patient's expectancy of help, then it should work best with those patients who have favorable expectations from medicine and, in general, accept and respond to symbols of healing. The scanty information available is consistent with this hypothesis. In the study of patients with surgical pain, placebo responders tended to be more dependent, emotionally reactive, and conventional, while the nonreactors were more likely to be isolated and mistrustful.[11] Psychiatric outpatients who showed strong responses to placebos, as compared with a group who showed no response, were more apt to take vitamins and aspirins regularly, were more outgoing, participated more in organizations, and were less cautious. These findings suggest that they expected medicines to help them, were better integrated socially, and were less mistrustful than nonreactors.

Thus it appears that the ability to respond favorably to a placebo is not so much a sign of excessive gullibility, as one of easy acceptance of others in their socially defined roles. This view is supported by the relation of placebo responsiveness of a group of schizophrenic patients to their subsequent clinical course.[12] Thirty-three who appeared at a follow-up clinic for a routine check-up shortly after their discharge from a state hospital were given placebos for three weeks. Their response was a remarkably good prognosticator of whether they would have to go back to the hospital or not. Of those who had to return within thirty days not one responded favorably, while of those who remained well enough to stay out of the hospital, four-fifths had felt better after receiving the placebo. Apparently placebo responsiveness was an indicator of the ability of these patients to trust their fellow man as represented by the clinic physicians, and this had something to do with their capacity to adjust to the world outside the hospital.

If part of the success of all forms of psychotherapy may be attributed to the therapist's ability to mobilize the patient's expectation of help, then some of the effects of psychotherapy should be similar to those produced by a placebo.[13] It has been possible to demonstrate experimentally that this is so. In an experimental study of the relative effects of six months of group, individual, and minimal psychotherapy with psychiatric outpatients, it was found that, while degree of improvement in social effectiveness was related to the amount of treatment contact, average diminution of discomfort was the same regardless of the form or amount of psychotherapy the patients had received. Moreover, the average amount of discomfort relief was the same for patients who had dropped out of treatment within the first month as for those who had received six months of treatment. It is perhaps more surprising, in view of the widespread belief among physicians that symptomatic relief is superficial and transient, that average diminution of discomfort persisted over a five-year follow-up period. That is, although some patients relapsed, the group as a whole maintained its gains.[14]

The fact that relief of discomfort was the same regardless of the type or duration of therapy and that it seemed to occur quite promptly suggested that it might be due to the mobilization of the patients' expectant trust. This would ordinarily not depend on the nature or length of treatment and should occur at the first contact of the patient with his physician. If this were the explanation, then administration of a placebo, the power of which presumably rests on the same factor, should have similar effects.

To test this, twelve patients of the original population were given a two-week trial of placebo at the time of their routine follow-up interview two to three years after their initial contact with the project. These patients had shown marked symptomatic improvement after the first six months and had slipped back only a little during the subsequent observation period, but they still were sufficiently distressed to desire further relief. The placebo produced just about as much relief of discomfort in these patients as had the six months of psychotherapy.[15]

This seems to confirm the hypothesis that part of the healing power of all forms of psychotherapy lies in their ability to mobilize the patient's hope of relief.

The intensity of the hope that can be elicited by psychotherapy must be but a pale shadow of that evoked by religious healing. It is therefore the more surprising that symptomatic relief following even minimal psychotherapy proved to be so enduring. The explanation may be that relief of anxiety and depression frees the patient to make better use of the healthy parts of his personality, so that he functions more effectively in general. As one writer puts it: "If the patient believes strongly in a cure . . . by his very belief he at once obtains sufficient moral support to *face all his problems* with some degree of equanimity."[16] Greater success in solving his problems, in turn, results in increased satisfaction and diminished frustration, further ameliorating his distress.

To forestall misunderstanding, it should be stressed that mobilization of the patient's expectation of help at best accounts for only a part of the effects of psychotherapy. In the experimental study, improvement in social effectiveness, in contrast to relief of distress, was clearly due to other factors. However, as suggested above, symptom relief and improved functioning are intimately related.

Nor should the ability of placebos to produce symptomatic relief under some circumstances be regarded as justification for their widespread use. In addition to the obvious consideration that this would cause them to lose their effectiveness and damage patients' faith in the medical profession, they have several serious drawbacks. Insofar as the doctor feels that he is deceiving a patient by giving him a placebo, this may undermine the doctor-patient relationship. For if the patient showed a good response, the doctor might lose respect for him as gullible; and if the patient failed to respond, he would have lost some faith in the doctor. The very power of the placebo makes it dangerous, for it may relieve distress caused by serious disease. This may cause neglect of diagnostic studies that would have revealed the condition and result in failure to give adequate treatment.

From the standpoint of psychotherapy, the psychiatrist by prescribing a placebo implicitly conveys that he considers medication the best treatment for the patient's condition. This decreases the patient's motivation to solve the personal problems that are the real source of his distress.

There are three conditions in which the use of a placebo may be indicated. Sometimes it can be helpful when an active agent for the patient's illness cannot be used or does not exist. It also may have a proper use with patients whose anxiety over their condition aggravates or prolongs it. To the extent that a placebo will relieve this anxiety, it is a genuine healing agent. Finally, for some patients treatment means receiving a medicine or an injection, and if they do not get it, they will not return. It may sometimes be advisable to meet the expectations of such a patient by giving him a placebo in order to hold him in treatment long enough to establish a therapeutic relationship with him.

But in most circumstances the physician can best arouse the expectant trust of his patients by his serious interest and competence and, where indicated, by the use of treatment measures that combat the pathological condition underlying the patient's symptoms. The chief value of the placebo will continue to be as a research tool to study some of the determinants and effects of expectancy of help, and to test the pharmacological action of new drugs.

SUMMARY

Experimental studies of the effects of the administration of inert medications by physicians demonstrate that the alleviation of anxiety and arousal of hope through this means commonly produce considerable symptomatic relief and may promote healing of some types of tissue damage. The relief may be enduring. The little that is known of personality attributes of those who respond favorably to placebos suggests that they are predisposed to accept and react to socially defined symbols of healing.

Comparison of the effects of psychotherapy and placebos on a group of psychiatric outpatients suggests that certain symptoms may be relieved equally well by both forms of treatment and raises the possibility that one of the features accounting for some of the success of all forms of psychotherapy is their ability to arouse the patient's expectation of help. These findings must not be interpreted as justifying widespread use of placebos or as explaining other more important, beneficial effects of psychotherapy that are clearly due to factors different from arousal of the expectation of help.

"Please your majesty," said the knave, "I didn't write it and they can't prove I did; there's no name signed at the end." "If you didn't sign it," said the King, "that only makes the matter worse. You *must* have meant some mischief, or else you'd have signed your name like an honest man." (*Alice's Adventures in Wonderland,* Chapter 12)

5 | Religious Revivalism and Thought Reform

So far we have reviewed phenomena that may be related to one aspect of psychotherapy—the relief of suffering through mobilization of healing emotional states, especially those linked to expectation of help. The goal of psychotherapy, however, usually is more ambitious than this. It seeks to bring about enduring modifications in the patient's assumptive world that will enable him to function more effectively. This chapter reviews two influencing procedures that may cast some light on this process—religious revivals and Communist thought reform. These procedures are difficult to consider dispassionately because they raise issues involving our deepest convictions. It should therefore be stressed that this chapter considers thought reform and revivalism only from the standpoint of their bearing on psychotherapy. Our interest is exclusively in their means of attempting to produce attitude changes and the determinants of their effectiveness. Questions about the desirability of the attitude changes, the moral implications of the methods, or the validity of the world views underlying them are ignored as irrelevant to our present purposes.

Thought reform will receive considerably more attention than religious revivalism because the issues it raises are not complicated by the question of supernatural intervention and because it has been intensively studied and reported upon by social scientists in recent years. But certain aspects of religious revivalism are similar enough to psychotherapeutic processes to warrant brief consideration.

RELIGIOUS REVIVALISM

The goal of religious revivalism is to produce conversions. In general terms a conversion may be characterized as a change in a person's assumptive world, involving inter-related shifts in his attitudes towards his God, himself, and the people significant to him. It can have any degree of scope, depth, and permanence. The term includes the rather undramatic re-discovery and re-affirmation of religious beliefs that had lapsed out of awareness, and the transient conversion of a person who "comes forward" at a revival meeting but is his former self again by the next morning. Our interest will be confined to sudden conversions characterized by drastic and far-reaching psychic upheavals, usually accompanied by strong emotion and leading to permanent changes in attitude and behavior.[1]

A sudden religious conversion is usually preceded by a period of misery, characterized by tormenting self-doubts, feelings of sinfulness, and self-castigation. The person feels himself to be a sinner, unable to find God or abandoned by him. At the moment of conversion he feels closer to God and confident of his favor. As with miracle cures, this experience is intensely emotional and may be followed by a sense of inner joy and peace.[2] The change in the convert's perception of himself in relation to the deity implies certain changes in his picture of himself and of others, and changes in his patterns of social participation. The invocation of supernatural forces to support certain attitudes may resolve certain intrapersonal conflicts and so promote personality integration. It also enhances the convert's sense of self-worth at the same time that he paradoxically feels a new sense of humility. The paradox is only apparent, however, for it is hard to conceive of a greater source of inner strength and personal security than the conviction that one is God's chosen instrument. Some persons for whom the convert previously had felt contempt or anger, such as a long-suffering spouse or parent, become objects of love and admiration. Others whom he had admired and emulated become persons to be shunned as evil, or targets for proselytizing. He forsakes his previous haunts and cronies and characteristically joins the group that converted him.

Persons who have conversion experiences in isolation usually, if not invariably, have previously had an intense relationship with a mentor or group[3] promulgating the ideology that the convert embraces. This person or group, moreover, is deeply concerned for the welfare of the penitent. General William Booth, the founder of the Salvation Army, is quoted as saying: "The first vital step in saving outcasts consists in making them feel that some decent human being cares enough for them to take an interest in the question whether they are to rise or to sink."[4]

In the modern Western world evangelistic revivals are important means of producing conversions. These events are characterized by high emotional intensity.[5] Before the evangelist comes to town, there may be a preliminary build-up through publicity and sermons, which creates some anticipatory excitement, arouses latent feelings of guilt, and holds out the hope of relief through salvation. The meetings themselves are highly emotional. The impact of the dramatic pleas, threats, and exhortations of the evangelist may be intensified through the singing of highly emotional gospel hymns by the entire audience, led by a choir and soloists. Billy Graham's revivals sometimes have a choir of fifteen hundred.[6] In susceptible persons the emotional excitation may be sufficient to produce manifestations of dissociation such as "speaking in tongues," shaking, and convulsions, similar to signs of "possession" in non-Christian religions such as voodoo.

The revivalist tries to arouse feelings of sin, guilt, and fear in his hearers by harping on their wickedness and the dire punishments that await those who do not repent. At the same time he dwells on the bliss that awaits them if they confess their sins, ask God's forgiveness, and mend their ways. The relative emphasis on these two contrapuntal themes seems to vary considerably with different evangelists and at different periods of history. Great evangelists of previous eras, like Jonathan Edwards and John Wesley, dwelt on the horrors of damnation, while some modern evangelistic movements, such as the Salvation Army, stress the joys of salvation.[7]

The effectiveness of revivalistic services varies in different epochs. At Billy Graham's revivals in Great Britain, an average of only about 2.5 per cent of the attenders "came forward," and only about half of these converts were active a year later.[8] Though no precise figures are available, Wesley's percentage of conversions must have been much higher. There are probably several reasons for this. God's wrath was much more vivid to man in the eighteenth than in the twentieth century, and emotionally Graham's revivals must be but a pale shadow of Wesley's. Moreover, Wesley recognized the importance of a like-minded group in sustaining the assumptive world of its members. Hence he placed great stress on continuing class meetings to consolidate and strengthen the new world view. He divided his converts into groups of not more than twelve, who met weekly under an appointed leader. Problems relating to their conversion and their future mode of life were discussed in agreed secrecy. The leader kept close watch for evidences of backsliding, and members who "grew cold and gave way to the sins which had long easily beset them"[9] were expelled from both the classes and the Methodist Society.

Very little can be said with assurance about the personal qualities that make for a successful evangelist. Some highly successful ones have led disorderly lives or been financially unscrupulous. Some great historical religious leaders might be considered psychotic by today's standards. Their delusions and hallucinations, however, must have been couched in terms that gained them wide cultural acceptance as veridical. Probably all successful evangelists have a deep religious conviction, a capacity for vivid, intense emotional experiences, which they can successfully communicate to others, sensitivity to audience response, and great organizational ability. Personal prestige may also contribute to an evangelist's success. Billy Graham, for example, gained a higher percentage of conversions during his English tour than did his assistants.

There is equally little firm knowledge concerning social and personal factors that might contribute to susceptibility to conversions. Revivalistic or messianic religions, whose adherents have dramatic, emotionally charged conversion experiences, flourish in societies that are in the throes of change, as in preliterate societies under the impact of contact with the West. The resurgence of religious revivalism in the Western world today may be a reflection of the confusion and anxiety elicited by the rapidly changing conditions of life created by atomic energy and vastly improved methods of communication and transportation, the end results of which no man can foresee.

Social conditions creating misery and frustration afford fertile soil for revivalistic cults. For example, voodoo, which is extremely emotional and involves possession by deities, is the dominant religion of a people the majority of whom "are doomed to a life without one moment's relief from the most desperate, nerve-wracking struggle to eke out daily subsistence."[10]

In affluent societies, though the evidence is inconclusive, there seems to be some tendency for evangelistic sects to flourish more among the economically or socially underprivileged. As adherents of these sects rise in the economic and social scale and have increased opportunities for worldly satisfactions, they tend to leave the sects, or the religious observances of the sects themselves become less dramatically emotional, as demonstrated for example by the evolution of Quakerism and Methodism in Western society.

It seems plausible that the ecstasies of evangelical religions provide outlets for pent-up emotional tensions, relief from the impoverishment and monotony of daily life, and a gratification of important psychological needs. This gratification includes a glimpse of an after-world in which the roles of oppressed and oppressor will be reversed. The ecstatic experience of union with God is a sign that the convert is "saved," and thus evidence of the intercession of infinitely powerful forces on his behalf. In these ways revivalistic religions probably help their adherents to maintain their personal integration in the face of widespread and enduring frustrations.

Individual personal attributes related to general susceptibility to influence seem to predispose to conversion experiences. Thus extroverts, hysterics, persons with low self-esteem, and those with undue fear of social disapproval, seem to be good candidates. As with miracle cures, the passionate skeptic may be quite susceptible. Many persons seem to have become suddenly converted at revival meetings while in a state of high indignation at the proceedings.[11] Only the emotionally detached are immune. In short, confusion, guilt, or frustration springing from personal characteristics or social conditions seem to heighten the attractiveness of revivalistic religions and enhance their effectiveness. This suggests that these feelings may increase a person's susceptibility to emotionally charged methods of influence that offer detailed guides to behavior, based on an inclusive, infallible assumptive world, which also strongly arouses hope.[12]

THOUGHT REFORM

It may seem odd that attempts by Communist governments to produce confessions could aid understanding of either religious revivalism or psychotherapy. Certainly, thought reform or brain-washing differs strikingly from each of them in many respects. Yet certain similarities of aims and methods are also marked and have considerable theoretical interest. The relevance for psychotherapy of both evangelical Christianity and communism lies in their heroic efforts to win converts, since these activities cast light on ways of inducing attitude changes. Proselytizing in both is motivated and guided by a systematic, comprehensive world view, which purports to govern every aspect of the thinking and behavior of its disciples. Though the Communist assumptive world has no place for supernatural powers, it incorporates a suprapersonal one that has many of the attributes Christianity invests in God. This is the Party, to which all Communists are expected to submit themselves willingly, absolutely, and unquestioningly. Through being the obedient instrument of this power, the individual gains a feeling of value in his own eyes and in those of his compatriots.

Thought reform resembles both religious healing and revivalism in utilizing emotional arousal and group pressures to achieve its goals. It differs from them in that its subjects are incarcerated, so all aspects of their lives can be controlled, and in that it is a prolonged process with open-ended goals rather than a brief one with a circumscribed goal.[13.] These properties lead to considerable differences in the means of emotional arousal and application of group pressures, and to much greater emphasis on the confession, which becomes a detailed life history, obtained in the setting of a prolonged intense relationship between subject and interrogator.

At first glance it seems hard to imagine anything more different than psychotherapy and thought reform. Psychotherapy is a form of treatment; thought reform is a method of indoctrination. Psychotherapy characteristically attempts to help persons in distress; thought reform creates distress in its objects as a way of facilitating the indoctrination process. Psychotherapists usually adhere to the same world view as their patients, and the success of psychotherapy may depend in part on the extent to which this is true.[14] The assumptive worlds of the person undergoing thought reform and his interrogator are opposed in essential respects. Outpatient psychotherapy exerts only the mildest overt pressures, if any. Practitioners of thought reform do not hesitate to apply the most extreme forms of pressure.

Although the differences between psychotherapy of outpatients who voluntarily seek help and thought reform are relatively clear cut, they are less distinct with regard to the treatment of patients hospitalized against their will[15] or of sociopaths. The latter group, especially, give one pause. Like persons subjected to thought reform, they are not in distress, and the goal of treatment is to modify their assumptive world in the direction of the psychotherapist's, who represents the larger society. It is also likely that such individuals can only be successfully treated—i.e., re-educated—if they are incarcerated and subjected to firm discipline, which characteristically creates considerable emotional distress in them. And this is a reminder that all psychotherapy tries to modify certain assumptive systems of its patients, along lines which, the therapist believes, will help them to function better, and that this process inevitably creates distress.

Finally the very respect in which thought reform differs sharply from revivalism is the one in which it most closely resembles psychotherapy—the detailed, open-ended review of past history in a setting of a prolonged, intense relationship between a distressed person and a person whom he perceives as having some control over his welfare. In this connection, the typical interrogator, as a convinced Communist, probably regards himself, in a sense, as a therapist. In his own eyes he is trying to help the prisoner become a better, more effective person by helping him to see the error of his ways and accept his penance, after which he is ready to become a full-fledged member of the new society. Moreover, like the psychotherapist, he may have considerable emotional investment in the prisoner's progress, not only because his success strengthens his own self-image and his confidence in his world view,[16] but also because his own security depends on getting results. In this he shows a faint parallel to the psychiatrist-in-training whose standing with his teachers and colleagues depends on his therapeutic success.

Under these circumstances, an intense relationship might develop between interrogator and prisoner, similar in some respects to that between patient and therapist in long-term psychotherapy. The prisoner might become very dependent on the interrogator, as his sole potential source of help, and the interrogator might be genuinely concerned at the prisoner's recalcitrance. There are even reports of prisoners confessing in order to help the interrogator out of a difficult situation. In addition, as in psychotherapy, each might come to project onto the other personal attitudes towards important persons in his own life—so-called transference and countertransference reactions.

These parallels suggest that scrutiny of thought reform might increase our understanding of certain aspects of psychotherapy. The account of thought reform which follows considers primarily the Chinese form, which has more points of relevance to psychotherapy than its Russian counterpart. In particular, it relies less on physical torture than on psychological pressures, especially the manipulation of group forces, and its goal seems to be to secure a genuine conversion rather than merely to obtain a confession. The following discussion is based on first-hand accounts and interviews with American military prisoners in the Korean war, Chinese civilian military prisoners, and Chinese intellectuals who underwent indoctrination in a

"revolutionary college." The last-named are especially interesting because they were not subjected to the physical hardships that tend to obscure the psychological features of the
process with prisoners. Material from first-hand descriptions
by Russian prisoners is mentioned where it seems pertinent.
Reports from all these sources confirm each other to such a
degree that they create considerable confidence in the general
picture that emerges from them.[17]

The account includes aspects of thought reform that appear
very different from most forms of psychotherapy, especially
the use of harassment and the mobilization of strong group
pressures. If the reader will be patient with these seeming
irrelevancies, their pertinence will eventually become apparent.[18]

The processes of thought reform can be conveniently grouped
according to three interrelated aspects—emotional arousal, total
milieu control, and the interrogation. Methods of thought reform attempt to produce an intense, disorganizing emotional
state in their subjects, to cut them off as completely as possible
from all social supports of their previous world view, and to
immerse them in a social milieu that consistently and uniformly represents the Communist one. The actual influencing
effort comes to a focus in the interrogation and confession,
which have both individual and group aspects.

The emotional build-up started some time before the arrest
when the marked person began to sense from his progressive
isolation that something was in the wind.[19] Friends stopped
visiting him, acquaintances crossed the street to avoid speaking
to him, and if he was a teacher he might discover letters by
his students in the newspapers criticizing his lectures. The
tension aroused by the premonitory period was heightened by
the method of arrest, which was calculated to intensify the
prisoner's apprehensiveness and demoralization. Russians
characteristically arrested persons secretly in the early morning
hours, when one is apt to feel most solitary and helpless.
Chinese tended to go to the opposite extreme, making arrests

in broad daylight with maximum public humiliation. A principal of a Jesuit college, for example, had to confront groups of jeering school children and pass through a denunciatory mob of his students.

American prisoners of war also underwent devastating emotional experiences before the actual indoctrination program began. These were precipitated by their capture, which led to a calamitous fall in their standard of living and an abrupt and drastic withdrawal of sustaining group forces. By the time they reached the prison camp, many had lost all sense of discipline or of responsibility to their fellow soldiers: "They refused to obey orders . . . . At first the badly wounded suffered most . . . the able-bodied refused to carry them, even when their officers commanded them to do so . . . the strong regularly took food from the weak. There was no discipline to prevent it."[20]

Once in prison, emotional tension was increased by both physical and psychological means. The degree of physical maltreatment varied considerably and sometimes, as with the Chinese intellectuals, was nonexistent, so it cannot be regarded as a necessary ingredient of thought reform. Also, much of it may have been inadvertent and simply reflected the generally less comfortable living conditions of the Chinese. Nevertheless, for many prisoners even the unplanned stresses were severe. They could not sleep on boards or stomach the food. But deliberate tortures were also used, especially with recalcitrant prisoners, such as depriving them of sleep,[21] beating them, manacling their hands behind their backs for long periods, and forcing them to stand until their feet were badly swollen and then applying pressure to them, which was excruciatingly painful.

Psychological harassment might be very severe. Its three major forms were the creation of uncertainty and anxiety about the future, personal humiliation, and manipulation of privacy. A distressing aspect of both military and civilian prison life was uncertainty about what would happen next. Lenient and harsh treatment alternated unpredictably. Civilian prisoners never knew when their confession was adequate, when they would be tried and sentenced, when they would be transferred to another prison, or even if they were going to be taken out and summarily shot. War prisoners feared that they might die, that they might never be repatriated, and that no one even knew they were alive. Thus present miseries were compounded by fear that the worst was yet to come, with death ever lurking in the background.

Personal humiliation took many forms. On admission to prison, civilians had to surrender their clothes and personal belongings, including all status identifications, and the treatment they received was determined solely by their "progress." Military prisoners were similarly deprived of all insignia of rank and the personal recognition accorded them was guided solely by the degree to which they collaborated or resisted. The details of prison life could be made occasions for severe humiliation. For example, when a person's hands are manacled behind his back, he has to eat like an animal and to depend on others to help him perform his excretory functions. Sometimes such a prisoner would be forced to stand for hours over the bucket used for excreta.

A powerful form of harassment was manipulation of privacy. Consistent with the differences in their methods of arrest, Russians and Chinese seemed to go to opposite extremes in this regard. Russian prisoners often had to undergo prolonged isolation. The prisoners of the Chinese, on the other hand, were placed in crowded cells, in which it was impossible to escape from one's fellows, even for an instant. For some this was probably at least as trying as isolation would have been, perhaps more so.

The emotion-arousing psychological pressures on the students in the revolutionary college were for the most part more subtle than those applied to prisoners, but, after an initial "honeymoon" period, apprehension about the future played some part, and group pressures might be extreme. In any case, some of the students, at least among those who defected (the only ones available for interviews) underwent considerable emotional turmoil and some felt deeply resentful.

Prolonged misery, frustration, and uncertainty tended to dull prisoners' critical faculties and weaken their capacity to withstand the continual and ubiquitous pressures to adopt the Communist world view. The Chinese immersed the prisoner or student completely in an "airtight communication system" characterized by "a highly charged morality and an absolute doctrinal authority for the 'correctness' of any solution or point of view,"[22] and permitted him to receive or send communications only in terms of this system. "Input" from the outer world was severely reduced and systematically manipulated so as to weaken his ties with his former groups. Communist literature was the only available reading matter. Prisoners learned only of Communist "victories" and American "atrocities." All incoming and outgoing mail was read, and only those communications allowed to pass in either direction that would estrange the prisoner from his loved ones or worry him about them. The Communists also attempted to make all of the prisoners' and students' "output" conform to their world view. Communications that indicated acceptance of the Communist position were rewarded, while all others were rejected. Prolonged, severe conflict between inner beliefs and outer behavior is hard to stand, so the enforcement of behavioral conformity tends eventually to bring about changes in one's belief system to harmonize with it.[23]

Measures were designed to prevent the formation of ties among prisoners that would strengthen their ability to resist.[24] The Chinese for example, fostered the breakdown of group cohesiveness in American prisoners of war. They watched for the emergence of structured groups and promptly transferred their leaders. They fomented mutual distrust by encouraging and rewarding informers. They would, for example, interrogate a prisoner about some aspect of his activities, no matter how trivial, obtained from an informer, show him a signed statement from another prisoner revealing information he had withheld, or bestow special favors upon noncollaborators as if they were collaborators. A public confession or a propaganda lecture by a prisoner was especially demoralizing, "because only if resistance had been *unanimous* could a man solidly believe that his values were correct, even if he could not defend them logically."[25] The encouragement of self-criticism and group confessions, considered below, inevitably led persons to reveal more than they had intended, however innocuously they might begin, and this would increase their motivation to get others to produce self-damaging material as well. In short, the Chinese "evolved a means of isolating every person emotionally from every other person, permitting each to turn only to the system for guidance and friendship."[26]

Furthermore, the Communists tried to present their society as affording better opportunities to achieve the prisoner's values than his own society did. With American prisoners of war they harped on the injustices and inequalities of American life and portrayed themselves as fighting for justice, decency, racial equality, and the like. Their manner and words were usually solicitous and sympathetic, and they played the role of "benevolent but handicapped captor."[27] They reminded the Americans that they were being treated just as well as the average Chinese. At the same time they never ceased to point out that American Air Force bombings were responsible for their inadequate supplies. Thus in a sense they tried to make the prisoners feel responsible for their own plight.

The focal point of the indoctrination process was the interrogation, which had individual and group forms. The general strategy of both was to obtain as much information from the prisoner as possible, including the apparently innocuous and irrelevant, and use it to undermine his own assumptive world and prevail upon him to adopt the Communist one. The preparation of a "confession" was the chief means to this end, as well as a way of gauging the prisoner's "progress." In its full-blown form, as required of the intellectuals at the revolutionary colleges and civilian prisoners, the confession was a detailed life history. Since wrong thoughts as well as wrong deeds were crimes, the confession included not only an account of alleged crimes and the events that led up to them, but also of attitudes and motives and their sources in the prisoner's early life. All of this had to be expressed in such a way as to demonstrate his complete and unqualified acceptance of the Communist world view.

Confessions were produced partly by group pressures, of which the most severe form was the "tou-cheng," or accusation process. In this, each group member had to criticize himself before the others, going into all his supposed misdeeds and his motives, while they hammered away at him to confess still more. Since the whole group was held responsible for the progress of each member, a recalcitrant one often was subjected to the severest pressure: "a 'tou-cheng' consisted of many gathering around a prisoner, shouting at him, insulting him, pointing fingers at him, while he usually stood with head down. Often a 'tou-cheng' lasted for hours. Few could stand it very long."[28] Mutual criticism, by keeping all the members angry at each other, incidentally helped to forestall development of resistance-strengthening bonds between members.

At the revolutionary college, the preparation of each student's confession was primarily a group process. With prisoners it was largely obtained through the interrogation, in which each prisoner was seen singly, although more than one interrogator might be present and usually there was a secretary taking notes.

The interrogator's attitudes were a combination of complete rigidity in some respects and equally complete ambiguity in others. He maintained an absolutely dogmatic and inflexible conviction of the prisoner's guilt, but gave no clues as to what the content of his confession should be: "Just confess your crimes and all will be forgiven! No one is clearly told what crimes he is charged with . . . but he must confess the crimes he is charged with."[29] Although never told what to confess, the prisoner might undergo any degree of punishment from mild disapproval to torture if the confession was not what the interrogator wanted. No matter what he confessed, it was never enough, but he was continually offered the hope that once he made a proper and complete confession he would be repatriated, if a war prisoner, or be permitted to start serving his sentence, if a political one.

The flavor of the interrogation process with a co-operative prisoner is conveyed in the following brief excerpt from the account of an American woman who, incidentally, was largely converted to the Communist viewpoint. The interchange is not too dissimilar from what might go on in long-term psychotherapy. Ostensibly the procedure is completely permissive—responsibility for producing pertinent material rests entirely with the prisoner. But there is an implicit threat of unfortunate consequences if she does not make a full and correct confession, perhaps analogous to the psychiatric patient's fear of not getting relief if he does not co-operate fully. In the end, the prisoner "voluntarily" comes to think of her past life in the conceptual framework of the Chinese and her conversion is well underway: " (The assistant interrogator) asked: 'Do you feel that you have finished, Li-Yu-An (the prisoner's Chinese name) ?' "

> "Yes," I replied. "I can think of nothing more."
> "Well, we feel there are some points you have missed, and we would like you to go on thinking a bit more . . . it is to the interest of both of you [the prisoner and her husband, also a prisoner but separated from her] that you get all possible details cleared up. We will not force you in any way, but we would like you to think about your history and your activities some more. Is there anything in your history that you have failed to make a clean breast of?"
> I stared at him hopelessly for a moment. "But I have thought and thought these past few weeks and there just isn't any more. Can't you give me a hint, or some line toward which to direct my thoughts?"

"That would be no help. You just think if there is anything at all that should be cleared up . . . ."

For the next six weeks I sat and thought . . . .

[I] began to look at our actions from the standpoint of the Chinese. . . . I tackled the problem from the standpoint of what I felt they wanted about us and not from what I considered wrong myself.[30]

Since everyone has thought or done things of which he is ashamed, a detailed review of his past acts and thoughts is bound to reveal some sources of guilt, and the interrogator played upon these. In addition, under the pressures of thought reform the prisoner almost inevitably committed acts in conflict with his ideals and his self-image, such as false denunciation of former associates, friends, and family members. "Everyone was required to denounce at least one other person who had 'recruited' him . . . and as many other people as possible whom he had himself . . . induced to commit political crimes. . . . [This] necessarily incriminated others and to the conscientious [it] presented a terrible moral problem."[31]

The interrogator harped on guilt from these and other sources, thereby demonstrating to the victim that his own ideology could not protect him and offering him one that would give him absolution. The interrogation thus tended to mobilize the prisoner's inner conflicts.[32] His confusion was further intensified by his state of physical and emotional exhaustion. In this condition he might be expected to seize on hints or suggestions of the interrogator that seemed to offer a means of resolving the conflicts and achieving some cognitive clarity.[33] At first he might be uncertain as to whether the idea was his or the interrogator's, especially since his mental alertness was reduced. The interrogator, however, by pointing out that the prisoner had said it first, could progressively persuade him to accept it as true.

Two other related aspects of thought reform deserve special mention because of their pertinence to psychotherapy—participation and repetition. Thought reform forces the person to participate actively in bringing about his own change of attitude. In the Russian form "the method of interrogation . . . consisted of making it the arrested man's primary task to build up the whole case against himself. . . . (He) . . . not only had to invent his own 'legend' but . . . to do his utmost to make it plausible in every detail . . . ."[34] In the Chinese revolutionary college "each group member had to demonstrate the genuiness of his reform through continuous personal enthusiasm and active participation in the criticism of his fellow students,"[35] and in the prisoner of war camps "some kind of verbal or written response was always demanded . . . . The Chinese apparently believed that if they could once get a man to participate . . . eventually he would accept the attitudes which the participation expressed."[36]

The repetitive quality of thought reform is apparent from the above descriptions of it. The same material was gone over again and again, and the interrogators never tired of repeating their demands or expressing the Communist viewpoint. Many prisoners of war stated that "most of the techniques used gained their effectiveness by being used in this repetitive way until the prisoner could no longer sustain his resistance."[37]

The cumulative effects of the influencing procedure in thought reform might be sufficiently intense to cause prisoners to confess sincerely to "crimes" that they could not possibly have committed. One, for example, described in circumstantial detail and with full conviction how he had tried to attract the attention of an official representative of his country who passed by the door of his cell, only to discover that no such person had been anywhere near his prison at the time.[38]

Completion of the confession to the interrogator's satisfaction meant surcease from torment and the re-integration of the prisoner's world view along lines that would enable him to become a valued member of the group. It was therefore often accompanied by a feeling of relief and even joy analogous to that following a religious conversion.

As with psychotherapy and revivalism the effectiveness of

thought reform with different types of persons is hard to evaluate. Under the enormous pressures exerted, no one could avoid complying to some extent, and even the most stout-hearted might sign and then repudiate several confessions. As one of these writes: "Almost every prisoner embarked on a program of confessing every possible crime he ever committed or could have committed."[39] That this forced compliance occasionally led to genuine internationalization of the new outlook, especially in Chinese prisoners, is suggested by the following passage:

"My cell mates were fired with the desire to be a part of the new China, and the feeling that they were criminals outside of it all weighed heavily on them . . . . No longer was it just a question of reforming simply to avoid punishment. Now there was a positive hope for a vital and fruitful future in helping the new country."[40]

Whether the attitudinal change was sustained or not probably depended to a large extent on whether it was supported by the world view of the group that the prisoner entered after his release. Presumably some Chinese remained loyal disciples of Chinese communism. Available data on repatriated military and civilian Americans, on the other hand, indicate that very few were fully converted to communism, and many who were partly shaken returned to their former value system after being reimmersed in American culture. Even the extreme pressures of thought reform seem unable in themselves to produce long-lasting changes unless they are sustained by subsequent group support.[41]

Finally, a word should be said about the kinds of persons who succumbed or resisted. Obviously, the greater the prisoner's conviction of the correctness of his world view and the more firmly it was anchored in his group identifications, the less likely would he be to become a convert. In fact, the harsh measures used against him might serve mainly to harden his resistance by mobilizing his resentment. Thus four years of extreme pressure served only to confirm a Jesuit more firmly in his rejection of the Communist viewpoint. The only statistical data available are on American prisoners in the Korean war, and they reveal nothing very startling. The collaborators, who comprised about 15 per cent of the prisoners, tended to occupy a low status position in American society, suggesting that they had grounds for dissatisfaction with it and would be more accessible to a philosophy apparently devoted to the welfare of the underdog. The 80 per cent on whom the Army had compiled no convincing derogatory information differed from both the collaborators and the 5 per cent who actively resisted in being more detached. They "withdrew from the prison environment . . . [and] . . . 'blended with the scenery' . . . and . . . came out of internment as see-ers, hearers, and speakers of less 'evil' or 'good' than their fellows."[42] Performance on various psychological tests tended to support the impression that the middle group was less emotionally involved than either the collaborators or the resisters.[43]

SUMMARY

As thought reform, revivalist religion, miracle cures, and religious healing in primitive societies have important common features that will be found to bear on psychotherapy, a brief recapitulation of these characteristics may be in order at this point. Since the English language lacks a common word for invalid, penitent, and prisoner on the one hand and shaman, evangelist, and interrogator on the other, the first categories will be referred to as sufferers and the second as persuaders. The sufferer's distress has a large emotional component, produced by environmental or bodily stresses, internal conflicts and confusion, and a sense of estrangement or isolation from his usual sources of group support. He tends to be fearful and despairing and to be hungry for supportive human contacts.

The persuader and his group represent a comprehensive and

pervasive world view, which incorporates supremely powerful suprapersonal forces. That communism identifies these forces with the Party, while religions regard them as supernatural is relatively unimportant for the purpose of this discussion. The world view is infallible and cannot be shaken by the sufferer's failure to change or improve. The suprapersonal powers are contingently benevolent in that the sufferer may succeed in obtaining their favor if he shows the right attitude. In return for submitting himself completely to them he is offered the hope of surcease from suffering, resolution of conflicts, absolution of guilt, and warm acceptance, or re-acceptance, by the group. The persuader is the point of interaction between the sufferer, his immediate group, and the suprapersonal powers. He guides the group's activities and embodies, transmits, interprets, and to some extent controls the suprapersonal forces. As a result the sufferer perceives him as possessing power over his welfare.

The means by which changes in the sufferer are brought about include a particular type of relationship and some sort of systematic activity or ritual. The essence of the relationship is that the persuader invests great effort to bring about changes in the sufferer's bodily state or attitudes that he regards as beneficial. The systematic activity characteristically involves means of emotional arousal, often to the point of exhaustion. This may be highly unpleasant, but it occurs in a context of hope and potential support from the persuader and group.

The activity requires the participation of the sufferer, persuader, and group and frequently is highly repetitive. The sufferer may be required to review his past life in more or less detail, with emphasis on occasions when he may have fallen short of the behavior required by the world view, thus mobilizing guilt, which can only be expiated by confession and penance. This serves to detach him from his former patterns of behavior and social intercourse and facilitates his acceptance by the group representing the ideology to which he becomes converted.

If the process succeeds, the sufferer experiences a sense of relief, peace, and often joy. His sense of identity is restored and his feeling of self-worth enhanced. His confusion and conflicts have diminished or been resolved. He is clear about himself and his world view and feels himself to be in harmony with his old group, or with a new one representing the new world view, and with the universe. Life regains its meaning or becomes more meaningful. He is able to function effectively again as a significant member of a group which, by its acceptance, helps to consolidate the changes he has undergone.

From the standpoint of psychotherapy, religious healing, revivalism, and thought reform all highlight the importance of emotions in facilitating or producing attitude change and in affecting one's state of health. Some degree of emotional involvement seems to be a prerequisite for susceptibility to any of these procedures. Maintenance of emotional detachment is the most effective form of resistance to them. Religious healing underscores the inseparability of mental and physical states. Thought reform and revivalism highlight the importance of a person's immediate social milieu in sustaining or shaking his self-image and world view. They also underline the function of detailed review of the sufferer's past history, with special emphasis on guilt-arousing episodes, followed by opportunity for confession and atonement, as a means of producing attitude modification.

"That's very important," the King said . . . . "*Un*important
your majesty means, of course," the White Rabbit said
in a very respectful tone, but frowning and making faces at
him as he spoke. "*Un*important, of course, I meant," the
King hastily said. (*Alice's Adventures in Wonderland,*
Chapter 12)

6 Experimental Studies of Persuasion

Far from the hurly-burly of the scenes described in
previous chapters psychologists in laboratories are patiently
teasing out the essential ingredients of the processes by which
one person influences another. Since, in psychotherapy, the
therapist tries to influence his patients, their experimental findings are pertinent to our interest.

In order to manipulate and control variables, experiments
must drastically simplify phenomena they study, so it is often
hard to evaluate the relevance of their findings to "real life."
But what they lose in general applicability they gain in certainty. The facts that the experimentalist turns up often seem
insignificant to the clinician, but at least one can be reasonably
sure that they are really facts and not misinterpretations resulting from the observer's bias.

Three areas of psychological research on the influencing
process seem especially relevant to psychotherapy: the effects of

participation on attitude change, changes in the content of a person's speech produced by very slight signals given by the experimenter, and the effect of an anticipated audience on memory.

All methods of promoting healing or attitude change through personal influence seem to require the object of the influence to participate actively in the proceedings. He must do much of the work himself. Moreover, characteristically the nature of his activities is not completely prescribed, so that he must take some initiative. The contents of his confession, for example, in religious healing, revival meetings, and thought reform are always up to him. The persuader merely keeps urging him to confess more, sometimes backing this up by stating that he already knows what the sins or crimes are, but without telling him what he knows. The universality of this procedure suggests that an individual may be more likely to change his attitude if he can be brought to participate in the process himself, and especially if he assumes some of the initiative. Some experimental studies support this hypothesis.

One experiment compared the effects on attitude change of playing roles and of observing others play the roles.[1] In role-playing, a person tries to act the part of someone else. He knows in general how that person should behave and what he stands for, but he is not told precisely what to do or say. For example, two persons might be asked to play the respective roles of an employer opposed to a closed shop and a union leader who wants to unionize the employer's business, as they try to reach an agreement. Since the behavior of each participant depends in part on the other's response to his previous act, the course of such an interaction is not fully predictable and role-players must do considerable improvising.

The experiment used three groups of fifteen college students in simple role-playing situations of this sort. In each experiment, two played the roles and the others observed. Each student was rotated through three experimental conditions. In the first he played a role. In the second he sat on the sidelines and tried to identify himself with the person playing the role, and in the third he was asked to be a strictly objective observer. After each session the students filled out a questionnaire and participated in an informal discussion led by the experimenter. Information obtained from these sources showed that the first condition caused the greatest susceptibility to change. That is, if a student assumed the role of a person with whom he disagreed, he was more likely to change his opinion to conform to that person's views than if he tried to identify with, or merely observed, someone else playing the role.

The finding that participation conduces to opinion change receives support from a rather elaborate but very carefully controlled experiment that attempted to influence the preferences of seventh grade children for jungle or fantastic comic books.[2] First, the children had to fill out a questionnaire in which they stated their preferences. Then a speaker gave a talk to the class in which he asserted that jungle books were more suitable than fantastic hero stories. Immediately afterwards the children were asked to write essays in favor of one kind of comic or the other. Three conditions of incentive were used. In all, the children were told that anyone who wrote in favor of fantastic hero stories (that is, against the speaker's view) would get a free book. One group, which served as a control, received no other incentive. The second received a high incentive to write in favor of jungle comics. They were told that anyone who did so would receive both a small and a large prize. The third was given a low incentive to write in favor of jungle comics, which also spurred them to competition. They were told that all who wrote in favor of jungle comics would be *eligible* for a large prize but only a few would get it. Thus each child in the low incentive group was confronted with the alternative of writing in favor of fantastic hero stories and being sure of a small prize, or of writing in favor of jungle comics and taking a chance on winning either a big prize or none at all. A week later all children were again given the preference questionnaire.

The experimenter was especially interested in the relative effects of the high and low incentive conditions on conformity and opinion change. Conformity was determined simply by whether the children wrote in favor of jungle stories, which the speaker advocated. Opinion change was measured by changes in answers to the preference questionnaire when it was given the second time.

The high incentive group showed the greatest conformity, but also more negativism and resentment. The low incentive group showed the greatest opinion change. Moreover, their stories were longer, of better quality, and showed more improvisation than those of the high incentive group. There are several possible interpretations of these findings.[3] For our purposes the significant point is that the increased effort elicited by the low incentive conditions (as judged by the better quality of the essays) was associated with greater attitude change. One source of the greater inner participation of the low incentive children was that they had to compete for a prize. Another may have been that they were offered balanced alternatives. Under these conditions, the child would be more likely to feel that his conformity resulted from his own free choice, whereas in the high incentive condition he would feel that he was yielding to external pressure. The finding that the low incentive children felt less resentment supports this view. In short, this experiment suggests that an influencing technique that is felt to be "permissive" and that mobilizes initiative and improvisation is more effective in producing internal attitude change than one that exerts obvious pressure towards conformity.

Another experiment demonstrating that causing a person to improvise is an effective way of influencing him was conducted with male college students.[4] Several months before the experiment their opinions were obtained, by means of a question-naire, about when they would be drafted and how long they would have to serve. In the experiment they were randomly divided into three equivalent groups. All received the same persuasive and personally meaningful written statement, which presented arguments in support of two main conclusions: that over 90 per cent of college students would be drafted within a year after graduation and that the majority of these would be required to serve a year longer than current draftees. Sub-jects in the first group were asked to study the script, put it aside, and then play the role of a sincere advocate of the view-point it expressed. Members of the second group were asked to read it aloud as effectively as they could. They were told that their talk would be tape recorded and presented later to a group of judges. The purpose was to give them as much incentive to do a good job as the first group, but to give them no opportunity to improvise. The third group simply read the statement to themselves. Immediately afterwards each student filled out the questionnaire he had received several months before. Opinion change was measured by changes in replies to the questions.

Only the first group, which had to improvise, showed a signi-ficant opinion change in the direction of the communication. By suitable analyses of the data the experimenters showed that this could not be attributable either to greater attention to the material or greater satisfaction with their performance than was experienced by the two control groups. They concluded that the crucial factor is improvisation. When a person has to improvise, he thinks up "exactly the kinds of arguments, illus-trations and motivating appeals that he regards as most con-vincing . . . [he] . . . is induced to 'hand-tailor' the content so as to take account of the unique motives and predispositions of one particular person—namely himself."[5] In improvising, the person not only emphasizes the arguments most convincing to him, but pays less attention to conflicting thoughts such as opposing arguments, doubts as to the persuader's trust-worthiness, and anticipations of unfavorable consequences that might follow from adopting the persuader's position.

The psychotherapist would like to know not only what conditions facilitate attitude change, but also what kinds of persons are most susceptible to these conditions. Everyone knows that some people are more suggestible or malleable than others, but it has proved difficult to define these characteristics precisely, and relate them to the person's tendency to yield to various forms of pressure. There are fragmentary experimental data, however, on personality attributes connected with the ease with which one is persuaded to change his opinion by the unanimous pressure of a group or by a written communication, which are worth a glance.

In the group pressure experiments, each subject heard other members of a group make a particular judgment before he was called upon to do so. Unknown to him, the other members were simply recorded voices. This technique permits precise manipulation of group pressures. In one such experiment subjects who had been given a paper and pencil test for submissiveness were asked to judge the number of clicks of a metronome. The most marked yielding to the uniformly incorrect answers given by the simulated group occurred in subjects rated as submissive on the test, when disclosure of personal identity was required. They showed significantly less yielding when allowed to remain anonymous. Rate of yielding for subjects rated as ascendant on the test was unrelated to disclosure of personal identity. The experimenters conclude that an important source of the susceptibility to group pressures of submissive persons is the possibility of being criticized or held accountable for deviations from the group.[6]

This finding seems consistent with the results of another study in which the entire process of persuasion was public. The design was similar to that of the improvisation experiment described above, except that three different communications and two different conditions of persuasion were used—passive reading and listening to the communication or active advocating of the viewpoint.[7] The students were divided into three groups in accordance with their persuasibility. The most persuasible were influenced by all three statements, the moderately persuasible by two, and the least persuasible by one or none. Personality differences among these three groups were sought in the clinic records of sixteen who had voluntarily sought psychological counseling and by statistical analysis of the scores of the entire group on a personality inventory that they had filled out.

The sixteen who had sought psychotherapy did not differ as a group from the sixty-six who had not. That is, coming to psychotherapy was not in itself related to persuasibility. Among the treated, however, those who were most persuasible had sought help "primarily because of social inhibitions and feelings of personal inadequacy," while the least persuasible had symptoms that the experimenter termed more circumscribed and fixed, such as hypochondriacal complaints, insomnia, and work inhibitions. Scores of the whole sample on the personality inventory showed a similar trend. Students who scored high in social inadequacy tended to be persuasible, those with fixed neurotic symptoms tended not to be.[8] Apparently persons in a public situation who feel generally unsure of themselves are more persuasible than those whose conflicts have jelled into clearly defined symptoms—a fairly obvious finding, but one that is especially pertinent to our interests because, as will be seen,[9] the qualities here found to go with persuasibility are similar to those of patients considered to be good candidates for psychotherapy.

In these experiments the subject knew what viewpoint the experimenter wished him to express and showed a stronger tendency to adopt it as his own if led to improvise arguments in support of it than if he was passively exposed to it. This raises an intriguing question. What would happen if the experimenter concealed from the subject both his own viewpoint and the fact that he was trying to get him to express it, but by using techniques of which the subject was unaware, caused the latter to say what the experimenter had in mind? One would expect this to be a powerful means of persuasion, since the subject would think that the viewpoint he expressed was really his own. Actually, such a technique does exist, and its implications for understanding aspects of psychotherapy may be far-reaching, especially since psychotherapists use it continually, albeit often unwittingly. A growing body of experimental findings, to which we now turn, suggests that a person can guide a speaker's verbal productions to a considerable degree by subtle cues of approval or disapproval without the speaker being aware of what is happening.

OPERANT CONDITIONING OF VERBAL BEHAVIOR

Much experimental research in animal psychology in recent years has utilized a technique termed "operant conditioning."[10] This technique, which produces very rapid learning, consists in promptly rewarding a spontaneous bit of behavior. For example, a hungry pigeon placed in a box will peck about at random. If he immediately gets a grain of corn on pecking at a certain spot, he quickly learns to peck at that spot only, and his rate of pecking can be manipulated in all sorts of ways by varying the schedule of reward. A few years ago a psychologist had the bright idea that human speech, being a form of spontaneous behavior, might be conditionable in an analogous manner. That is, a person might be able to influence what another person said by giving signs of approval after he made statements in certain categories. If human speech were subject to operant conditioning, as time went on an increasing proportion of the speaker's statements should fall into the approved categories.

To demonstrate that this occurs, the speaker would have to be unaware of the approval signs given by the experimenter. Otherwise, changes in his speech following these signs might mean nothing more than conscious compliance with the experimenter's wishes. Actually, much of all communication between persons goes on at the edge of awareness. Words are expressed with different emphases and intonations and are accompanied by a constant stream of gestures and facial expressions. These cues, of which speaker and hearer may be scarcely conscious, often determine the meaning of the message more than the content of the words themselves. That a person's speech can be influenced by signals of approval or disapproval, of which he is unaware, was first demonstrated by the following experiment.[11] Some graduate students were told to say any words that came into their minds, and say as many as they could, for about an hour. The experimenter sat behind the subject, writing down what he said, but exerting no ostensible control over him. In accordance with a preconceived plan, however, every time the subject named a plural noun he grunted, with either an affirmative or negative inflection. Although the subjects were unaware of what he was doing, he was able to show by statistical analyses that affirmative grunts caused them to name more plural nouns, and negative grunts had the opposite effect.

This experiment inspired an increasing series of studies that are gradually tracing out the conditions under which verbal behavior can be affected, using a variety of communication situations, categories of statements, and types of approval.[12] Since many of the studies have used an interview-type situation with psychiatric patients as subjects, their findings, fragmentary as they are, are worth a brief review for the light they may cast on aspects of psychotherapy.

The success of operant conditioning of verbal behavior depends on characteristics of the subject, the persuader, and the relationship between them. Subjects for the most part have been graduate students in psychology or patients in mental hospitals, and persuaders have been fellow students, psychologists, or psychiatrists. Results seem to be more consistently positive when the persuader has some prestige or power in the subject's eyes. Thus graduate students are less consistently influenced by each other than by their instructors, and patients are quite responsive to members of treatment staffs. This suggests that some of the effectiveness of operant conditioning rests on the subject's caring about the persuader's opinion of him. In this connection, an experiment with college students, too complex to be described here, found that subjects to whom the experimenter had previously behaved in a hostile fashion showed less verbal conditioning than those to whom he had been sympathetic.[13]

With regard to characteristics of the subjects related to their susceptibility to this type of influence, two studies have shown that hospitalized mental patients with high anxiety are more conditionable than those with low anxiety. Presumably the former are more eager to please the interviewer.[14] In another study patients who were rated as "compliant" by their therapists conditioned more readily than those rated as relatively noncompliant, while those rated as highly "defensive" were relatively nonconditionable.[15] In a third study adolescent delinquents who were not anxious about their dependency feelings could be readily conditioned to increase the number of confiding statements they made to the interviewer. Boys who were anxious about their dependency feelings showed no such conditioning.[16] In conjunction, these experiments suggest that ease with which verbal behavior can be conditioned is related in part to the subject's dependence on the experimenter.

Of particular pertinence to psychotherapy is the question of the relation of the subject's awareness of the cues emitted by the experimenter to the conditioning of his speech. This proves to be a more complicated matter than the initial experiments suggested. Studies have consistently yielded two apparently contradictory findings. The first is that for the cues to be effective they must have some meaning or connotation that enables the subject to associate them with the correctness or incorrectness of his response. The second is that they may be effective even when the subject is not consciously aware of this association.

A few examples may clarify these statements. A flashing light will condition graduate students to say more plural words under the conditions of the experiment reported above.[17] Confronted with an essentially meaningless task, they are probably especially sensitive for clues as to what the experimenter really wants, and the light could be interpreted as such a clue. A flashing light, however, does not affect productions of patients being interviewed by a hospital staff member. When asked what they thought it meant, patients said that it was either some sort of timing device or an effort to distract them.[18] Similarly, affirmative grunts tend to be effective conditioners in an interview situation, but were ineffective when uttered in the course of a telephonic interview.[19] "Mm-hm" in a face-to-face interview tends to signify approval; at the other end of a telephone it probably conveys little more than that the interviewer is still there.

Though the cues must bear a potentially meaningful relation to the response in order to be effective, the responder does not seem to be aware of them or, if aware, to understand their relation to what he is saying. Roughly 95 per cent of the subjects of operant conditioning experiments indicated no awareness that they were being conditioned.[20]

One experiment has investigated the relationship between awareness and conditioning in some detail. Graduate students were the subjects, and plural nouns were reinforced by "mm-hm" as in the original experiment. After it the subjects were carefully questioned as to their consciousness of the experimenter's actions, and each was rated with respect to this on an eleven-point scale. Those subjects who thought "mm-hm" was meant as encouragement increased their use of words followed by this clue. Those who thought it meant they were going too fast or were giving the wrong kinds of words decreased their use of these words. Although all knew that the experimenter said "mm-hm" now and then, none could state precisely what the relationship was between the grunt and the kind of word he gave. The average subject suspected that there might have been some sort of relationship, but could not state it. Further-

more, there was no correlation between the level of the subjects' awareness and the amount of conditioning they showed.[21]

To make the matter still more complicated, subjects may be
more aware of what is going on than they are willing or able
to report after the experiment is over. Thus in one study that
attempted to condition the word "mother" by a suitable grunt,
one patient remarked during the conditioning period that the
interviewer seemed to be interested in this word and promptly
stopped using it. But at the end of the experiment he denied
any awareness of what the interviewer had been doing.[22]

This much, at least, seems safely established: One person can
influence the verbalizations of another through very subtle
cues, which may be so slight that they never come to the center
of awareness. These cues are effective, however, only if they
have some connotation of approval or disapproval and the extent of their influence is related to how much the subject cares
about the interviewer's attitudes towards him.

Since in psychotherapy the patient cares desperately about
what the psychiatrist thinks of him, it seems plausible that his
productions will be influenced to some extent by cues given by
the latter. Thus, if the therapist has a predilection for certain
categories of response, he may influence the patient to give the
kinds of material he favors. Since very subtle cues can be
effective, this may occur without either of them realizing that
this is happening. Some objective evidence supports these
suppositions.

One study suggests that psychotherapists do tend to approve
or discourage statements by patients that are related to their
own personality characteristics. Twelve psychotherapists of
parents in a child guidance clinic were rated by the research
staff, on the basis of prolonged social and personal contacts,
with respect to their ability to express hostility directly and
their need for approval. Those who could express their hostility directly were more likely to make an encouraging response after a hostile statement by a patient, than those who

could not give vent to their hostility or those who sought approval. The patients responded to the therapists' leads. Encouraging responses were followed by a continuation of hostile responses 92 per cent of the time, discouraging ones only 43 per cent of the time. In this study, most of the therapist's encouraging or discouraging responses were fairly obvious, but, consistent with the findings on studies of operant conditioning, there was no relation between their obviousness and their effectiveness. A subtle sign of approval such as reflecting the patient's feeling was just as encouraging as open expression of approval, and simply ignoring the hostile content of a patient's remark discouraged him as effectively as suggesting a change in topic.[23]

That psychotherapists influence patients' productions by operant conditioning even when they are unaware of this is strongly suggested by an analysis of a treatment record, published as an example of "nondirective therapy," in which the therapist supposedly simply encouraged the patient to speak by his supportive attitude without influencing his productions in any way. Two startling findings emerged. The therapist's responses could be reliably categorized without difficulty as approving or disapproving, that is, he was conveying his attitudes in spite of himself. Furthermore, the patient's productions were strongly influenced by this implicit approval or disapproval. Statements in categories disapproved by the therapist fell from 45 per cent of the total number of statements in the second hour to 5 per cent in the eighth, while over approximately the same period statements in approved categories rose from 1 per cent to 45 per cent.[24]

Although the effects of operant conditioning on patient's productions seem to be impressive, three important limitations of reported data should be emphasized. First, in operant conditioning experiments the experimenter tries to produce specific alterations in the subject's speech. In many forms of psychotherapy the therapist consciously tries not to influence the patient's productions, but instead only to follow his leads. Since very slight hints may influence the patient, however, it is possible that the therapist may emit them without knowing it. That this occurs is strongly suggested by the content analysis of a therapy protocol reported above,[25] but the extent of this influence remains to be determined. Second, experiments on the conditioning of verbal behavior cast no light on the relation between the strength of a patient's personal commitment to certain topics or attitudes and his susceptibility to this type of influence. The experimental studies, for the most part, used categories in which the patient had no emotional investment. It made little difference to him if he used more plural nouns or third person pronouns or said "mother" more often.[26] Moreover, in the reported analyses of psychotherapeutic interviews the categories showing change—for example, "hostile statements"—do not refer to actual topics of discussion. Thus the extent to which statements of views anchored in personal convictions can be influenced by this means is unknown.

The third major limitation of the reported findings is that they apply only to what a patient says. The extent to which this corresponds to how he actually feels remains unknown.[27] As with thought reform, it is important to keep in mind the distinction between compliance and internalization.[28] Operant conditioning clearly produces some degree of compliance, but that is as far as one can safely go at present. It should be added, however, that one's attitudes are probably affected by one's own words. As pointed out in the discussion of thought reform, most persons cannot indefinitely tolerate a discrepancy between their words and their underlying attitudes, especially when they must improvise what they say, and under some circumstances the attitudes may yield.[29] Furthermore a technique of influence of which the person is unaware may be especially effective because he has no incentive to mobilize his resistance against it. These questions will be discussed further in the detailed consideration of psychotherapy below.[30]

THE INFLUENCE OF AN ANTICIPATED
AUDIENCE ON RECALL

In conclusion, two experimental studies exploring the effect on one's recall of anticipation that one will have to present material to a biased audience deserve mention. They are pertinent to psychotherapy because the therapist is an "anticipated audience" between sessions. His patients are likely to think of him from time to time, wondering how he would handle a problem they have encountered, how he would react to certain of their thoughts, or what they will tell him at the next session. Some even consciously rehearse what they will say, despite the therapist's efforts to discourage this. The studies reviewed to this point suggest that the therapist may exert considerable influence on his patients' productions when they are in direct contact. The two to be described accord with the clinical impression that his influence continues to operate when they are apart.

In the first study[31] the experimenter told groups of students that she was seeking persons to speak before an organization on the subject of teachers' pay, and that the following week they would be asked to write sample speeches on this topic. She told half the groups that she represented the "Taxpayers' Economy League," which wanted to save the taxpayers' money, and the other half that her organization was the "National Council of Teachers," which was interested in improving the teachers' lot. She then read a short passage of information and arguments they could use in their speeches. Half the students in each group heard a passage that supported a rise in pay; half heard one opposing it. Immediately afterwards the students were asked to write the passage from memory. A week later they were asked to write it again, as literally as they could. There was no difference in the amount of material recalled from the two passages by the different groups immediately after hearing them. After a week, however, students remembered significantly more of the passage that represented the same viewpoint as that of their anticipated audience than of the passage that expressed the opposing view.

A simpler experiment on a larger scale confirmed this finding.[32] College students were told that they would be asked to prepare speeches on voting age. The best speech was to receive a prize. Half of the students were told that the organization offering the prize opposed lowering the voting age, the other half that the organization advocated this. All students were given the same set of balanced arguments to read and told to remember them because they would be asked to write the speeches a week later. At that time they were given a memory test which revealed that they recalled significantly more arguments on the side represented by the organization they were to address.

These studies suggest that images of future audiences affect the way in which a person organizes and retains new, incoming information. Since the psychotherapist is such an audience between sessions, the patient's image of him could well influence his recall of experiences happening between sessions. The experiments have no bearing on whether images of anticipated audiences similarly affect recall of earlier experiences, which form the bulk of many psychotherapeutic interviews, but the possibility is not excluded.

SUMMARY

Experimental studies of the influencing process confirm impressions gained from real-life persuasive procedures that participation increases a person's susceptibility, especially if the situation requires him to assume some initiative. Perhaps more unexpected is the experimental demonstration that the content of a person's speech can be influenced by faint cues of approval or disapproval given by his listener, and that the amount of this influence is independent of how aware he is of it. Relevance of these findings to the influencing process in psychotherapy is limited by differences in the attitudes of experimenter and therapist, the nature of the material influenced, and the question as to the relationship between changes in what a patient says and changes in his feelings. Nevertheless, some findings strongly suggest that even the most "nondirective" therapist may influence the patient's speech in the direction of his own wishes, without the awareness of either. Finally, a bit of experimental evidence that an anticipated audience influences recall of new information raises the possibility that the psychotherapist may indirectly influence the patient's productions in therapeutic sessions by affecting his recall of happenings between interviews.

"You're thinking about something, my dear, and that makes you forget to talk. I can't tell you just now what the moral of that is, but I shall remember it in a bit."

"Perhaps it hasn't one," Alice ventured to remark.

"Tut, tut child!" said the Duchess. "Everything's got a moral, if only you can find it." (*Alice's Adventures in Wonderland*, Chapter 9)

7 | The Psychiatrist and the Patient

The time has now come to examine psychotherapy in the light of the observational and experimental data reviewed in the preceding chapters. As we have defined it,[1] psychotherapy is a form of help-giving in which a trained, socially sanctioned healer tries to relieve a sufferer's distress by facilitating certain changes in his feelings, attitudes, and behavior, through the performance of certain activities with him, often with the participation of a group. It is convenient to separate the therapeutic process into two parts—the relationship between psychiatrist and patient, and the therapeutic activities they jointly perform—even though these obviously affect each other.

The psychotherapeutic relationships in different forms of psychotherapy seem to have certain common features that may outweigh their differences.[2] Since help flows from psychiatrist to patient, the course of the interaction is largely determined by the former, although as in all interpersonal activities, some influence flows the other way, especially since the therapist tries to guide his activities by his understanding of the patient's needs, as revealed by the latter's communications.

The therapist's power is based on the patient's perception of him as a source of help, and it tends to be greater the greater the patient's distress and his faith in the therapist's desire and ability to help him. The attitudes of the therapist that seem to contribute most to the patient's trust in him are a steady, deep interest, an optimistic outlook, and dedication to the patient's welfare. These attitudes enable the patient to talk about any aspects of himself, however shameful they may be, with confidence that the therapist will maintain his interest and concern.

The shared expectancy that the patient will be helped is probably healing in itself, as considered earlier.[3] In addition, the therapist's consistent interest strengthens the patient's self-esteem by implying that he is worthy of the therapist's efforts. This helps him to find the courage to give up habitual but unsatisfactory perceptual and behavioral patterns and search for better ones.

The patient's perception of the therapist as a healer depends in the first instance on the latter's sociocultural role, including his training. Other properties of the therapeutic relationship are determined largely by personal qualities of therapist and patient. This chapter reviews information pertinent to these aspects of the therapeutic process as a background for consideration of the therapeutic activities that characterize the various forms of psychotherapy in America today.

All of the material that follows comes from naturalistic forms of psychotherapy, that is, treatment in offices, clinics, and hospitals by professionally trained persons operating within a naturalistic rather than a supernatural conceptual framework. Reflecting the background and experience of the writer, interest will center on psychiatrists and persons who regard themselves, and are regarded by others, as psychiatric patients; but data from related situations, such as counseling, will be considered when pertinent.

THE SOCIOCULTURAL ROLE AND TRAINING
OF THE PSYCHIATRIST

The psychiatrist's ability to help a patient depends in part on the latter's image of him as the possessor of knowledge that gives him healing powers. This image is partly determined by the psychiatrist's role in the society to which both he and the patient belong. The complexity and diversity of American culture result in certain ambiguities about the psychiatrist's position, which has both advantages and drawbacks from this standpoint.

One problem is created by the multiplicity of the psychiatrist's public images, some of which are mutually contradictory. Different segments of American society may view him quite differently. Furthermore, perhaps reflecting his dual heritage from religion and medicine, the psychiatrist may be invested with attributes of both witch doctor and physician, causing him to be overvalued in some respects and undervalued in others. Some persons regard him as the possessor of unusual wisdom and, at times, almost magical powers. At parties some guests may become uneasy in his presence and speak half-seriously of their fear that he will read their minds. Many of his patients expect him to resolve their lifelong problems in a few sessions. An important psychiatric skill is the ability gently to disabuse them of their exalted expectations without losing their confidence.

A psychiatrist may be called upon to function not only as a physician, but as a criminologist, educator, spiritual adviser—in short, as an expert in all human affairs. There is justification for this to the extent that all people are more alike than they are different, so that the understanding gained from working with psychiatric patients may be relevant to all human problems. But as many psychiatrists have discovered, not all human activity, especially when it involves organized groups and institutions, can be explained in terms of psychiatric theory or modified by psychotherapeutic techniques. One of the occupational hazards of the psychiatrist is the temptation to let himself be seduced into pretending to be an expert about matters in which he has no special competence, often with unfortunate effects, both on his own self-esteem and on his public image.

For hand in hand with the overevaluation of the psychiatrist by patients and public goes derogation. He is the butt of endless jokes, the target of much irritation, and he is viewed by many, including quite a few of his medical colleagues, as something of a quack who promises more than he can perform. Thus with some patients his initial task is to overcome their skepticism, rather than to find a way of climbing down gracefully from the pedestal on which he has been placed.

In preliterate societies with a single, all-encompassing world view and a correspondingly unified social structure, the shaman gains much of his power through his universal recognition as a healer, and through being a representative and transmitter of the values and assumptive systems of the group. Since American society is neither unified nor dominated by a simple, universal assumptive world, the psychiatrist cannot gain the same amount of power from these sources as the shaman, but it is likely that some of his healing ability still derives from his membership in the group to which his patients belong or aspire to belong. As a representative of this group, the psychiatrist's willingness to make a great effort to help the patient regardless of the latter's deficiencies and delinquencies implies the group's potential acceptance as well, thus strengthening the patient's self-esteem and his sense of being restored to harmony with his social world. Moreover, because the psychiatrist represents the attitudes of the group, the patient can use his reactions as a touchstone to evaluate the acceptability of his own behavior and attitudes.

A virtue of the diversity of American society for psychotherapy is that it tolerates a considerable variety of assumptive systems, thereby affording a multitude of routes to mental health. Certain psychiatrists can find group support for the rejection of widely held values such as conformity and social prestige, which may contribute to their ability to help patients who share these views, or who would gain improved mental health by progressing in a similar direction. Patients can achieve personal integration in terms of values that are not widely shared and without having to achieve harmonious relationships with any particular group. In this connection, although Americans place much emphasis on conformity, one of their basic values is the worth of the individual, and obedience to the dictates of one's own best self is a highly regarded virtue. So the psychiatrist who helps his patient achieve greater inner freedom and self-fulfillment, even at the expense of conformity, is not running counter to many important group values, and the patient may gain in respect and admiration from others what he loses in popularity.[4]

On the negative side, the complexity of American society makes it possible for psychiatrists and patients to differ widely in background and socioeconomic position. The greater the class discrepancy between them, the greater is apt to be the difference in their value systems and therefore the more difficulty they may have in communicating.[5] Furthermore, much of the meaning of verbal communications depends on the connotations and feeling tones attached to words rather than their dictionary definitions, and these nuances are determined by the usages of a person's group. Hence differences in group membership may impede the development of mutual understanding. In psychotherapy, this can be a serious obstacle to the development of the intimate, confiding relationship that is a prerequisite for successful psychotherapy,[6] although skillful psychotherapists are sometimes able to overcome it, especially in long-time therapy.

As physicians, psychiatrists have been born into or achieved middle- or upper-class status and share the attitudes and values of these groups. In private practice, where the economic hurdle largely restricts the psychiatrist's clientele to members of his own class, this creates no problems; but in clinics, which are available to all, the class discrepancy between psychiatrists and patients may have important consequences.

Many forms of psychotherapy, having been devised by middle-class psychiatrists, attribute considerable healing power to self-knowledge and, to this end, require the patient to verbalize his inner feelings and personal problems. This activity may be totally unfamiliar to lower-class persons, and they cannot perceive it as treatment. Nor do they attach any value to increased self-understanding.

These considerations probably account for the consistent finding that in clinics the class position of a patient affects the kind of treatment he receives and his acceptance of it. For example, in one university clinic it turned out, to the surprise of the staff, that the higher the patient's social class, the more likely he was to be accepted for treatment, to be treated by the more senior staff members, and to be treated intensively over a long period.[7] Apparently the senior physicians, who assigned patients, unwittingly chose those of the higher classes for themselves. Furthermore, in clinic settings patients who remain in psychotherapy tend to be higher socially, educationally, and economically than those who drop out. It must be added that these factors are related only to acceptance or rejection of psychotherapy, not to improvement for patients who stay in treatment. For these, class position seems to be irrelevant to outcome.[8]

More important than his general social position in determining the psychiatrist's effectiveness is the method by which he has acquired his healing powers. In America, all psychiatrists are physicians. A small proportion have received additional specialized training in a particular body of theory connected with a special method of treatment, in an institute conducted by practitioners of this method. These "analytic institutes"[9] have had an important influence on the pattern of psychiatric training and practice in America. Therefore some discussion of their place in the contemporary scene seems in order.

The psychiatrist's self-confidence and the patient's faith in him rest in the first instance on his being a physician. Medical training is the accepted route to the acquisition of healing powers and confers a high prestige in American society. The basic training of psychiatrists is the same as that of all physicians and includes a general or medical internship. Almost all follow this with three years of residency training, corresponding to the training programs of other medical specialties. Psychiatrists can be divided roughly into two more-or-less well-defined groups according to their subsequent careers.[10] These groups, which have been termed the directive-organic and analytic-psychological, differ markedly in many ways and do not associate much with each other. The directive-organic consider their training to be completed when they finish their residencies, and they identify themselves primarily as physicians. They are apt to be trained in neurology and basic biological sciences, remain active in medical societies, and handle their patients as any physician would. They wear the white coat of the doctor in office and hospital, perform medical and laboratory examinations, and readily prescribe drugs or other forms of physical treatment. They see their patients relatively briefly and infrequently in a setting like that of the usual doctor's office and tend to rely on nonspecific psychotherapeutic methods such as advice, reassurance, and persuasion, which all physicians use.

Analytic-psychological psychiatrists have undergone an intensive and prolonged training in a special institute that teaches psychoanalysis or one of its derivations, and this becomes the center of their professional lives. Although they maintain their status as physicians by keeping membership in medical societies, their identification as physicians may be relatively weak. Some analytic institutes even train nonphysicians and accept them as members. Analytic-psychological psychiatrists do not do their own medical or laboratory examinations, are reluctant to prescribe drugs, see their patients in offices that do not resemble those of the usual physician, and wear ordinary business suits. Their pattern of treatment differs markedly from ordinary medical practice. The patients may lie on a couch instead of facing the physician. Their treatment methods usually involve long and frequent interviews and stress gain in self-knowledge through detailed examination of the patient's present and past interpersonal relationships.

The aim of analytic training is to confer mastery of these techniques and of the theory on which they are based. Training methods emphasize maximal participation of the trainee. The core of the process is the detailed continuous supervision by faculty members of his treatment of patients and a personal analysis through which he experiences the method at first hand. These activities are supplemented by lectures and seminars in which pertinent literature and theory are studied, and the treatment of certain cases is followed in detail.

The training program is prolonged, laborious, and expensive. It lasts at least four years and costs thousands of dollars. Since it does not replace the psychiatrist's usual activities but runs concomitantly with them, it reduces his mobility and seriously cuts into his free time. It usually requires that he go into debt, or that his wife work to supplement his income. Thus, in several ways it may require considerable sacrifices by both the trainee and his family.[11]

Although psychoanalysts do not claim any superiority for their method as therapy,[12] they enjoy a high prestige, and analytic institutes attract many of the ablest young psychiatrists, who are undeterred by the sacrifices involved. What are the reasons for this? Partly they lie in the appealing features of analytic theories. Other theories may explain certain aspects of human functioning more satisfactorily, or be more easily verifiable, but none approach analytic theories in scope or brillance. Moreover, many analytic concepts have been incorporated not only into theories of mental illness and treatment, but also into all aspects of America's intellectual and cultural life, so that mastery of these doctrines gives one the satisfaction of being thoroughly familiar with theories that others know only indirectly or partially.

Another attraction of analytic training is personal analysis, which gives the trainee an intimate knowledge of the method from the standpoint of the patient and may lead to enhanced feelings of personal security, greater self-understanding, and increased inner freedom.[13]

Finally, completion of training is signalized by admission of the trainee to membership in the institute, which assures acceptance by his colleagues and mentors and a source of patient referrals, thereby yielding both financial security and status.

Whether these values are sufficient to explain the attractiveness of analytic training with all its hardships, especially in the absence of demonstrable superiority of the method over simpler or briefer ones, is problematical. It suggests that an additional factor may be involved, the indoctrinating power of the training procedure. Viewed from this standpoint comparison with a form of indoctrination discussed earlier, thought reform, may be illuminating.[14]

The analytic institute is a tight little cultural island in which the trainee comes into prolonged intensive contact with other trainees and the teaching staff. The teaching program is guided by a conceptualization of human psychic life that is all-inclusive and is not susceptible of disproof. Analytic theories do evolve and change in the light of accumulated experience, but the changes involve elaborations, accretions, and shifts in emphasis rather than clear abandonments of earlier positions. Teaching seminars in institutes subject their theories to critical scrutiny, but the limitations of the critique are suggested by the fact that no training institute has yet disbanded because it reached the conclusion that its theory was inferior to that of another school.

A striking example of the essential irrefutability of psychoanalytic doctrine is afforded by Freud's handling of his discovery that his patients confabulated infantile memories, in itself strong evidence for the influencing power of his techniques. As he was quick to see, "this discovery . . . serves either to discredit the analysis which has led to such a result or to discredit the patients upon whose testimony the analysis, as well as the whole understanding of neurosis, is built up." This is a bleak predicament indeed, from which Freud extricates himself by a *tour de force*. He points out that "these phantasies possess *psychological* reality in contrast to *physical* reality" and "*in the realm of neurosis the psychological reality is the determining factor.*"[15] Therefore the fact that these infantile experiences were phantasies rather than actualities, far from refuting his theories, actually confirms them.

Analytic theories of human behavior rest on more solid evidence than real or fabricated infantile memories, of course, and Freud's point may well be correct. But the type of reasoning illustrates a characteristic not only of psychoanalysis but of many theories underlying psychotherapy which may be an important source of their power—that they cannot be refuted by the patient's productions. Nor is the inexperienced and youthful analytic trainee in a position to challenge the validity of the theory. His teachers have high prestige in his eyes from the start, and their opinion of him becomes increasingly important as training continues. The greater his investment becomes, the more desirable completion of training appears, and the more strongly he may be impelled to conform to the views of his teachers in order to achieve this. For their decision on his readiness to graduate is based on his demonstrated comprehension and acceptance of the theory, mastery of the method of treatment associated with it, and the completion of his own training analysis.

The training analysis is probably the core of the indoctrination process. It consists of the application to the trainee of virtually the same technique as is used with patients. This technique will be considered more fully in the next chapter.[16] It involves a detailed review of the trainee's current thoughts and feelings in relation to his life history, interpreted consistently by the training analyst in terms of the doctrines of the institute. Since the initiative in the production of material resides with the trainee, the method fosters improvisation and participation. As it lasts for several years, the same material is reviewed repeatedly. As we have seen, improvisation, participation, and repetition are important in producing attitude change in other situations.[17] The training analysis is not complete until the student produces memories, thoughts, and feelings in a form that confirms the doctrines of the institute.

There can be little doubt that the training analysis, regardless of its other effects, which are considered more fully below, is a method of indoctrination. As a leading psychoanalyst has written: "It is scarcely to be expected that a student who has spent years under the artificial . . . conditions of a training analysis and whose professional career depends on overcoming 'resistance' to the satisfaction of his training analyst, can be in a favorable position to defend his scientific integrity against the analyst's theory and practice . . . for according to his analyst, the candidate's objections to interpretations rate as resistance. In short, there is a tendency in the training situation to perpetuate error."[18]

The conceptual scheme is reinforced by the patient's productions in treatment. As suggested earlier,[19] operant conditioning tends to take place in therapy, causing the patient's productions to conform to the therapist's theory. The analyst tends to guard himself from the impact of a patient's behavior or statements that do not conform by describing them in terms suggesting that the patient is wrong, such as "resistance." Patients' criticisms of the therapist can be dismissed as based on "transference," implying that they are entirely the result of the patient's distorted perceptions. Faced with such behaviors the young analyst is admonished not to become "defensive," i.e., not to admit, even by implication, that his viewpoint requires defending. The conceptual scheme is further protected through the selection of patients for treatment. The analyst tries to select only those patients suitable for analysis, but the criteria of suitability are similar to those that would make the patient a good prospect for any type of psychotherapy.[20] Like the shaman, the psychoanalyst maximizes the likelihood of success by his selection of cases for treatment.

Failure to improve can be readily attributed to the patient's unsuitability for analysis.[21] Since the length of treatment is indeterminate, the analyst may take refuge in the position that the patient broke off too soon, which incidentally may be a reason for the increasing length of psychotherapy mentioned earlier.[22] As long as a patient is still in treatment, the therapist need not admit failure. Occasionally he may entertain the possibility that he applied his technique incorrectly, but failures rarely lead him to question the technique itself or the premises underlying it. As one young psychiatrist in training put it: "Even if the patient doesn't get better, you know you're doing the right thing." Thus, as in other forms of healing and influence, successful cases strengthen the underlying conceptual scheme while failures do not shake it.

The conceptual scheme is reinforced by the trainee's colleagues, who also are in process of becoming indoctrinated. The more deeply they become immersed in their training, the more they tend to confine their associations to each other. This may be partly because they learn a specialized vocabulary, the terms of which are fully grasped only by members of the same school, partly through the development of a common body of shared experience. The cohesiveness of each group is heightened by the lack of sympathy of other rival groups and of large segments of the medical profession. Like other specialists, after their training is completed, analysts continue to associate primarily with their own group. This serves to reinforce the conceptual scheme, in a fashion similar to Wesley's classes, especially since members who come to doubt the theory usually tend to drift out of the group. Finally the magnitude of the sacrifices the trainee has made to master certain methods and doctrines, and his public adherence to them, create a strong incentive for belief. For if the analyst were to abandon his position, his sacrifice would have been in vain and he would be under the painful necessity of admitting that he had been wrong. In this connection the very fact that the method may not work very well and that the doctrine is open to question may tend paradoxically to strengthen the analyst's dogmatic adherence to them as a way of stifling his misgivings.[23] It probably also contributes to the perpetuation of analytic institutes, irrespective of the actual merits of what they teach. For one of the best ways to allay self-doubts is to try to convert others to one's point of view, thereby gaining confirmation of its correctness from them. Conceivably this may be one factor in the energy devoted to the propagation of analytic doctrines.[24]

The indoctrination aspect of training has facilitated psychiatric progress in some ways. The support of analytic institutes has enabled analysts to persist in their trail-breaking explorations of the human psyche in the face of widespread and often vehement opposition of influential segments of society, including many of their medical colleagues. Many physicians were made uneasy by aspects of human nature revealed by psychoanalysis, the strangeness of analytic terminology, and the content of its theories. As a result, for decades analysts had to pursue their studies and their teaching outside medical schools, with all that this meant in terms of absence of academic status, financial insecurity, and lack of access to students. They persisted, and as a result psychoanalysis and its derivatives have had an invigorating and liberating influence that it would be hard to overestimate, not only on psychiatry but on all scientific disciplines concerned with human beings, and on many forms of creative activity.

Nevertheless at the present stage of psychiatric development, the influence of psychoanalytic institutes has certain potentially unfortunate implications, which must be considered in any attempt to evaluate their position in the current scene.

They exert a strong pressure on young psychiatrists to go into private practice, partly because they are run by private practitioners and are therefore oriented to it and partly because private practice is the easiest way for the psychiatrist to recoup the expenses of his training. This leads to a disproportionate expenditure of effort on a small segment of the patient population—those who can afford to pay for long-term therapy. Within this group, attention tends to become concentrated on those who are considered to be most suitable for analytic therapy. These prove to be persons with good adaptive capacities who are intelligent and verbally skillful, that is, patients who might well benefit equally from simpler and briefer procedures. To the extent that able psychiatrists devote themselves to this group, their energies are diverted from psychiatric patients who present a much greater social problem—the indigent and the hospitalized insane.

The lure of private practice also tends to draw analytic psychiatrists from teaching and research, which cannot compete in financial rewards. This is particularly unfortunate now that most medical schools in contrast to their earlier policies of exclusion are eager to obtain the services of analytically trained psychiatrists.

The analytic conceptual framework also has certain serious drawbacks from a research standpoint. Like all theories, it has fostered interest in certain areas at the expense of others that may be equally important. In particular, it has focused on psychological factors in mental illness to the relative neglect of biological assets and liabilities on a congenital or other basis. It has also stressed the role of personal life experience, especially in childhood, in molding personality, to the relative neglect of sociocultural forces. Finally, it has emphasized early life experience rather than current faulty interaction patterns as sources of difficulty. Modern analytic theory has endeavored to encompass the factors it initially neglected, but not being constructed to explain them, it has not dealt with many of them adequately.

The most serious drawback of analytic concepts, however, lies not in their content but in their formal characteristics. As attempts at inclusive formulations of all human thinking, feeling, and behavior, they have to be able to explain everything that happens. The validity of analytic hypotheses cannot be tested by making predictions from them and determining whether the predictions are confirmed. For no matter how the test comes out, analytic theory can explain the results.[25] The type of imagination-catching, aesthetically appealing, all-inclusive conceptual scheme exemplified by psychoanalysis represents a necessary early step in the exploration of a new field. It directs attention to new data, shows their importance, and offers a framework for thinking about them. This type of theory, however, becomes a handicap at a later stage, and psychiatry today may be ready to move ahead to the formulation of more rigorous, experimentally testable hypotheses.[26]

This general discussion of sociocultural aspects of the psychiatrist's role may be brought to a focus by a brief consideration of its implications for the preparation of the patient for psychotherapy. Because of the diversity and the ambiguities of public conceptions of mental illness and psychotherapy, psychiatric patients reach the psychiatrist's office with a wide variety of attitudes and expectations. Only the most sophisticated are perfectly clear about why they are there and what they expect. A major source of difficulty is their inadequate preparation by the referring source. As a result they often experience referral to a psychiatrist as a "brush off," an indication that their doctor believes that their complaints are imaginary and is tired of hearing them. This plays into any feelings they may have that psychiatric illness is a disgrace, so they arrive at the psychiatrist's office feeling humiliated and confused.

The psychiatrist, therefore, often must take measures to acquaint the patient with the true nature of psychotherapy and, implicitly, to impress him with his authority and competence. This process may begin even before he meets the patient. Private practitioners urge their referring sources to prepare the patient properly for the psychiatric consultation by carefully informing him of its purpose and what it will be like. Clinics usually put the patient through some sort of intake procedure. Traditionally this consists of one or more interviews with a social worker, the purpose of which is to determine the patient's suitability for psychotherapy and prepare him for it. Implicitly it may also heighten the importance of the psychiatrist and psychotherapy in the patient's eyes by appearing like a probationary period to determine his worthiness to receive this form of treatment. In this sense it may not be too far fetched to liken the intake procedure to the preparatory rites undergone by suppliants at faith-healing shrines, with the social worker in the role of acolyte and the psychiatrist as high priest.

Once in the presence of the psychiatrist, the patient's image of him as a help-giver and authority figure is reinforced by certain culturally established symbols.[27] The clinic or hospital office automatically is identified with the healing activities of the institution.[28] The private office of the psychiatrist who keeps his identity as a physician contains all the trappings with which the patient is familiar: the framed diploma and license, examining table, stethescope, ophthalmoscope, reflex hammer, doctor's white coat, and so on, Analytic-psychological psychiatrists, whose medical identification has been weakened, also display diploma and license, but they have developed special symbols of their healing art. These include heavily laden bookcases, couch with easy chair, and usually a large photograph of the leader of their particular school gazing benignly but impressively on the proceedings.

Thus the intake procedure and the therapeutic setting, viewed from a sociocultural standpoint, implicitly or explicitly combat patients' unfavorable attitudes and enhance their expectations of help.

PERSONAL QUALITIES OF THE PSYCHIATRIST

The effectiveness of the psychiatrist depends not only on his training and on other sociocultural determinants of the patients' image of him, but also on certain personal qualities and attitudes. This section reviews the scanty data relevant to this important matter, utilizing studies of nonmedical psychotherapists as well as of psychiatrists, since all findings are consistent.

It is generally agreed that the success of a psychotherapist depends in part on his really caring about the patient's welfare,[29] and the odds are that he can invest more of himself, other things being equal, in patients he can like and respect, if not for what they are, then for what they can become. Freud expressed this clearly in his first publication on psychotherapy: "[Psychoanalysis] presupposes in [the physician] . . . a personal concern for the patients . . . . I cannot imagine bringing myself to delve into the psychical mechanism of a hysteria in anyone who struck me as low-minded and repellent, and who, on closer acquaintance, would not be capable of arousing human sympathy."[30] Thus the psychiatrist's predilections based on personal qualities may tend to influence his choice of patients and his success with different types. Some experienced psychiatrists, recognizing this, will not attempt to treat alcoholics, while others avoid hysterics; some believe they do especially well with depressed patients, others regard their forte as schizophrenics.

The scanty objective studies of personal qualities of the good therapist are of three sorts. The first define a psychotherapist's competence in terms of the judgments of his colleagues or superiors; the second in terms of the opinions of his patients; the third in terms of his actual success.

The good therapist emerges from the first type of study as a good person in general—he is intelligent and responsible, has good judgment, and is creative.[31] He is also judged to be sincere, energetic, and able to display controlled warmth to his patients, that is, to let himself become somewhat emotionally involved without losing his objectivity.[32] Moreover, the type of relationship he offers his patients probably tends to be consistent with his general pattern of social behavior. One study that rated the attitudes of two group therapists toward the same patients—they took turns leading the same groups for a few sessions—found that the one whom colleagues and subordinates described as more tolerant, respectful, supportive of others, and self-confident offered his patients the better relationship.[33]

If qualities like self-confidence and energy are believed to contribute to a psychotherapist's success, then anxiety should militate against him, and one study found this to be true. Forty-two young psychotherapists in four clinics, all of whom were clinical psychology students, rated each other and themselves on a variety of personality traits and also received ratings of therapeutic competence from their supervisors. Those who were judged more anxious by their colleagues tended to be judged less competent by the supervisors. It is interesting that the degree of the therapist's insight into his own anxiety made no difference. His uneasiness probably militated against the patient developing confidence in him, whether he knew its cause or not.[34]

All studies relying on judgments of therapists' competence by their colleagues or supervisors are measuring what a good therapist should be, or how he should behave, not his actual therapeutic ability. Hence they must be viewed with caution.[35] That these studies may have some validity is suggested by the fact that judgments of therapists made by clients or patients agree with those of colleagues as to the personal qualities associated with therapeutic success. One study made a beginning of exploring clients' feelings about counselors' personal attributes and behavior. Analysis of interviews with 150 clients (none of whom were patients) immediately after their first interview with a counselor revealed that their expressed willingness to see him again was based on personal liking for him, while their acceptance of his advice depended on their estimates of his competence, technical skill, and anticipated thoroughness. Both attitudes were favorably influenced by the clients' "felt progress, experienced freedom to reveal himself, interest of the interviewer in the helping situation and understanding of each other's communication."[36]

Another study explored the problem by means of interviews with two college students who had made significant improvement following short term psychiatric treatment. Each was asked to state what he believed had helped him, and these evaluations were compared with similar ones prepared by the psychiatrists. The discrepancies between the two evaluations are of particular interest. Both psychiatrists stressed insight into the correlations of childhood experiences with current symptoms, and the bringing to awareness of unconscious feelings as the sources of therapeutic gain. That is, they attributed their success to their therapeutic method. Neither patient mentioned these. Instead, both stressed the psychiatrists' indirect reassurance (in one case by granting an emergency interview and in the other by offering factual information as to the nondangerous nature of the patient's symptoms) and the encounter with an authority figure who was both firm and completely accepting. These findings are highly tentative, being based on only two cases, but as far as they go they confirm that emotional support, kindly guidance, and the feeling of being accepted by the psychiatrist—qualities related to the psychiatrist's personality rather than his technique—are therapeutically important.[37]

The strongest support for the therapeutic importance of the psychiatrist's attitudes is supplied by a series of studies that related the actual results of treatment to aspects of the therapeutic relationship.[38] The patients were hospitalized schizophrenics; the therapists were psychiatric residents. It was found that those who showed "active personal participation" with their patients obtained a very much higher improvement rate than those who showed a less personalized and understanding attitude. Insulin coma treatment, moreover, had no effect on the improvement rate obtained by the first group, but greatly improved the results obtained by the second. Examination of the data suggested that insulin treatment, which may endanger the patient's life and increases his tendency to reach out actively for help, caused the more impersonal doctors to enter into more active personal interactions with these patients; that is, it helped them to act more like the successful doctors, and this was reflected in improved therapeutic results.

From the personality standpoint, doctors in the two groups showed striking differences in interest patterns. The interests of the successful group coincided to a high degree with those of lawyers and were not at all like those of high school mathematics teachers. The interests of the less successful therapists were exactly the reverse. Thus the interests of the good therapists were similar to those of persons whose career involves personal dealings with others and the ability to understand and represent their interests in a resourceful way. Therapists in the second group, on the other hand, had interests like persons whose work tends to be routinized, to leave little room for imaginativeness, and to be relatively impersonal.

To this point the training of the psychiatrist and his personal attributes have been considered as if they were independent of each other. This distinction is artificial in the case of psychoanalytic training, since its goals are not only to teach technique and theory, but to bring about changes in the trainee's personality and attitudes believed to make him a better therapist.

The major means of producing these changes is the training analysis, which tries to enhance the trainee's self-knowledge, thereby freeing him of certain emotional conflicts and vulnerabilities and enabling him to guard against the effects of those he cannot eliminate. Through the training analysis the trainee becomes more objective, more sensitive to and tolerant of the attitudes and feelings of his patients. This is essential because prolonged psychotherapy often creates a highly charged emotional relationship between patient and therapist. Unless the latter is himself emotionally secure and clear about his own feelings and motives, he may fail adequately to meet the challenges thus created, and even perhaps harm his patients through his own reactions.

Analytic training may be especially desirable for physicians, whose medical training has taught them to protect themselves from the emotional impact of their patients by viewing them as specimens of bodily disease rather than persons. A training analysis, by helping the physician to dispense with this type of shield and relate in a personal way to his patients may help him to be not only a better psychotherapist but also a better doctor.

Whether the personality changes fostered by analytic training are always desirable however, is questionable. While cultivation of self-awareness, tolerance, and objectivity may be valuable in physicians who are deficient in these qualities, it may hamper the therapeutic effectiveness of those who are aloof, passive, or overintrospective. For there is only a fine line between objectivity and coldness, self-awareness and morbid introspection, tolerance and passivity. Thus psychoanalytic training may reduce the capacity of some physicians for active personal participation with their patients, which seems so important for the success of a therapeutic relationship.

PERSONAL QUALITIES OF PATIENTS RELATED TO RESPONSIVENESS TO PSYCHOTHERAPY

The outcome of a psychotherapeutic encounter depends on personal attributes of the patient as well as the therapist. Clinical impressions and controlled observational studies agree as to the personal qualities of patients related to their acceptance of psychotherapy and their ability to respond favorably to it. Unfortunately most reports do not specify whether the attributes described are related to remaining in therapy, improvement, or both. A patient cannot benefit from a treatment unless he takes it, so remaining in therapy is a prerequisite for improvement. On the other hand, he can remain in treatment indefinitely without improving, so the distinction may be important.[39]

Since psychotherapy endeavors to relieve the patient's distress and improve his adaptation to life through personal influence, his adaptive capacity and susceptibility to influence would be expected to be related to his ability to profit from it. With respect to general adaptive capacity, patients who are persevering and dependable tend to remain in therapy, while impulsive patients tend to drop out. That is, persons who tend to stick to any task despite difficulties and disappointments also persist in psychotherapy. This trait, however, is nowhere mentioned as related to improvement.

High intelligence, verbal skill, and capacity for self-understanding besides being generally useful equipment for the battle of life, fit patients well for therapies that stress self-examination and the verbalization of feelings, so patients possessing these assets can participate relatively easily in analytic therapies.[40] Many do well, but others who appear equally well endowed do not, indicating that other personal attributes must also play a part in the outcome of treatment.

Patients whose symptoms are clearly related to environmental stress probably have greater adaptive capacity than those who have become ill in the absence of obvious external pressures, and the former are believed to have a better prognosis.[41] In actual fact the disturbance for which they seek psychiatric help may often be a normal reaction to stress.

Disaster victims typically undergo emotional turmoil, often with psychic and bodily concomitants indistinguishable from those shown by psychiatric patients, and the absence of these responses may be a more ominous sign than their occurrence. Persons shaken by disaster, if tided over the immediate crisis by simple supportive measures, recover rapidly and completely.[42] Analogously, of those patients whose distress is linked to environmental pressure, a considerable proportion may need only a little help to regain their emotional equilibrium, and whatever brand of psychotherapy the therapist uses receives credit for this outcome. The controlling factor in the recovery of these patients is the severity and modifiability of the environmental pressure under which they have broken down.

Patients who seek psychotherapy under situational stress not only may have better adaptive powers than those who collapse with such stress, but they also tend to have two other characteristics probably related to responsiveness to psychotherapy. These are influencibility and emotional reactivity. That these patients are involved with other persons and respond to them is suggested by the fact that in civilian life most stresses involve interpersonal disturbances such as marital, familial, or work conflicts or traumatic terminations of intimate relationships through death or separation. Emotional reactivity is implied by the fact that the stress upsets them sufficiently to cause them to seek treatment.[43]

With regard to susceptibility to interpersonal influence, there is some evidence that suggestible persons tend to stay in treatment longer than nonsuggestible ones and that persons who participate in group activities and generally get along well with others seem to do better than antagonistic, mistrustful ones who tend to be isolates or nomads.

The relevance of emotional reactivity to psychotherapy lies in the fact that emotional arousal seems to be a prerequisite for attitude change and also to accompany it.[44] That emotional responsiveness is closely related to dependency on others is suggested by the somewhat complex relationship between the severity and nature of the patient's expressed misery and his responsivity to therapy. Patients seeking psychotherapy show a great range of distress. Some are absolutely desperate, and most are sufficiently troubled so that they wish to change and are predisposed to look to the psychiatrist for help. But there are many reasons for coming to a psychiatrist, and some psychiatric patients are not a bit upset.[45]

The importance of emotional distress in the establishment of a fruitful psychotherapeutic relationship is suggested by the facts that the greater the over-all degree of expressed distress, as measured by a symptom check list, the more likely the patient is to remain in treatment, while conversely two of the most difficult categories of patients to treat have nothing in common except lack of distress. One consists of certain so-called sociopathic personalities, who seek or are forced into treatment to escape the consequences of their misbehavior and inwardly are relatively content. The other category consists of intellectuals or people from the upperclass who look to psychotherapy to help them overcome vague self-dissatisfactions or to find more meaning in life. In the same group may be included many analysts in training, whose discomfort springs chiefly from having to submit to a time-consuming and expensive procedure. The psychiatrist's usefulness to these types of persons depends in part on his creating or unearthing some source of distress or otherwise convincing them that they are ill. As one writes: "Without a full-hearted acknowledgment of the sense of illness a patient can go through only the motions of treatment."[46] One is reminded of the effort to create distress by revivalists and interrogators as part of the endeavor to produce attitudinal change.[47]

The specific nature of the patient's expressed distress also seems related to his responsiveness to psychotherapy. Patients who express their difficulties in interpersonal terms, thereby indicating an acceptance of psychotherapy, tend to stay in treatment longer than those who complain primarily of bodily symptoms. The latter also do less well in treatment than those who evince anxiety or other psychic symptoms. Anxiety heightens a person's dependency on others, as seen, for example, in the greatly increased susceptibility to hypnosis of soldiers with battle reactions.[48] Absorption with bodily complaints, on the other hand, is often best understood as an attempt to retreat from involvement with others. Such patients would therefore be expected to find it difficult to relate closely to the therapist. In addition, bodily complaints are ordinarily treated by a physician, not a psychiatrist, so that the mere presentation of these as leading symptoms may be a sign that the patient does not expect to be helped by psychotherapy. And this illustrates another relevant point. A patient's willingness to admit distress, especially in conjunction with personal problems, implies a willingness to make humiliating self-revelations, which in itself is evidence that he trusts the psychiatrist and expects to be helped by him. It also implies dissatisfaction with oneself, hence motivation to change.[49]

The close relationship between degree of expressed anxiety,

dependency on others, and acceptance of psychotherapy has been beautifully demonstrated by some experimental and statistical studies, which have many thought-provoking implications.[50] Girl college students were led to expect a painful shock after a ten-minute delay and were given the choice of waiting with other students in a similar predicament or staying by themselves. Their anxiety was simultaneously measured by asking them to rate how they felt about being shocked and by giving them a chance to withdraw from the experiment if they wished to do so. Presumably those who were not willing to go through with it were more anxious than those who said they would see it through. Actually the experiment terminated before the shock was administered. By ingenious manipulations of the experimental conditions and statistical analyses of the results, the experimenter demonstrated that the desire to be with others was related to the degree of anxiety produced by anticipation of a painful stimulus and that the level of anxiety was higher for subjects who were only and first-born children than for those who came later in the family. Moreover, first-born subjects with high anxiety had a stronger desire to be with others than later-born subjects with the same degree of anxiety.

The experimenter then analysed the statistics of a nearby Veterans Administration Mental Hygiene Clinic, and these indicated that patients who were first-born or only children accepted psychotherapy when it was offered, and stayed in it longer if they accepted it, than did those who were later-born. It should be added that the first group were no "sicker" than the second, that is, ordinal position in the family was unrelated to degree of psychological disturbance. In view of the experimental results, a very plausible explanation of this finding is that first-born tend to be more dependent on others to relieve their distress than are later-born. There is considerable theoretical support for this along the lines that parents of first-born children are both more inexperienced and more anxious than they are when the subsequent children arrive, and they can give the first child undivided attention. Thus they tend to over-protect him and to handle him inconsistently, both of which patterns would, on theoretical grounds, be expected to increase dependency.[51] Parents have progressively less time for later-born children the farther down the line they are, and also, having become experienced, they handle them more consistently. Moreover, later-born children have to compete with their brothers and sisters for the parents' attention. On both counts one would expect them to be less likely to see others as a source of help when they are in distress. We may tentatively conclude that dependency is related both to acceptance of psychotherapy and susceptibility to anxiety. That all three of these turn out to be related to order of birth is a fascinating finding, which, if confirmed, will open interesting vistas for further study.

As our survey to this point has shown, knowledge of personal qualities related to responsiveness to various forms of personal influence is tantalizingly sketchy, and it would be foolhardy to attempt to draw any firm conclusions from it. It does seem safe to say, however, that personal attributes affecting responsiveness to psychotherapy seem generally similar to those that have been identified as related to influencibility, and none are contradictory. Accessibility to the influence of others appears as extroversion in those susceptible to religious conversions, dependency and good social integration with placebo responsiveness, and compliance in the conditioning of verbal behavior. Isolation and mistrustfulness militate against acceptance of the latter two forms of influence. Intense distress, with its implication of emotional responsiveness enhances susceptibility to thought reform and religious revivalism. Feelings of personal inadequacy or dissatisfaction, which would be expected to contribute both to distress and dependence on others, seem to heighten susceptibility to conversion and persuasion, as well as to psychotherapy.

That persons with circumscribed bodily complaints are less susceptible to influence than those with general anxiety appears from studies of placebo responsiveness, conversion, persuasibility and verbal conditioning. Finally, ordinal position in the family is related to susceptibility to anxiety dependence on others when anxious, and acceptance of psychotherapy. In short, this review of attributes of therapist and patient that militate for or against the success of psychotherapeutic transactions between them supports the notion that this relationship has much in common with other forms of interpersonal influence.

SUMMARY

This chapter has considered psychotherapy with regard to sociocultural position and training of the psychiatrist and personal attributes of psychiatrist and patient. From the sociocultural standpoint the tendency of psychiatrists to be overvalued in some respects and undervalued in others creates problems with certain patients. The multiplicity of world views and groups in American society creates the possibility that psychiatrist and patient may belong to different socioeconomic classes, impeding communication between them, and patients from the lower class may be unable to perceive a therapy based on middle-class values as helpful. Moreover, the psychiatrist is deprived of the prestige possessed by healers whose role is sanctioned by the entire society to which they and the patient belong. The major advantage of the diversity of American society for psychotherapy is that it permits a variety of routes to improved personal integration and social adjustment.

The psychiatrist's status as a physician enables him to inspire confidence in his patients and to strengthen their self-esteem through his acceptance of them. Some psychiatrists, in addition, have undergone analytic training, which teaches a particular body of doctrine linked to a special technique, affords extensive experience in the use of the method, and includes an analysis of the trainee. This training has many values, including mastery of an inclusive and penetrating theory of human nature and enhancement of the analysts' self-knowledge, but the superiority of analytic treatment over other methods remains to be demonstrated. This suggests that part of the popularity and persistence of analytic training may lie in its effectiveness as an indoctrination procedure. In this connection similarities of analytic training to thought reform are pointed out.

From the standpoint of personality, the good psychotherapist has qualities such as self-confidence, energy, and controlled emotional warmth. These enable him to offer his patients a pattern of active, personal participation, which arouses their expectation of help and facilitates attitude changes.

Favorable personal features of patients appear to be good adaptive capacity and attributes similar to those found to predispose persons to acceptance of other forms of personal influence, such as religious revivalism, thought reform, administration of a placebo, and operant conditioning of verbal behavior. These include accessibility to other persons, self-dissatisfaction, and emotional distress, especially in the form of anxiety.

"Where do you come from?" said the Red Queen. "And where are you going? Look up, speak nicely, and don't twiddle your fingers all the time." (*Through the Looking Glass,* Chapter 2)

"Would you tell me, please, which way I ought to go from here?" "That depends a good deal on where you want to get to," said the Cat.
"I don't much care where—so long as I get *somewhere*," Alice added as an explanation.
"Oh, you're sure to do that," said the Cat, "if you only walk long enough." (*Alice's Adventures in Wonderland,* Chapter 6)

8 | Individual Psychotherapy

PSYCHOTHERAPY AND THE PRODUCTION OF CHANGE

Having reviewed certain cultural and personal characteristics of psychiatrists and patients that influence their ability to enter into a psychotherapeutic relationship and affect its outcome, we are now in a position to look more closely at the therapeutic encounter itself. Before psychotherapeutic procedures are considered in detail, however, it seems advisable briefly to consider the major processes involved in the production of therapeutic change. For convenience, components of the psychotherapeutic process may be roughly grouped as emotional, cognitive, and behavioral, though, as will be seen, these features are closely interrelated.

Psychotherapeutic methods influence the patient's general emotional level as well as his qualitative emotional experience. Considerable experimental evidence suggests that there is an optimal level of central nervous system excitation for the facilitation of learning.[1] If psychotherapy is viewed as a learning process,[2] it might seem desirable to bring about this optimal level in patients. Actually, some psychiatric treatment methods, like other forms of healing and influence, produce arousal that seems to be well above the ideal intensity. The value of these methods may lie in their production of a central excitatory state so intense as to be disorganizing, thereby paving the way for a new reorganization of attitudes.[3]

Certain it is that emotionally shocking procedures have always played a part in the treatment of the mentally ill. Back in the first century A. D., Celsus wrote of certain patients showing abnormal behavior: "When he has said or done anything wrong, he must be chastised by hunger, chains and fetters . . . . It is also beneficial in this malady, to make use of sudden fright, for a change may be effected by withdrawing the mind from that state in which it has been."[4] Brutal treatment of the mentally ill continued through the intervening centuries, often in the guise of exorcising demons. In the nineteenth century, even the great humanitarian Pinel, who struck the chains from the insane, believed that fright was an effective remedy, and "scientific" treatments included submerging the patient until he was almost drowned or spinning him in a chair until he lost consciousness as means of restoring him to his rational senses. Today we use pharmacological and electrical methods, the main therapeutic effectiveness of which may lie in their power to produce severe physiological upheavals in the patient analogous to those caused by beatings and duckings.[5]

Modern medications can be used not only to stir patients up but to calm them down. They can make patients more accesible to interpersonal influence by dampening their overactivity and reducing their anxiety so that they become not only able to sustain a relationship with someone else, but to remember and report painful past experiences.[6]

In this connection, patients' responses to some psychopharmaceutical agents are strongly influenced by the psychological atmosphere surrounding their administration, includng the at-titude of the person administering the drug. And the patient's reactions may, in turn, affect the attitude of his physician. This is seen most dramatically in insulin coma therapy, the efficacy of which (as of the ducking stool) may lie partly in its threat to the patient's life, which compels the physician to give him a lot of attention.[7]

Psychotherapy can influence the patient's general emotional level even without pharmaceutical aid, but more significant is its ability to combat disintegrating emotions that hamper the patient's ability to profit from new experiences and to fos-ter those that facilitate experimentation and personality inte-gration.[8] This helps the patient to substitute hope for despair, courage for fear, self-confidence for feelings of inferiority.

As will be discussed in more detail presently, different types of psychotherapy tend to arouse patients emotionally in dif-ferent ways. Among these are the requirement that the patient place himself in situations, or carry out acts, that he fears; the facilitation of emotional reliving of traumatic early life ex-periences; the therapist's failure to respond to the patient's maneuvers as the latter expects; and the evocation of "trans-ference" feelings to the therapist. At this point it seems ap-propriate to call attention to an often neglected aspect of most psychotherapeutic methods, which may stir patients emotionally in a helpful but nonspecific fashion. This exciting feature is their novelty. Novelty is pleasantly exciting in itself, as evidenced by our constant search for new experiences, and it also tends to inspire hope. It is a medical truism that all forms of treatment work best just after they are introduced. The major reasons for this seem to be the physician's emotional in-vestment in the success of a procedure he has initiated and the ability of something new and untried, especially when recom-mended by an authority, to arouse the patient's hopes. Thus all new remedies, merely because they are new, tend to create favorable emotional states analogous to those aroused under favorable conditions by placebos.[9] In addition, of course, the hopes of patient and physician may cause both to overestimate the effectiveness of a new treatment, leading to overoptimistic claims for it.

Psychotherapeutic techniques such as hypnosis, free association, or a free-interaction group may retain their novelty for many generations of patients. If a form of therapy such as psychoanalysis or hypnosis becomes very well known, however, it loses its novelty for increasing numbers of patients because they have read about it and seen it portrayed on stage and screen. This may have something to do with the oft-repeated observation that new forms of psychotherapy report their highest rates of success shortly after they are introduced. It may also be related to the increasing length of treatment such as psychoanalysis and "client-centered therapy."[10] There are various possible explanations for this, including growing sophistication with increasing experience as to what constitutes a satisfactory outcome. But diminution of enthusiasm and hope in both therapists and patients as the novelty wears off cannot be excluded.

Cognitively psychotherapeutic methods supply the patient with new information about himself, or with a new way of conceptualizing what he already knows, which helps him to develop a more workable assumptive world, including his image of himself. Though different forms of psychotherapy differ widely in their conceptualizations, each has a definite rationale that helps the patient to organize his life more effectively by helping him to discover relationships he had overlooked and supplying a consistent way of interpreting his experiences.

For psychotherapy to be successful, these emotional and cognitive changes must eventuate in actual behavioral changes. To facilitate this, all forms of psychotherapy offer a relatively sheltered environment in which the patient can experiment, with little if any penalty for failure because he is not required to commit himself. The experimentation is carried out within the framework of a more or less structured task that requires the patient to participate in certain repetitive activities, certain of which are reinforced in more or less subtle ways.

The psychotherapeutic task, whatever its specific nature, is an integral part of the patient-therapist relationship and enhances certain beneficial aspects of it. The therapist's mastery of a particular therapeutic technique heightens his self-confidence and qualifies him in the patient's eyes as an expert. In both these ways it enhances the patient's confidence in him. Furthermore, the technique helps the therapist to maintain his interest, especially during dull or unrewarding stretches, thereby sustaining the therapeutic relationship.

The success of any form of treatment depends in large part on the extent to which the changes it has accomplished are supported by the patient's subsequent life experiences. A patient's attitudes must not only be changed, but the new ones must be "frozen,"[11] or he will slide back again. Little attention has been paid to this aspect of psychotherapy, apparently on the assumption that the changes produced by treatment will automatically be reinforced because they tend to lead to more gratifying experiences than the old patterns.

The emotional, cognitive, and behavioral changes that psychotherapy seeks to effect are obviously closely intertwined. If all goes well, each reinforces the others. A more workable assumptive world leads to behavior that is more successful and less frustrating. This reduces the patient's anxiety and fosters emotions that increase the flexibility of his thinking and behavior. This in turn leads to new behavior which, if successful, further strengthens the new assumptive systems. This happy state of affairs is rarely, if ever, fully achieved of course, but it affords a useful model for thinking about the methods and goals of different forms of treatment.

CLASSIFICATION OF PSYCHOTHERAPIES

In order to discuss different therapeutic activities, some simple way of classifying them is required. It is convenient to consider them from two standpoints—their target, and whether the therapeutic task is primarily directive or evocative. With respect to the target, there is a continuum from exclusive attention to the individual patient, through focus on the patient as a member of a group, to major emphasis on the group to which the patient belongs. The first two types of treatment try to modify the patient directly. Treatment contacts are intermittent, never more frequent than one hour a day and usually much less, and occur in an office setting. The last type, which may be termed milieu therapy, tries to change the patient primarily by manipulating his total environment. It therefore requires an institutional setting and ideally should control the environment twenty-four hours a day.

These categories are, of course, not mutually exclusive. Most hospitals include some individual or group treatment as part of the treatment program. Hospitals in which patients spend only the day or only the night represent forms of milieu treatment that do not operate around the clock. Therapy of families on an outpatient basis[12] may be viewed as a kind of intermittent milieu therapy. These intermediate forms may possess greater promise than the traditional therapies.

The extent to which the patient's dependence on the therapist for help is forced or voluntary loosely parallels institutional versus office settings and public versus private support. Most patients in public mental hospitals have no choice in the matter, while most patients of private practitioners come of their own free will and, in fact often have had to overcome considerable obstacles to get treatment. Some patients enter public hospitals voluntarily, however, and some private patients have been forced into treatment by more or less subtle but powerful family or social pressures. Patients in public outpatient settings cover the entire range, but only the few who are in legal difficulties and have been told to seek treatment as an alternative to jail lack all voluntary motivation.

This chapter and the two that follow consider individual, group, and milieu therapy, respectively. Each focuses on the most common settings and types of patient. Since the bulk of individual therapy is conducted with voluntary patients, whether in private offices or clinics, the present chapter concerns itself primarily with them.

Therapeutic methods can be loosely classified as directive or evocative. The former try directly to bring about changes in the patient's behavior which, it is believed, will overcome his symptoms or resolve the problems for which he sought treatment. Evocative therapies, often inaccurately termed "permissive,"[13] try to create a situation that will evoke the full gamut of the patient's difficulties and capabilities, thereby enabling him not only to work out better solutions for the problems bringing him to treatment but also to gain greater maturity, spontaneity, and inner freedom, so that he becomes better equipped to deal with future stresses as well as current ones.

Except for one form of directive therapy,[14] the goals of directive treatment tend to be circumscribed, and those of evocative techniques, open-ended. Both types attach importance to an understanding of the nature of the patient's problems, but directive forms emphasize the therapist's understanding while evocative ones stress the patient's. Directive therapies focus on the patient's current adjustment problems and review his past only sufficiently to enable the therapist to reach an understanding of his present difficulties. Evocative methods cast a wider net, exploring in detail current problems, past experiences, dreams, and phantasies. They may pay special attention to the patient's feelings toward the therapist, which are viewed as closely related to the therapeutic process. Directive therapies tend to take these feelings for granted and proceed essentially as if the relationship were the conventional one between doctor and patient. In keeping with differences in their goals and approaches, directive therapies tend to be briefer than evocative ones.

These brief introductory comments may serve as sufficient orientation for the more detailed examination of certain directive and evocative forms of psychotherapy that follows.

DIRECTIVE INDIVIDUAL PSYCHOTHERAPIES

These forms of treatment are characterized by direct efforts of the therapist to correct the patient's symptoms or maladaptive behavior patterns through advice, persuasion, and exhortation, often coupled with special techniques such as hypnosis or relaxation exercises.[15] The following example of successful treatment of a subjective symptom and a behavioral difficulty by "rational psychotherapy" may serve as representative. The unusually favorable outcome of this case should not be regarded as typical. Many patients with sexual deviations do not respond to this or any other form of psychotherapy.

The patient was a thirty-five-year-old man who was exclusively homosexual and also had periodic attacks of chest pain and palpitation. His homosexual activities had been going on for sixteen years. He also was emotionally overdependent on his parents, which was related to his having reluctantly and resentfully abandoned his teaching career to take over his father's business after the latter had suffered a stroke. The therapist first attacked his homosexuality, since this concerned the patient most. He made clear that his goal was not to cause the patient to surrender his homosexual desires, but to overcome his irrational block against heterosexual behavior. After determining that the patient never once made the initial homosexual advance, the therapist told him that his outstanding motive for remaining homosexual was fear of rejection, springing from his illogical belief that being rejected, especially by a girl, was a terrible thing. "His fear of rejection, of losing approval, of having others laugh at and criticize him was examined in scores of its aspects, and revealed to him again and again . . . [and] scornfully, forcefully *attacked* by the therapist."

Concomitantly the patient was encouraged to date girls so that he could overcome his fears by actual experiences with them. The therapist instructed him how to behave with a girl, what to expect, how to avoid being discouraged by rebuffs, and when to make sexual advances. After seven weekly sessions the patient had heterosexual relations that were mutually satisfying. By the twelfth week he was "virtually a hundred percent heterosexual. All his walking and sleeping fantasies became heterosexually oriented and he was almost never interested in homosexual outlets."

The patient's psychosomatic symptoms and vocational problems were attacked and overcome in a similar manner, as a result of which he was able to resume his interrupted academic career. It should be noted that some basic issues in the patient's life, such as his resentful overattachment to his mother and his probable jealousy of his father's hold over his mother, were virtually never discussed during the entire therapeutic procedure.

The patient discontinued treatment after nineteen sessions. A letter from him three years later revealed he was married, was completely uninterested in homosexual activity, held a university teaching post, and was free of the heart symptoms with which he came to therapy.

As this example illustrates, the directive psychotherapist operates within a clear and definite conceptual framework. He takes enough of the patient's history to formulate a diagnosis of the maladaptive attitudes and behavior patterns responsible for the patient's distress and sets the goals of treatment on the basis of his understanding of these. The goals are more or less circumscribed and characteristically involve resolution of current interpersonal difficulties. To achieve this the therapist guides the patient to new ways of behaving, typically involving more direct expression of aggressive and affiliative drives, and improvement in communication skills.

In considering the sources of effectiveness of these forms of treatment, it is convenient to view their emotional, cognitive, and behavioral aspects separately, although, as already suggested, they are closely interwoven. Emotionally, from a quantitative standpoint the therapist has various ways of maintaining an optimal state of emotional tension in the patient. He can influence the intensity of anxiety or anger by his manner and the amount of pressure he exerts to cause the patient to carry out activities that are initially anxiety-producing. He uses relaxation or hypnotic techniques to reduce emotional tension when this is indicated.

With respect to the qualitative nature of the patient's emotions, the therapist inspires his hopes by behaving like a physician initially. That is, he takes a history which, though different in emphasis, is similar to the usual medical history, forms a diagnostic impression, and recommends a plan of treatment. He promptly demonstrates his competence to the patient by using his special techniques. The patient gains confidence from the feeling that he is being given a specific remedy for what ails him.

By assuming so much overt responsibility for the conduct of therapy, the directive therapist may perhaps temporarily weaken the patient's self-confidence and increase his feelings of inadequacy. But these effects are partly counteracted by his deep and serious interest in the patient, as conveyed by the efforts he makes on his behalf. And they are more than compensated if the patient succeeds in overcoming his symptoms and disabilities.

Directive therapies foster cognitive clarity by concentrating on a few major issues and attempting to formulate as clearly as possible their nature, and precisely how they can best be resolved. From the behavioral standpoint, the tasks of directive therapies all require maximal participation by the patient and all are highly repetitive, as in other methods of persuasion. To the extent that they are clearly defined the patient can readily judge his progress, which affords an additional source of encouragement. An important aspect of the tasks of directive therapies is that the patient must apply the techniques he learns in treatment to his daily life. For example, he must carry out relaxation exercises at home as well as in the therapist's office and is urged to be more assertive with the headwaiter as well as with his therapist.

As already indicated, published analyses of results do not permit any conclusion as to the relative over-all effectiveness of directive therapies as compared to other forms of treatment.[16] It should be stressed, however, that although the immediate goals of directive treatment are limited their achievement may have far-reaching and permanent consequences, as in the example cited. A switch from an exclusively homosexual pattern to a fully heterosexual one ultimately leads to changes in almost every aspect of a person's life through changing his associates, making it possible for him to marry and become a parent, and so on. That is, changes introduced by this form of treatment may become progressively reinforced through the new life experiences to which they lead. One follow-up study of forty-five patients categorized as apparently cured or much improved after receiving any of a variety of directive therapies found that after two to seven years forty-four had maintained their improvement or improved further without formal aid.[17]

EVOCATIVE THERAPIES

Evocative approaches, which dominate the American psychotherapeutic literature, can be traced back to Freud's psychoanalysis, though many now deviate markedly from it.[18] All share the psychoanalytic aim of helping the patient to achieve increased insight into his feelings and behavior and stress his ability to express his insights in words. They thus tend to appeal especially to the more educated members of our society who place a high value on self-knowledge and verbal skills. Since these persons also tend to belong to the higher socioeconomic strata, this may account for the higher prestige enjoyed by evocative methods as compared to directive ones.

Evocative therapies tend to de-emphasize alleviation of the patient's complaints, viewing them as merely symptoms of general adaptational difficulties. They try to help the patient to become more mature, creative, and spontaneous, so that he will be able to gain more success and satisfaction from all aspects of living.

The essence of evocative methods lies in the fostering of a particular type of relationship between patient and therapist that promotes enlargement of the former's self-knowledge, thereby enabling him to discover and achieve the type of change that is best suited to his own particular personality and circumstances. To facilitate this process, the therapist encourages the patient to express himself with complete freedom. No matter how humiliating or unpleasant the patient's revelations, the therapist maintains an attitude of serious, consistent, impartial interest. His attitude is one of attempting to understand the patient, to follow his leads, and to talk about what is on the patient's mind rather than on his own. He not only accepts, but may encourage, opposition. He makes no claim to omniscience or infallibility and, in fact, may explicitly disclaim any such powers and openly admit his ignorance or his failure to comprehend. In these ways he seeks to prevent the patient from developing an unrealistic dependence and to strengthen his sense of autonomy.

Feeling himself accepted by someone he admires, and to whom he feels increasingly close by virtue of the intimacy of his revelations, the patient, it is claimed, dares to reveal more and more of the shameful or frightening aspects of himself that he has pushed out of awareness. These include the feelings that cause his distress. As, through this process, his self-understanding increases and his self-esteem becomes stronger, he is able to become more spontaneous and his interactions with persons important to him become successful and satisfying. This further enhances his self-confidence, and so he continues to progress. In short, through psychotherapy the patient learns progressively to trust his therapist, and this may be the first step to the development of greater faith in his fellow man and in himself.

While fully recognizing that much of this process, and perhaps its most important part, occurs as the patient tries out his new insights in his relations with persons in his daily life, evocative therapists in accordance with their philosophy seldom explicitly instigate changes in the patient's behavior. They reason that as he becomes inwardly more free such changes will occur automatically.

The patient's communication of his feelings and thoughts as freely and honestly as possible leads to an ever-widening exploration of his psychic life. To facilitate this process Freud devised the method of free association, in which the patient is instructed to report everything that comes into his mind without exercising any selection. To minimize distractions introduced by the reactions of the analyst, and also to encourage relaxation, which fosters the free flow of thought, he had the patient lie on a couch and sat out of his line of vision. Many current practitioners of evocative therapy believe these arrangements to be unnecessary and simply conduct a face-to-face conversation.[19]

One influential school of evocative therapy believes that the therapist's entire function is to maintain an attitude of "unconditional positive regard," while encouraging the patient with simple signs of interest. This is deemed sufficient to enable the patient to discover, reveal, and re-integrate ever more deeply hidden or rejected aspects of himself.[20] Analytical schools, while concurring as to the importance of the analyst's impartial attitude, believe that he can facilitate the therapeutic process by interpretations of the patient's productions, as discussed below.

Analytic schools differ somewhat in the areas of the patient's mental life that receive the chief scrutiny. Some make much use of dreams, others deemphasize them. Initially great emphasis was placed on the recovery of upsetting experiences with the patient's immediate family in infancy and early childhood, thought to have been the sources of the anxieties and distorted assumptive systems responsible for his current difficulties. Many modern schools focus more sharply on the patient's contemporary problems, delving into the past chiefly to elucidate these. All agree that in an intimate, prolonged relationship with the therapist, the patient eventually shows feelings and behavior towards him similar to those making trouble for him outside of therapy. Some evocative therapies put great weight on the mutual exploration by patient and therapist of these "transference reactions," as the major route to increased self-knowledge.

Evocative therapies may bring about beneficial changes in patients in a variety of ways, all of which cannot be fully encompassed in this essay. We shall consider only those features that seem analogous to those encountered in other forms of interpersonal influence, while recognizing that this may be but a small part of the story.

Evocative therapies may well influence patients as much as directive ones.[21] Evidence was presented in Chapter 6 that the content of the patient's utterances in nondirective therapy may follow the therapist's unconscious leads. It has long been known that dreams may be "produced in a form that will best please the analyst."[22] The kind of improvement reported by patients in evocative forms of therapy also tends to confirm the therapist's theory. Patients in psychoanalysis, which relates mental health to the extent of the patient's self-knowledge, express increasing amounts of hitherto unconscious material as therapy progresses. Those who improve in client-centered therapy show on suitable tests that the discrepancy between their perceived self and ideal has been reduced, which is the change the theory underlying this form of treatment equates with improvement.[23] Therapists who view ability to sense and express one's feelings directly as a sign of progress find that their patients are better able to do this as therapy progresses.[24] One experimental study found that patients who improved under evocative treatment showed a shift in certain of their values towards the therapist's;[25] another, that patients treated by therapists of different evocative schools explained their improvement in terms of the methods of these schools.[26]

It is unnecessary further to belabor the point that evocative therapies, like directive ones, are influencing techniques. Let us instead turn to a closer analysis of the sources and modes of their persuasive power. These prove to be more subtle than those of directive therapies and probably take longer to reach full effectiveness.

The conceptual framework underlying evocative therapies may contribute to their influencing power in several ways. Since the therapist believes that he does not influence the patient's productions, he can regard them as independent verification of the theory. As all of us try to gain support for our assumptive systems by getting others to confirm them, the therapist may be tempted to induce patients to produce such material, especially since his theory enables him to conceal from himself the fact that he is doing so.[27]

The claim to objectivity of evocative treatment methods may paradoxically heighten their influencing power with some patients because this implies that they are scientific, and science has high prestige. Many patients have more confidence in a therapist who appears to be scientifically open-minded than in one who is dogmatic, and therefore they are more susceptible to his influence. Since the therapist uses no obvious techniques of persuasion, the patient's thoughts appear to be his own. Common sense as well as experiments cited earlier[28] suggest that a person is more likely to adopt ideas that he believes he has thought of himself than those that he believes are imposed upon him.

Although the theories underlying evocative therapies do not claim infallibility, as described in Chapter 7, they seem to have retained certain characteristics of the self-consistent, irrefutable conceptual schemes underlying other forms of psychic healing and influence. Many psychiatrists recognize that their concepts are tentative and preserve a detached, critical attitude towards them in theoretical discussions, but for the purposes of therapy the concepts are not open to question. In the actual therapeutic situation the patient's feelings and behavior are interpreted in terms of the psychiatrist's particular view of human functioning, and treatment is expected to continue until the patient somehow acknowledges the correctness of the interpretation. The theory may assume that the patient's troubles are due primarily to repressed intrapsychic conflicts or to an unrealistic self-image, to take two examples. Therapy is not complete until the patient produces data confirming this assumption and, presumably as a result, modifies his behavior in the direction deemed to represent improvement. The possibilities that his psychic life does not contain the phenomena in question or that they may be irrelevant to his illness are not entertained.

The therapist's activities in evocative therapies have strong persuasive components. In accord with the emphasis of these methods on objectivity, the psychiatrist is apt to conclude his initial interview by offering the patient an opportunity to explore his problems further, but to refrain from any explicit claims that this will be helpful. That the patient nevertheless maintains his expectancy of help, which contributes to his susceptibility to influence, is indicated by his willingness to persist in treatment, even at the cost of considerable time, effort, and sometimes emotional distress.[29] Mere curiosity about his inner life would scarcely supply sufficient motivation for this. In the initial phases his expectancy of help is probably maintained by the cultural forces discussed in the previous chapter.[30] If, as often occurs, the therapist takes a history not too dissimilar from a medical one, concluding with a formulation of the patient's problems, this links him in the patient's eyes with other physicians. If he does not, the patient's hopes may be sustained by the symptomatic improvement that so often occurs early in treatment, or perhaps by signs emitted by the therapist, such as evidence of deep and continuing interest, which belie his overt reluctance to claim therapeutic power. In any case, there is no reason to think that evocative techniques are less successful in mobilizing the hope of recovery in patients who accept them than are other healing methods.

As therapy progresses, the therapist's behavior may be at variance with the patient's expectations, and this may contribute to its influencing effect. He differs from the usual physician in offering no prescriptions or advice and in his willingness to admit uncertainty, or even error. At the same time he differs from persons familiar to the patient by failing to respond to his provocations. He does not react to criticism by either anger or contrition, to complaints by sympathy or impatience, or to seductive behavior by amorousness, embarrassment, or rebuff. He thus disconfirms aspects of the patient's assumptive world, tending to cause the patient to modify them. This therapeutically important process is usually accompanied and facilitated by emotional reactions as indicated earlier, leading to the use of the term "corrective emotional experience" for it.[31]

The therapist's steadfast refusal to assume active leadership tends to create an ambiguous situation for the patient, who has only a vague idea of what he is supposed to do, how long he is to keep it up, and how he will know when he is finished. In response to the patient's attempts to gain clarification the therapist does nothing at all or may make noncommittal encouraging sounds or ask noncommittal questions. The resulting unclarity of the situation may enhance its influencing power. As outlined in Chapter 2, everyone constantly tries to form stabilized and clear assumptions by which to guide his behavior. Therefore a person in an ambiguous situation is impelled to try to clarify it, that is, to assume the initiative in trying to find out what is expected of him and then do it. In therapy this leads him actively to participate in the treatment process. Thus participation is as important in evocative therapies as in other forms of healing and influences.

To the extent that a person cannot unaided construct a clear set of expectations in a situation, he tends to look to others for direction.[32] This may explain the finding that confusion increases suggestibility.[33] In evocative therapy, the patient's tendency to scrutinize the therapist for clues as to what is expected of him may be heightened by his belief that relief from his suffering depends on his doing or saying the right thing. Therefore he is likely to be acutely aware of the therapist, even when he sits out of sight, as in psychoanalysis, and subtle signs such as the analyst's shifting in his chair, and so on, may serve as cues that affect his productions.

Ambiguity or unclarity tends to arouse unpleasant emotions such as anxiety and resentment, which heighten the patient's desire for relief, thereby increasing his influencibility. The relation of ambiguity to anxiety is obvious.[34] Nothing is harder to stand than uncertainty as to how to proceed, especially when making the correct choice seems vital. Resentment may be aroused by the patient's mounting feelings of frustration as the therapist consistently refuses to satisfy his implicit or explicit demand for help. This occurs particularly in classical psychoanalysis, in which the therapist may remain virtually silent for long periods. As a leading analyst puts it:

> The patient's sense of frustration affords a continuing provocation to resentment. For, as the days go by, there develops in the patient a growing suspicion that there exists between him and his therapist what an economist would call "an unfavorable trade balance." The patient has "cooperated," he has obeyed instructions, he has given himself. He has contributed information, exposing his very heart, and in addition to all this he has paid money for the sessions in which he did it. And what return has he gotten from the physician? Attention, audience, toleration, yes—but no response. No "reaction." No advice. No explanation. No solution. No help. No love.[35]

The analyst's refusal to come to the patient's rescue may serve many valuable functions. The state of mind it produces, although unpleasant, may facilitate attitude change, not only by arousing the patient emotionally, but by helping him to recognize his unrealistic expectations of the therapist and so achieve a more objective attitude towards others.

Evocative therapies in the analytic tradition place considerable weight on detailed exploration and interpretation of the patient's psychic life, including his past history. That this may be an influencing process is suggested by its similarity to procedures in thought reform and primitive healing rites.[36] In all prolonged influencing procedures, the same historical material is reviewed repeatedly, in the presence of someone who maintains a consistent attitude towards it, and this repetition seems important for learning new patterns of response.

Exploration of the patient's past is much more than a fact-finding expedition—an effort to help him gain insight into his current maladjustments by uncovering their historical sources. From the emotional standpoint, detailed exploration of past history tends to mobilize guilt. In the absence of overt direction from the therapist, the patient is tempted to become ever more self-revealing, partly in the hope of producing something that will gain a supportive response. Since he knows he is supposed to bring up troublesome and painful experiences, he does so, and many of these may make him feel guilty, as described in the following quotation, which incidentally clearly suggests an analogy between this process in psychotherapy and in thought reform.

"Sooner or later . . . the confessions and confidings . . . begin to include material which the patient had not been aware of any need to confess . . . he soon gets into the position of 'betraying' himself and implicating others. He finds himself telling tales out of school and admitting things which he had previously denied—perhaps even to himself. So, whereas at first he had been relieved by the diminished pressure of his confessions, now new pressures develop because of them . . . ."[37]

Guilt tends to facilitate attitude change by alienating the patient from the experiences and attitudes that produce it. At the same time the therapist's continued impartial interest in the face of guilt-arousing material tends to be experienced as a kind of implicit forgiveness. Since the therapist in some sense represents society, this may help to counteract the patient's sense of isolation and enable him to feel more closely integrated with his group. Thus the phenomena of guilt, confession, and absolution, which play such an important part in religious healing, conversion, and thought reform, have analogies in evocative psychotherapy.

From a cognitive standpoint, even in prolonged therapy a patient recalls only a minute fraction of all his past experiences, so the question arises as to what principle of selectivity he employs and the extent to which his choice may be influenced by the psychiatrist's expectations. Man is a time-binding creature whose self-image includes expectations about his future and is supported by his picture of his past. A social psychologist has suggested that a patient's account of his life might be appropriately termed an *apologia*, "an image of [a person's] life course, past, present and future—which selects, abstracts, and distorts in such a way as to provide him with a view of himself that he can usefully expound in current situations."[38] To change a person's image of himself today, it is necessary to change his view of his future. But the future is not here yet, so his view of it can only be changed by a re-interpretation of his past.

If this viewpoint is correct, then the review of past history may be primarily a means of modifying the patient's self-image. He comes to treatment with an apologia that justifies and supports an unsound picture of himself. To this end, he has blotted certain experiences out of his memory and overemphasized others. Supported and implicitly guided by the therapist, he recalls some of the forgotten material and re-interprets some of it. In the process he gradually reconstructs a new apologia that gives him a more favorable view of the future and sustains a new and better self-image. Thus "insight" should probably be viewed as the result of a reworking of the past that leads not only to the discovery of new facts and of new relationships between previously known ones but also to re-evaluation of their significance.[39]

In most forms of evocative therapy the therapist from time

to time interprets the patient's productions. In directive therapies, interpretations are explicit modes of persuasion and form
the basis for specific advice. In evocative ones, their aim is to
foster self-revelation and insight, and the patient is expected
to draw his own implications for his conduct from them.
Though many interpretations do have a purely evocative function, they are probably the chief means whereby the therapist
influences the patient, and they are considered only from this
aspect here.

The simplest form of interpretation consists of repeating
something the patient has said, perhaps with some change in
emphasis, so that he becomes more clearly aware of it. In a
roughly ascending scale of degree of inference and amount of
complexity, other forms of interpretation are summarizing,
in order to co-ordinate and emphasize certain aspects, verbaliz-
ing the feelings that seem to lie behind the patient's utterances,
and confronting him sharply with attitudes implied by his statements that he had not recognized. Complex interpretations
may indicate similarities between a patient's feelings toward
significant persons in his past and toward important contem-
poraries, including the therapist. They may also suggest symbolic meanings of his statements or link them to a theoretical
scheme.

Interpretation of the attitudes and feelings of the patient
towards the therapist, the so-called "transference reactions,"
have received increasing emphasis in recent years. They color
the patient's reports about all aspects of his life. At a simple
level he may exaggerate his suffering if he believes the therapist
can be won over by arousing his sympathy, hide material that
he thinks will arouse the therapist's contempt, and so on.
Therefore his productions can be properly evaluated only in
the light of his attitudes towards the therapist and the treatment situation.

The major significance of transference reactions lies in the
fact that they afford valuable clues to the patient's feelings and
behavior towards persons important to him outside of therapy.

If the patient can be brought to see how his reactions to the therapist are caused by a confusion of the therapist with other persons, this highlights the inappropriateness of the responses and also increases his ability to detect the inappropriateness of similar reactions outside treatment. If he discovers that in some respects he is reacting to the therapist as if he were his childhood image of his father, for example, he then may find that he is doing the same to other "father figures," such as employers. By identifying his maladaptive behavior and feelings, he becomes more able to modify them.

The possibility that interpretations might directly influence the patient's productions has long been recognized. Psychoanalysts in keeping with their emphasis on therapeutic objectivity have sought to deny that interpretations can operate as suggestions in this sense.[40] Evidence from psychoanalysis itself casts considerable doubt on this contention. Freud's well-known statement that "we are not in a position to force anything on the patient about the things of which he is obtensibly ignorant or to influence the products of the analysis by arousing an expectation"[41] was made before his discovery that patients fabricated infantile memories in accord with his theories. A leading analyst once went to some lengths to draw a distinction between correct and incorrect interpretations, agreeing that the latter might operate by suggestion but offering elaborate reasons why the former did not. That he did not entirely convince himself is suggested by the following quotation, from an article written some twenty years later: ". . . despite all dogmatic and puristic assertions to the contrary, we cannot exclude or have not yet excluded the transference effect of suggestion through interpretation."[42]

Even when couched in noncommittal terms, interpretations may convey information about the therapist's competence and his attitudes that may affect the patient. Through interpretations he demonstrates his ability to understand the patient, his skill at drawing inferences, and his command of both theory and technique. The therapist's interpretative ability therefore arouses and maintains the patient's confidence in him as a master of a special healing art. Incidentally, a good interpretation also reassures the therapist as to his own competence, which may tempt young and inexperienced practitioners to offer too many and too elaborate ones to allay their self-doubts.

Interpretations may subtly convey the therapist's acceptance or rejection of the patient's productions. Labeling a patient's feeling for example may convey that the therapist is not afraid of it, that it is familiar to him, and that he will continue to accept the patient in spite of it. Such an interpretation has an enabling function—it encourages the patient to continue further in the same direction. Other interpretations, especially those that point out some inappropriateness of the patient's feelings or perceptions, are implicit criticisms. By indicating that an aspect of the patient's psychic life is maladaptive, the therapist implicitly suggests that he do something else. Such an interpretation differs from a conventional suggestion in that it does not tell the patient how he should change, but only that change would be desirable. Thus its effect is to inhibit certain lines of feelings or conduct and encourage the patient to develop more acceptable ones.

Interpretations may affect the general level of the patient's emotional tension and also arouse specific emotions. Tension tends to be reduced by any interpretation that heightens the patient's faith in the therapist. Merely naming a hitherto inchoate feeling may have the same effect by bringing it out of the realm of the vague and mysterious into that of the clear and commonplace, thereby increasing the patient's sense of mastery. Interpretations that indicate the therapist's understanding and acceptance of the patient's feelings may work either way. They may induce a feeling of relief and relaxation on the one hand, or encourage the patient to let himself feel and express the emotion more fully on the other. Neutral interpretations may heighten tension if they confront the patient with feelings he would prefer to disavow. Interpretations that are implicitly critical may have a similar effect.

The same type of interpretation may enhance the self-esteem of one type of patient and weaken that of another. Thus a patient who is overwhelmed with feelings of guilt may gain considerable support from interpretations that imply that these feelings were inevitable reactions to the actions of others and he is not to blame. Such a formulation might aggravate the condition of patients who are already too prone to transfer responsibility for their difficulties to the shoulders of others. They often feel a powerless resentment, as if they were pawns at the mercy of a malignant fate, and so may gain support from interpretations that highlight their own contributions to their predicaments. By implying that the patient brought his troubles on himself, this type of interpretation may suggest that he has the power to resolve them, and thus it is reassuring.[48] The same interpretation might heighten the guilt of the patient who already feels over-responsible.

Complex interpretations that relate the patient's productions to a body of doctrine or give them symbolic meanings also may have useful emotional by-products. The therapist's ability to link the patient's personal troubles to an established set of concepts implies that he is not unique, thereby diminishing his sense of isolation, especially when the same concepts are applied to normal persons. Such interpretations enable him to reconceptualize his problems in terms that simultaneously make him feel closer to his fellow man and his society. Moreover, some conceptual schemes, notably those in the Freudian or Jungian tradition, have a highly dramatic quality. The patient is no longer an insignificant creature but becomes a battleground of titanic forces or a storehouse of the accumulated myths and wisdom of the ages. There may be a slight echo here of the linkage of the individual to suprapersonal forces, which seemed to be important in thought reform as well as conversion and religious healing. In any case, such interpretations heighten a patient's sense of importance and so may help to bolster his morale.

Interpretations have important influencing effects at a cognitive level. The verbal apparatus is the chief tool of analysis and discrimination, so that getting feelings and attitudes into words enables patients to test their appropriateness. Analytic theory stresses this function of interpretations. Some analysts feel that the core of the analytic process is the confrontation of the patient's adult self with the distortions he has unconsciously carried over from childhood. Once he clearly sees their inappropriateness to his current life situation, he may be able to modify them.[44] At a more complex level interpretations that offer a patient concepts by which to comprehend and organize his feelings help him to reconceptualize his past and present experiences into a more satisfactory "apologia."[45]

A final form of influence exerted by evocative therapies arises simply from the fact that they involve a long-term relationship between a person and someone on whom he feels dependent. This fosters identification. Just as children learn adult roles partly through identifying with their parents, so patients may identify with their therapists.

While the conditions determining identification are still poorly understood, there is no doubt that in long-term therapy patients may more or less unwittingly use the therapist as a model. They may unconsciously copy his mannerisms, for example. Often the identification extends considerably deeper, to include aspects of the therapist's value system or his way of approaching problems. His ability to be mature, tolerant, and flexible may help the patient to become so. In this connection his willingness to admit his limitations without becoming insecure may help the patient to accept his own imperfections more easily. Since he may serve as a model, it behooves him to have his own emotional house in order. This is a major reason for the requirement of many schools of evocative therapy that the therapist himself undergo psychotherapy.

This brief survey of the influencing processes of directive and evocative therapies indicates that the latter are more indirect and may be expected to take longer to reach their full effects. The influence exerted through interpretations and identification, for example, would take longer to be apparent than that exerted through direct commands or advice. By giving the patient at least the illusion of autonomy, evocative therapies may be less apt to foster unhealthy dependency, although this consideration must be balanced by the recognition that the very duration of the treatment process may habituate the patient to reliance on the "therapeutic hour," if not directly on the therapist, to an extent that impedes his growth towards genuine independence. In any case this review suggests that it is unsafe to assume, as is so often done, that evocative therapies influence their patients less than directive ones.

SUMMARY

        Psychotherapy may be viewed as an influencing process that has emotional, cognitive, and behavioral facets. Emotionally it tries to produce and maintain a degree of arousal optimal for learning, to foster hope, self-confidence, and trust, and to combat despair, insecurity, and suspicion. Cognitively psychotherapy helps the patient to achieve new and more accurate understanding of his problems and ways of dealing with them. From the behavioral standpoint, it requires that the patient participate repetitively in some form of activity that leads to behavioral changes outside the therapeutic situation.

Psychotherapies can be classified according to whether they deal primarily with the individual patient alone, with the patient as a member of a group, or with the patient's total milieu. This chapter considers individual therapies, which can be roughly classified as directive or evocative. In the former, the therapist tries by direct intervention to alleviate specific symptoms or to bring about limited changes in the patients' behavior. In the latter he tries to evoke and explore a wide range of the patient's feelings and attitudes as a means of increasing the accuracy and extent of his self-knowledge, so that he becomes better able to function in all aspects of his life.

The conceptual frameworks underlying both directive and evocative forms of treatment are essentially irrefutable, like the theories underlying other types of persuasion and healing. Directive therapies can heighten the patient's level of emotional tension through the amount of pressure they exert on him to carry out anxiety-producing activities and can lower it through, for example, hypnosis or relaxation exercises. The directive therapist inspires the patient's hope by behaving as a physician and offering specific remedies for his problems, attempts to achieve cognitive clarity by focusing on only a few areas of the patient's life, and at the behavioral level requires that the patient promptly put into practice the techniques he has learned.

Viewed solely as methods of persuasion, evocative therapies may paradoxically heighten the therapist's incentive and ability to influence the patient through their stress on his neutrality and objectivity. This tempts him to induce the patient to express material that confirms his theories, because he can regard it as independent evidence for them; and the patient is induced to accept the therapist's formulations because he believes them to be his own.

From the emotional standpoint, the failure of the evocative therapist to respond as the patient expects can sharply disconfirm the patient's assumptive world and so lead to a corrective emotional experience. His refusal to tell the patient what to do creates an ambiguous situation that may increase the patient's suggestibility and also arouse his anxiety and resentment, which, if not too intense, may act as incentives to change. Detailed review of the patient's psychic life may mobilize guilt that helps him to detach himself from certain attitudes, and the therapist's noncondemnatory attitude may represent a form of forgiveness that helps him to overcome feelings of isolation. Cognitively, review of the patient's experiences, including his emotional reactions to the therapist, also helps him to reconceptualize them so that they sustain a more viable self-image. This process is guided by the therapist's interpretations, which, as the chief tools of evocative treatment, are means of demonstrating his competence, thereby raising the patient's expectancy of help. They also guide the patient indirectly by subtly conveying the therapist's approval or disapproval. At a cognitive level they heighten the patient's ability to analyze and reconceptualize his feelings by getting them into words. They may also influence the patient's emotional state by indirectly diminishing his feelings of isolation, strengthening his sense of mastery, increasing or decreasing his sense of responsibility for his condition, and dramatizing his problems. In addition to influencing the patient through these means, evocative therapies because of their long duration afford an opportunity for the patient to use the therapist as a model. Much of a therapist's influencing potential may lie in this process of identification, which occurs more or less unconsciously.

"I'm glad they've come without waiting to be asked," she thought; "I should never have known who were the right people to invite!" (*Through the Looking Glass,* Chapter 9)

9 | Group Psychotherapy

Group therapies, by virtue of the fact that they attempt to modify the attitudes and improve the health of many sufferers simultaneously, are more obviously analogous than individual forms of treatment to the forms of healing and persuasion reviewed earlier. Methods of primitive healing utilize group forces mobilized by well members of the community. Methods of mass conversion and certain types of religious healing, represented by Lourdes, exploit powerful group forces created by the simultaneous participation of many persons with common problems, sufferings, and goals. Group psychotherapies differ from these group forms of healing and influence in bringing the same patients together intermittently over a considerable span of time. Ordinarily the participants are patients, and the healthy segment of the community is represented by the group therapist, sometimes supplemented by a co-therapist or observer. Some groups consist solely of patients, as will be described presently. This chapter considers only outpatient groups. In the next chapter, groups of hospitalized patients will be considered as components of the total therapeutic program of the hospital.

The principles and methods of group therapy that are identical with those of individual approaches will not be considered again. This chapter will concentrate on the differences between individual treatment and group therapy introduced by the participation of fellow sufferers.

As indicated in Chapter 2, each person constructs his assumptive world through interactions with others and has a strong need to check the validity of his perceptions and feelings against theirs. At first, the child is mainly influenced in this respect by parents and other elders whom he perceives as possessing superior power and knowledge. In many societies, as he grows older and becomes aware of the split between generations, he becomes increasingly influenced by his age mates, whom he perceives as being more like himself and as having more experiences in common with him than his elders do. Most persons remain quite dependent on the groups with which they identify themselves as sources of validation of their own feelings, and group-belongingness is a major means of maintaining one's sense of self-identification and self-esteem. Ostracism is regarded as a particularly severe form of punishment, and re-acceptance by one's group is apt to produce a powerful surge of joy and relief. Therapy groups attempt to utilize these properties of groups to help patients help each other.

EXAMPLES OF GROUP THERAPIES

Like individual forms of psychotherapy, group therapies can be roughly grouped as directive and evocative.[1] Group forms of directive therapy can be applied to groups consisting of as many as fifty or more members, although the groups are usually smaller. All firmly guide the transactions of the members, either through the direct leadership of the therapist or through the group code that he has established. Thus these groups offer members certain selected ways of relating to others that combat their perceptual distortions, lift their spirits, and help them to develop and practice social skills. Many forms explicitly cultivate a strong sense of group-belongingness through rituals, testimonials, and formal group-recognition of members' progress.[2]

A particularly successful example of directive group therapy is Alcoholics Anonymous, which is said to help about three-fourths of those who join.[3] This movement is run solely by and for alcoholics. Group meetings are devoted almost entirely to inspirational testimonials by members who describe the horrors of life as an alcoholic and tell how much better things are since they stopped drinking. As alcoholics are comfortable only with each other, they tend to congregate in bars, where their drinking habits are re-inforced. The groups of Alcoholics Anonymous afford them the same type of companionship in a group whose standards support total abstinence. Other health-promoting standards are the insistence that the alcoholic admit that the craving for alcohol is stronger than he is, which combats his unrealistic feelings of omnipotence, and the requirement that he make restitution to those he has harmed, which counteracts demoralizing feelings of guilt and remorse and helps restore his self-respect. Members reinforce their good resolves by seeking out and trying to help other alcoholics, which not only strengthens their self-esteem but reminds them vividly of the fate in store for them if they resume drinking.

A similar type of directive group conducted by the members themselves is Recovery Incorporated.[4] Originally members of this movement consisted of ex-hospitalized patients, and the groups were conducted by the late Dr. Abraham Low. After his death the movement has continued autonomously, using his writings as its guide. Membership has come to include all types of mental patients who are able to function in the community. Meetings start with a reading from Dr. Low's book, followed by testimonials in which members describe how the principles of Recovery Incorporated have helped them to handle certain problems more effectively. These testimonials and the subsequent discussion follow a prescribed form and make much use of slogans. This type of group gives direct guidance and fosters group solidarity through repeated affirmation of common values and the use of a common language. Like Alcoholics Anonymous it encourages a hopeful outlook through the use of testimonials.

A set of group therapeutic methods that combine directive and evocative techniques is known by the term "psychodrama." In these methods, originated by Dr. J. L. Moreno, the patient acts out, or watches others act out, a personal problem.[5] Other patients and therapists serve as both actors and audience, and the patient's therapist is the stage director. To a varying degree he helps the patient choose the problem, selects the other players, suggests the dialogue and action, and guides the discussion in which the audience participates.

With institutionalized patients, psychodrama tends to be highly structured, as described in the next chapter. With outpatients, the psychodrama is often primarily evocative. A patient is encouraged to improvise the acting out of a personal problem involving persons emotionally close to him such as parents or spouse. He calls on others to help him and tells them how to play the roles that he assigns them. As the playlet proceeds, the participants become increasingly spontaneous and emotionally involved. Frequently members of the audience participate vicariously so that the situation may develop an intense emotional impact for many of the participants, which forms the basis for the discussion following the psychodrama.

Evocative group therapies strive to promote members' self-knowledge through encouraging free discussion and honest self-revelation.[6] This requires small, face-to-face groups, con-

sisting of not more than eight members in which free interaction is encouraged. Through mutual examination of their
transactions with important persons in their lives, with each
other, and with the group leader in a supportive emotional
atmosphere, patients gain insights that help them to correct
aspects of their assumptive worlds. The absence of formal
structure allows considerable latitude for experimentation,
while the emphasis on honesty helps to assure that members
report their reactions to each other accurately. Thus they
have a chance to learn how they appear to each other, make
suitable modifications in their behavior, and carry these over
into their daily lives.

An example of the kind of therapeutic experience that
can occur in a free-interaction group is the following.[7] The
group consisted of six housewives with neurotic difficulties.
The meetings soon became very lively, with much interaction
among the members and free expression of feelings towards
each other and the male psychiatrist who conducted the group.

Mrs. Smith, the central patient of this episode, was a thirty-
two-year-old housewife who complained of nervousness, gag-
ging, and fullness in the stomach. She connected her symptoms directly with her mother, a demanding, complaining
woman who, the patient felt, favored her younger sister. The
mother brought all her complaints to the patient, asked her
advice, then rejected it. She expressed strongly ambivalent
feelings toward her mother: "I love her so much, I resent
what she is doing." She could not tell her mother how she
felt and was ashamed of her attitude. Her stomach cramps
and jittery feelings came on when she felt anger at her mother
and was unable to express it. She often had anxiety attacks
when her mother criticized her. Her general attitude seemed
to be that "you must not show your feelings or people will take
advantage of you."

In the group she participated actively from the start, at first
in a superficial way. She frequently spoke of problems with
her mother and gradually came to identify Mrs. Jones, an

older woman, with her. As the result of certain experiences in the group, she came to resent Mrs. Jones for not appreciating her, but could mention this only when Mrs. Jones was not present. At the same time she wanted to help her, thus practically duplicating her attitudes toward her mother.

In the course of months Mrs. Smith's symptoms improved. Her feelings toward her mother had eased to the extent that "I don't get sick when she makes the same old nuisance of herself," yet she still could not express her resentment. She took the lead in focusing the group discussion on sexual difficulties, over the protests of Mrs. Jones.

The day before the seventy-second meeting (in the nineteenth month of treatment), Mrs. Jones called Mrs. Smith and told her she wasn't coming to the group because Mrs. Smith talked about sex all the time. In reporting this to the group, Mrs. Smith said that Mrs. Jones was acting exactly like her mother and that she had felt frightened and resentful after the telephone conversation. She added that she still felt extremely guilty and could only talk this way because Mrs. Jones was absent. Scarcely had these words left her lips when Mrs. Jones walked in, looking deeply distressed. She wore no make-up, her hair was stringy, and, as she collapsed in her chair, she seemed about to weep. Mrs. Smith's tension visibly mounted until suddenly she burst into tears and began screaming hysterically: "I caused it, I know it's my fault! I caused it, I caused it! I know it's my fault!"

To reduce the almost unbearable tension the doctor asked Mrs. Smith why she felt as she did. Mrs. Smith said: "It's the way I feel about my mother. I know I caused her to feel the way she does." Mrs. Jones listened carefully and then said calmly: "What makes you think you caused this? It's something entirely different." She then described some recent temper outbursts against her husband and son, then resentment at her husband for his indifference. While she spoke, Mrs. Smith brightened up more and more as she came to see that her assumption of responsibility for Mrs. Jones' upset was baseless. At the following meeting, Mrs. Smith said she felt a good deal better after having discovered that Mrs. Jones had not been mad at her but was upset at something else. The next week she indicated that she no longer felt obligated to listen to her mother's complaints or give in to her demands.

It was not until two months later that Mrs. Smith was able to criticize Mrs. Jones to her face. She did so by laughingly telling Mrs. Jones, who was complaining, that she was just trying to make everyone feel bad because she was feeling bad. Some weeks later the doctor noted: "Mrs. Smith can take Mrs. Jones much better and there is a good deal of warm exchange between the two."

In this example Mrs. Smith, under the impact of her group experiences, gradually became less fearful of and guilty toward Mrs. Jones, who represented her mother, until finally she was able to defy her openly by continuing to discuss details of her sexual difficulties. Mrs. Jones' emotional upset seemed to confirm her worst fears, but this was immediately followed by the startling discovery that Mrs. Jones was really disturbed about something quite unconnected with Mrs. Smith. This experience, which helped Mrs. Smith to see that her feelings were not as destructive to others as she had feared, was followed by her increasingly direct criticism of Mrs. Jones, leading to a much better relationship between them. Concomitantly, she gained increased emotional independence from her mother.

DYNAMICS OF GROUP THERAPIES

Both directive and free-interaction group therapies share many features that distinguish them from individual therapies on the one hand and ordinary social groups on the other. The following discussion focuses on free-interaction groups. Directive groups are specifically mentioned only in connection with those aspects that distinguish them from free-interaction groups. The presence of peers implies that the therapy group more closely resembles daily life than does individual treatment. Fellow group members are more like the persons each member meets outside than is the psychiatrist, who is specially trained and has a professional role. The group may be viewed as a society in miniature, which makes it a good testing ground and enables its members more readily to transfer to daily life behavior that is successful in it.

This, however, is obviously not enough, for group patients have not been able to benefit from their everyday group associations. The therapeutic power of therapy groups depends on two properties that set them off from the usual groups to which patients may belong. The first is that the group code fosters free, honest expression of feelings and attitudes. Members are encouraged to indulge in "uninhibited conversation."[8] In free interaction groups there are no limits to topics that may be discussed. Although directive groups may set certain limits—one type, for example, excludes discussions of religion —they require the same honest revelation of attitudes about topics that are discussable.

In fostering direct and open expressions of feelings therapy groups resemble families, and this may be an important source of their attractiveness. The rootlessness of many Americans has deprived them of the emotional support formerly provided by the intimate, free interactions of the large family unit. The shallow and shifting sociability of the residential development, the office, the committee, and the club is not an adequate substitute because it is tainted with an undercover competition for popularity and prestige. Therapy groups value honest expression of feeling more than poise, politeness, and apparent self-assurance, and the opportunity they offer members to be themselves is an important aspect of their healing power.

The second novel aspect of the therapy group is closely related to this: its values are unique in placing no weight on success or achievement.[9] In fact, the ticket of admission is precisely that one has failed in meeting certain problems of living. When persons first enter a therapy group, they tend to evaluate each other according to the standards prevailing in the wider society, and these standards never completely vanish, but, as a group continues, members gain status less on the basis of outside accomplishments than on their sincerity and ability to discuss their own and each other's problems constructively. Acceptance by their fellows is based more on what they are than what they do.

The combination of relatedness to the outside world, encouragement to speak honestly and freely, and de-emphasis of success in the usual sense has two widely found consequences. The first is that members of all therapy groups from derelicts to civic leaders report that one of the main values of the experience is the discovery that others have troublesome problems too, thereby diminishing their secret sense of inadequacy. Apparently people are readily deceived by each other's appearance of competence and poise. Each tends to accept the other as he presents himself while having secret doubts about his own adequacy. Under these circumstances the mutual self-revelations of the therapy group, after the first shock, can bring enormous relief.

The second consequence of the unique combination of attributes of the therapy group is that discussion of a problem in a group may lead the patient to change his assumptive world and behavior even after repeated discussion of the same material with the psychiatrist privately had no effect. A striking example of this not uncommon occurrence is afforded by Mr. Angelo, a thirty-year-old married man who had had individual treatment for about three years before entering a group.[10] His major complaint was that he had "no urge to live" because he knew that he suffered from progressive familial loss of hearing. Several members of his family were already severely affected. It soon appeared that the main source of his distress lay not in the disability itself but in his family's attitude towards it, which he shared. All of them regarded it as a disgrace, to be concealed from others. As a result they were often teased or scorned for their seeming inattentiveness, and they misinterpreted these reactions as confirming their conviction that their affliction was disgraceful.

Although Mr. Angelo learned a lot about himself in individual treatment, and this particular problem was discussed repeatedly, his chronic depression did not lift, and he continued to try to conceal his handicap. In the group his reticence very gradually diminished, and finally in the thirty-sixth meeting he finally overcame his fears sufficiently to reveal the whole story. In the process he mentioned a new fear that had never come up in individual sessions, namely that when he became completely deaf he would be helpless and his wife would abandon him. As he spoke, he burst into tears. Of course no one in the group mocked him, and no one saw his affliction as disgraceful. Instead they were supportive and reassuring. The very next day he left on vacation (the imminence of a break in treatment may have precipitated his self-revelation), and in sharp contrast to previous occasions he immediately told some new-found acquaintances about his disability. He enjoyed his vacation as never before. Thereafter he gained ground steadily as he accepted the idea of dealing with his deafness like any other handicap. His long-standing depression lifted almost completely in spite of the fact that his hearing was obviously deteriorating, and he soon terminated therapy.

Apparently the attitudes of the group convinced Mr. Angelo, as the doctor could not, that his conviction that others regarded his loss of hearing as a disgrace was unfounded. On the basis of this, he experimented outside the group and the experiment was successful, leading to his progressive recovery.

This example illustrates several other points. Mr. Angelo was aided to speak out by his knowledge that the group did not derogate admissions of weakness and difficulties and by the group code, which stressed honest revelation of feelings. This also helped him to trust the responses of his fellow members. Since the group represented the larger society, he could easily generalize this experience to other situations. The aspect of confession of a guilty secret followed by re-affirmation of the group's acceptance, which plays such a large part in religious healing, was also implicitly present. The upshot was a major beneficial change in the patient's assumptive world.

The example also shows how an interpretation that brings out a patient's own responsibility for a difficulty that he had previously attributed exclusively to a malign fate may increase his sense of power to do something about it.[11] Finally, it exemplifies a point made earlier,[12] namely that the distress caused by a chronic disease may be due more to its effects on the patient's attitudes than to the actual extent of his handicap.

A group operating under a code that facilitates honest expression of feeling and does not strongly penalize failure tends to have certain emotional, cognitive, and behavioral effects on its members differing in some respects from those produced by the individual therapy situation.

All therapy groups tend to arouse their members emotionally. Merely attending a group is apt to be felt as more stigmatizing than going to a doctor privately, because it is a public acknowledgment that one needs psychiatric help. Initial sessions are characterized by the tension felt by any group of strangers thrown together for the first time. This is heightened by their knowledge that they are expected to reveal intimate and damaging details of their lives to other persons whom they tend to distrust and derogate. For to the extent that each feels contemptuous of himself, he is likely to have contempt for others perceived to be like himself. Since psychiatric illness characteristically involves chronic difficulties in getting along with others, more members of therapy groups than of other groups are apt to behave in irritating or upsetting ways. Individual members display arrogance, insensitivity, hypersensitivity, self-dramatization, self-pity, and other patterns of behavior that stir the emotions of others.

In addition to the emotion-arousing attitudes patients bring into the group, the situation itself has provocative components. Patients become involved in various sorts of rivalries for the therapist's attention and status in each other's eyes. These rivalries may be intensified by the fact that the prize is a position that only one member can have at a time, such as the "sickest" member, the therapist's "favorite," or the group leader. As differences in life experience and world view become revealed, they may become sources of antagonism. It is difficult, for example, for a southern white woman and a Negro in a group to discuss desegregation dispassionately, or for an employer and a union leader to see eye to eye about labor questions.

As the group continues and patients get to know each other better, tensions develop based more strictly on the distorted views of themselves and each other related to their illnesses. Two common sources of strain are so-called "mirror"[13] and transference reactions. The former term refers to the tendency to detect and disapprove of a trait in someone else that one dislikes in himself, before one recognizes it as his own. An example from a group was the mutual antagonism of two members of a minority group, one of whom ostensibly gloried in his group identification and the other of whom tried to deny it. After bitterly criticizing each other for months, each recognized that he secretly entertained the same feelings he was attacking in his antagonist. By "transference" is meant the tendency to transfer to an inappropriate object feelings that were once appropriate to a member of one's family. An example was an interchange in which one group member described his pleasure in fantasying different roles, especially after a few drinks, and another became unreasonably angry at him for living in a "dream world." It soon turned out that the second had an alcoholic mother who lived in a dream world and whom he had been trying in vain to reform for years. She was the real target of the feelings aroused by his fellow group member. Group members offer multiple stimuli for transference and mirror reactions while individual therapy offers only the therapist.[14]

The ability of therapeutic groups to arouse their members

emotionally heightens their therapeutic potential, but it is a two-edged sword. For unless anxiety, resentment, guilt, and similar feelings are counteracted by more rewarding ones, the situation may become so unpleasant for a member that he quits. Since more positive feelings tend to come to the fore only as the group develops, as considered below, the drop-out rate tends to be very high at the start of a group's life[15] unless the leader makes deliberate efforts to ease initial tensions. Since directive groups limit the interactions of members to certain prescribed forms and the leader actively guides and protects them, severely uneasy or disturbed patients may tolerate them better than the free interaction type.

On the positive side, therapy groups diminish the members' sense of isolation, heighten their hopes, and increase their self-esteem by means differing in some respects from those of individual therapies. At the most primitive level, the mere fact that a patient feels himself to be taken seriously by persons who, unlike the therapist, are not professionally required to accept him, may lift his morale. A mental patient is usually used to being pitied, scorned, or ignored by those about him. For him, even an angry blast from another member may be felt as supportive, for it demonstrates that the latter takes him seriously enough to get angry at him.

In successful therapy groups, members derive support from a feeling of group belongingness, which slowly develops from a growing body of shared experience in free interaction groups and is actively cultivated in directive groups through participation in more or less ritualistic activities, the use of a special language, and so on.

The psychological effects of belonging to a group depend in part on whether membership in it is viewed as desirable or not. In this sense it is somewhat paradoxical that many patients gain enhanced self-esteem from membership in a group composed of other patients. Several factors seem to operate to bring this about. They may cling to the point that group membership makes them superior to other patients who did not have the good sense to join a therapy group. In addition, membership in a cohesive group enhances each member's feeling of personal power, for the group in some way represents an extension of himself. Each member exerts an influence on the functioning of such a group, if only by the fact that his absence makes a difference. The sense of shared responsibility for the group's activities enhances each member's feelings of competence and may account for the fact that dependence on a therapy group does not seem to be as demoralizing to patients as a similar degree of dependence on the psychiatrist would be.

In therapy groups, members' hopes may be raised by observing improvement in each other and hearing progress reports. This means of lifting morale is deliberately exploited in certain directive group therapies that permit patients to give only favorable reports publicly. Since free interaction groups have no such safeguard, members may freely express discouragement, and this may damage morale. By his attitudes, however, the therapist can usually enhance the effects of favorable reports and diminish those of unfavorable ones, and in time there tends to develop a group standard that effectively inhibits undue complaining.

More important as a source of heightened morale is the fact that members display faith in each other's capabilities. Since psychiatrists, like all physicians, are trained to focus on disease rather than health, patients may detect assets in each other that the leader has overlooked. This may lead a member to venture into activities or assume responsibilities of which he thought himself incapable.

Perhaps the most potent way in which therapy groups strengthen members' self-esteem is by gving them an incentive and an opportunity to help each other.[16] Altruism combats morbid self-centeredness, enhances the individual's feelings of kinship with others, and strengthens his sense of personal worth and power. As noted earlier, many forms of primitive healing require that the patient do something for others, and shrines like Lourdes place great stress on the fact that pilgrims pray not for themselves but for each other.

Everybody needs to feel that he is needed. Mental patients

characteristically have felt, or have been made to feel that they are a burden to others. Individual therapy offers no opportunity to dispel this feeling through actions. For in it help flows only from the therapist to the patient; the relationship is a complementary one. There is little the latter can do in return except pay his bills promptly and gratify his therapist by reporting improvement and recommending him to his friends. Rarely, the therapist may be willing to accept a present.

In group therapy, relations between patients are reciprocal; each can give as well as receive help. They find they can help each other by comparing experiences or giving useful insights or advice. This discovery is often a great aid to regaining a sense of personal worth.

As is apparent, patients' interactions in therapy groups have both supportive and stressful features, and one of the hazards of group treatment for certain patients, especially in free interaction groups, is that the stress may outrun the support, causing the patient to drop out, and perhaps even harming him. An example is afforded by a middle-age spinster who had devoted her life to caring for other family members, at considerable emotional cost to herself. She dealt with her resentment and frustrations by complaining constantly about her health. Her complaints made life tolerable by eliciting some attention and affection from her relatives and enabling her to express her anger indirectly. This martyr-like behavior, however, was unacceptable to the group members, who persistently ignored or criticized her. At the same time group discussions stimulated her repressed hostile and sexual feelings. Her anger at her mother reached the point that she struck the senile old lady on two occasions, creating intense guilt, which the group did not assuage. At this point she needed an operation, which enabled her to stop group treatment without loss of face. Her group experience, which stimulated her unacceptable feelings without offering the emotional support necessary to enable her to deal with them, could scarcely be considered helpful.

Therapy groups facilitate or hinder cognitive and behavioral changes in their members in some ways that differ from individual treatment. In these groups each member has many therapists. Patients as models, instructors, and guides have certain advantages and disadvantages over the psychiatrist. Their mere multiplicity is an advantage because it gives each member several possible models. Since patients are personally involved in the proceedings and have had no special training in understanding human problems, their interpretations and advice are apt to be strongly biased by their own preconceptions and concerns, and their degree of tolerance for each other tends to be lower than that of the therapist. On the other hand, a patient may be able to sense what a fellow patient feels and express it in a more comprehensible way than the psychiatrist can, simply by virtue of being more like him, or having had similar experiences himself. This also sometimes makes it possible for patients to transmit the therapeutic concepts of the group leader to each other more successfully than the leader himself can do it.

Since patients lack the therapist's authority, a recipient of another patient's unhelpful advice or interpretation can reject it more easily than advice from the leader. On the other hand, if the interpretation is appropriate, the patient may be able to accept it more readily because it comes from someone whom he feels to be more like himself than the therapist and therefore better able to understand him.

The fact that patients resemble each other and have had similar experiences is not always entirely advantageous, since it also enables them to support each other in "resisting" an attitude or interpretation advocated by the therapist. It may be difficult to get a group to accept and act in accordance with therapeutic mores such as tolerance for certain impulses and feelings and emphasis on impartial self-exploration.[17]

The value the group places on honest expression does not always succeed in overcoming patients' feelings of reticence about emotions or experiences that they regard as shameful and that they can talk about more easily with the doctor in private. This is especially true of activities that have a criminal connotation in American society, such as homosexual behavior. In a long-established group, however, no topic is too "hot" to handle.

One important set of feelings that are more easily expressed in a group than in an individual setting are those towards the therapist. Group therapy has highlighted the extent to which some patients distort the psychiatrist into a dangerous, unpredictable, and powerful figure to a degree that severely inhibits their expression of hostile or affectionate thoughts to him. They fear that he may retaliate for the former feelings and take advantage of the latter. In prolonged, intensive individual therapy all these attitudes come out eventually, but there seems little doubt that most patients can express them more readily in the group. This is probably because they feel both protected and supported by the other patients. One who speaks up against the therapist may regard himself as a spokesman for others as well, and the public character of the proceedings is a good guarantee against the leader's feared retaliation. In two different groups, for example, a patient whose parents had been brutal and unpredictable never sat next to the psychiatrist. He always made sure that at least one other patient intervened. When asked about this, both patients said they did it to preclude the psychiatrist's striking them. One added that he thought the therapist kept a loaded revolver in his desk drawer! Neither had been able to mention these feelings in individual sessions.

It might seem that the opportunity for members to support each other in "resisting" or attacking the group leader would handicap treatment, but this seems seldom to be the case. Since the members feel dependent on the therapist for help, they cannot afford to demolish him. A therapy group cannot remain cohesively hostile to its leader for long, and if he maintains his poise he soon finds members coming to his defense. Interactions revolving around attitudes to the therapist may be especially helpful in illuminating members' attitudes to authorities or help-givers.

The structure and code of the therapy group greatly enhance opportunities for learning from antagonisms and conflict.[18] Patients' internal conflicts are often reflected in conflicts with others. They are apt to be especially sensitive to issues about which they are inwardly conflicted and so become embroiled with others over them. Individual therapy helps the patient to develop more harmonious relations with his fellows through helping him to resolve his internal tensions. Group therapy offers an opportunity to reduce inner tensions by working through their externalized manifestations. Although this may sound like a reversal of cause and effect, it need not be so, because the feelings of anger and frustration produced by chronic unresolved conflicts with others may be the chief impediments to resolving the corresponding internal ones.

In individual treatment the therapist is the only available target for the patient's hostile feelings. In group therapy he often is not, which gives him much greater flexibility. He can support both antagonists or protect the weaker patient if indicated. His presence is a guarantee that the conflict will not be allowed to get out of control, so that each feels relatively free to express his feelings. In most real-life situations, mutual antagonism leads to progressive disruption of communication, making it increasingly difficult to resolve the basis of the hostility, or for the antagonists to learn anything from each other.[19] Therapy groups exert pressure on antagonists to maintain communication even in the face of prolonged conflict. Since in such a relationship each protagonist is apt to bring up more and more material to bolster his position, conflict affords unique opportunities for each to learn about his methods of defending himself and for unearthing hitherto hidden feelings. Thus conflicts between group patients, in addition to their emotionally stimulating quality, may help the protagonists to learn about themselves and each other and to correct mutual distortions. From the behavioral standpoint, they may help the rivals to develop more effective ways of resolving disagreements or prevailing in interpersonal conflicts outside of therapy.

Finally, a therapy group has aspects that enhance the likelihood that the changes it produces in its members will endure. This is because of the tendency to "internalize" the standards of the groups with which one identifies himself. Even when a member is away from the group, he carries it around inside himself, as it were, and when the need to make decisions related to the group standards arises, these are apt to influence his choice. This may occur without his awareness, or he may be consciously influenced by a desire not to let his fellow members down, and this may be reinforced by his anticipation of having to confess his deviation at the next meeting.

The extent to which group members internalize group standards is probably closely related to the strength of their feelings of membership in the group. That is, the more cohesive a group is, the more it influences its members.[20] Since therapy groups are composed of emotionally ill persons, the question arises as to why they do not develop unhealthy standards. The major safeguard against this may be that the group can become really cohesive only by incorporating the standards of the therapist. It cannot become cohesive against him because, in the last analysis, members depend on him for help. In any case, clinical experience clearly suggests that group patients tend to reinforce each other's healthy reactions and correct each other's neurotic ones.[21]

In conclusion of this survey of the therapeutic dynamisms of group therapy, a major difference between individual forms of treatment and group methods should be mentioned, the significance of which is as yet unclear. In therapy groups, each patient must continuously cope with the real or anticipated reactions of others. When he speaks, he is aware that others want the floor, and he must be prepared for a variety of responses to whatever he says. Moreover, the group has little patience with private worlds; members prefer to discuss topics in which all have an interest. The therapy group is not a suitable place for the detailed examination of an individual member's past history or his phantasy world.

In individual treatment, the patient is assured of the undivided, serious attention of the therapist for the duration of the treatment session. He can take his time, relax, let himself go in describing dreams or phantasies, secure in the knowledge that nothing he says will stimulate someone else to interrupt with his own problem.

Thus group therapies may be unduly strenuous for patients who are easily hurt by criticism or have difficulty holding their own in a competitive atmosphere, and may impede the progress of patients who need to retreat from others and solve their problems by unhurried meditation or indulgence in phantasy in the presence of an understanding partner. It may be that the ideal form of psychotherapy would utilize both individual and group methods. Group and individual sessions may interfere with each other under some circumstances, for example, by leading patients to withhold material in one setting, knowing that they can bring it up in the other. On the other hand, they can usefully supplement each other. For this reason, when time and resources are available, most group therapists also see group members individually from time to time.[22]

In this connection it may be relevant that primitive healing rituals often include a private session between patient and shaman,[23] and thought reform combines both individual and group methods of influence.

SUMMARY

The persuasive power of therapy groups resides basically in the tendency of each person to look to others for validation of his feelings and attitudes. Therapy groups differ from individual therapy chiefly in their greater nearness to everyday life. They differ from ordinary social groups in their encouragement of honest expression of feeling and in granting status for reasons other than achievement. This combination of factors helps patients to discover unsuspected similarities,

which counteracts their sense of isolation and facilitates production of attitude change. Therapy groups arouse patients
emotionally through their pressure to self-revelation, through
differences in outlook, and through rivalries arising from differences in life experiences and from stimuli in the group situation itself. They increase members' hopes and heighten their
self-respect through fostering a sense of group-belongingness,
affording examples of progress to each other, and giving them
opportunities to help each other. They promote cognitive and
behavioral change through the provision of multiple models,
encouragement to express and examine feelings towards fellow
group members and the therapist, and pressures to maintain
communication despite conflict. Changes produced in the
group are stabilized by the members' internalization of group
standards, which usually are healthier in some respects than
those of the individuals composing the group.

The greatest potential drawback of therapy groups is the
tendency not to supply sufficient support, especially in early
meetings, to enable members to cope with the stresses they
generate. They also afford no opportunity for the production
of attitude change through detailed unhurried examination of
personal experiences and phantasies, in the presence of an
understanding partner whose attention is exclusively devoted
to the patient. These disadvantages may often be counteracted by suitable combinations of group and individual sessions.

"We're all mad here. I'm mad. You're mad."

"How do you know I'm mad?" said Alice.

"You must be," said the Cat, "or you wouldn't have come here."

Alice didn't think that proved it at all.

(Alice's Adventures in Wonderland, Chapter 6)

10 | Institutional Group Influences— The Traditional Mental Hospital and the Therapeutic Community

With the exception of thought reform and certain types of religious healing, this book has focused on forms of healing and persuasion that are brought to bear on patients intermittently, in the setting of their daily lives. It now remains to glance briefly at the healing and influencing forces operating on patients who are placed in a special environment around the clock. The hospitalized patient is separated from all his usual contacts and immersed in a new culture, all aspects of which may affect him. The effects of the social structure of hospitals, of their routines, and of personal contacts of staff with patients, staff with staff, and patients with patients have been extensively studied in recent years, leading to progressive changes in their organization.[1] Adequate consideration of these matters lies beyond the scope of this book. We shall be concerned only with those aspects of the treatment of hospitalized patients that involve principles operative in the forms of healing and persuasion already considered. Of particular interest is the contrast between the old-fashioned mental hospital and the concept of the "therapeutic community."

Although the traditional mental hospital is rapidly changing, it probably still represents the dominant pattern of care for hospitalized patients and also illustrates the operation of some of the principles of influence considered earlier. The basic assumption underlying its structure and organization is that mental patients are irresponsible and therefore liable to harm themselves or others. Furthermore, most patients are viewed as suffering from chronic illnesses that are unlikely to improve, so that they will require lifelong care. These assumptions have led to the building of mental hospitals in rural settings at a distance from the communities they serve, where patients are cared for behind locked doors, economically and out of harm's way.

The social structure of the mental hospital resembles that of the general hospital. The treatment staff forms a complex hierarchy, with physicians at the apex, professionally trained ancillary personnel such as nurses and social workers next, and aides or attendants at the bottom.[2] The patient's role is to submit to treatment and take orders without question. Since he is presumed to be irresponsible, he does not know what is good for him and must therefore accept the judgment of the staff. Thus patients tend to be treated as objects rather than persons. Their communications with treatment personnel are strictly limited, and the nature of the communications is chiefly determined by the staff.

Because of the very small ratio of physicians to patients, the physicians spend most of their time wth those newly admitted patients who seem most likely to respond to treatment.

Others, such as senile patients, are placed immediately in custodial wards, to be joined by those who, failing to respond promptly to therapy, must make room for newcomers. Thus the hospital becomes an end station for most of its inmates, where they are expected to spend the rest of their lives. It shelters, feeds, clothes, and protects them, but they are no longer regarded as objects of treatment or candidates for return to the community, and they receive minimal attention from the treatment personnel. They pass their lives under conditions of extreme monotony in an atmosphere of hopelessness.

Any environment that engulfs a person completely is bound to influence him for better or worse, and the traditional mental hospital is no exception. Its basic assumptions, social structure, and activities exert emotional, cognitive, and behavioral effects on patients that deserve brief consideration. At the risk of stretching an analogy, they may be conveniently compared with those operative in thought reform.[3]

The similarities between hospitalization for a mental illness and thought reform are already present in the prodromal phase. The path to the mental hospital too often is at least as emotionally unsettling as that to the prison. The patient may go through a period of progressively severe embroilment with or alienation from his work associates, friends, and family before he is hospitalized. Before this climax he may be subjected to such humiliations as arrest, court appearance, even a night in jail. Although these experiences are fortunately not typical, hospitalization always requires some sort of formal procedure, which emphasizes the importance of the step and the patient's relinquishment of control over himself to others.

Involuntary procedures, known as certification or commitment, are based on the assumption that the patient is incapable of making rational decisions about his welfare, so legally constituted authorities must take this responsibility. Though commitment procedures differ widely among states, physicians participate in all. Most state hospitals and all private ones also have a voluntary admission procedure in which the patient formally requests hospitalization in writing and promises to give the hospital authorities several days' advance notice of his intention to leave. Though overt coercion is absent, the patient often seeks voluntary admission only in response to strong family pressure, and the procedure impresses him with the importance of the step he is taking and emphasizes the staff's control over him while he is hospitalized. If properly conducted, the interview culminating in voluntary admission can heighten the patient's hope of benefit from his stay and his confidence in the hospital's staff. Involuntary commitments ordinarily do not present this opportunity.

The actual admission to the hospital may have various emotional implications. At best the patient welcomes it as the first step towards his recovery. At worst, the family may have deceived him as to his destination to get him to go quietly, or he may be put to sleep with sedatives and wake up amidst strangers in the unfamiliar environment of the hospital. Even if everything has been explained to him, he may dread the loss of personal freedom and share the popular image of the mental hospital as a "snake pit" peopled by maniacs and brutal guards. Thus, even more than the prisoner in thought reform, he may enter the hospital badly frightened and demoralized, feeling abandoned and betrayed by his loved ones. This emotional state, if used by the treatment staff as a means of leverage, may facilitate his progress, but also, it can be very damaging, perhaps even lethal, as suggested earlier.[4]

As with thought reform, the patient must meet the desires of the treatment staff in order to gain release from the hospital. Although this statement is not strictly or universally true, in that there are legal means by which a patient may attempt to force his release and his family can remove him without the staff's consent, most patients feel themselves to be in the power of the hospital staff. Even in voluntary hospitals, the three days' notice stipulation enables the authorities to hold over the patient the implicit or explicit threat of arranging for involuntary commitment if he persists in his insistence on leaving.

In the traditional mental hospital, as in thought reform, the patient may be subjected to a "mortification of the self," which strips him of the usual supports of his personal identity and his self-esteem. He is divested of his personal belongings and may have to ask permission to carry out the simplest activities, such as smoking. He must show signs of respect for the staff, including the lower echelons, whom he may feel to be beneath him. In addition, channels of communication with his former world are severely restricted through limitation of visiting hours and censorship of outgoing mail. These measures intensify his feelings of dependence on the treatment staff and his awareness that he must meet their requirements to gain release, but he often has no clear ideas as to what these requirements are, other than that he cause no trouble.

Despite its demoralizing aspects the conventional mental hospital exerts some sort of helpful influence on the patients at cognitive and behavioral levels. Cognitively, the staff is guided and informed by a poorly articulated but irrefutable conceptual scheme concerning mental illness and its cure. According to this scheme, everything that is done to the patient has therapeutic intent, even though a specific measure, such as transfer from an open to a locked ward, might be perceived by the patient as a punishment. Furthermore, as in thought reform, nothing the patient does or says can shake the staff's assumptive world, especially since the patient is viewed as irresponsible. If the patient demurs at a procedure, he is apt to be met with the "institutional smirk," implying that the staff knows better than he does what is good for him. Despite its shortcomings, the conceptual scheme of the mental hospital is essentially oriented to the patient's welfare, so that his acceptance of it probably helps him to re-integrate himself.

At the behavioral level the mental hospital influences the patients both indirectly and directly. Indirect influence is exerted through more or less adequately supervised, organized, goal-directed activities. These include housekeeping or maintenance chores, occasional social and recreational functions, and often some occupational therapy. Direct guidance is afforded by a systematic scale of privileges and penalties, meted out in accordance with the patient's behavior. In large state hospitals the essential criterion for the granting or withdrawing of privileges is whether or not the patient conforms to regulations. This probably has some steadying value. In private hospitals, the criterion of conformity tends to be tempered by recognition that a given form of behavior may represent progress for one patient and retrogression for another, so that a patient's behavior is evaluated not only from the standpoint of its effect on hospital discipline, but also with respect to whether or not it represents a move in the direction of health for him. In any case, the privilege system serves to mold the patients' verbalizations and behavior along lines deemed desirable by the staff.

In concluding this sketchy account of influencing features of the conventional mental hospital, the point should be made that its authoritarian organization may be beneficial to certain patients. It may counteract the anxiety of some patients by reducing the ambiguity of the environment to a minimum, and by not presenting them with any challenges or problems requiring decisions. While it contains very few sources of helpful stimulation, it is unlikely to expose patients to problems that might overtax their capacities and cause them to have demoralizing failure experiences. By sheltering the patients it gives spontaneous recuperative forces a chance to operate and it interferes minimally with them. Through its unpleasantness it may increase a patient's motivation to "pull himself together" and so gain his release. It is not rare for patients to improve promptly on transfer from a private hospital to a state institution, suggesting that what these particular ones needed most was to be left alone. If a patient has not progressed under such a regime in a few months, however, its continuance is self-defeating, since it leads to progressive loss of his sense of personal identity and demoralization, through separating him from his former contacts and activities.

THE THERAPEUTIC COMMUNITY

Ever since World War II, mental hospitals have been undergoing a quiet but massive revolution from essentially custodial institutions to active treatment centers, involving progressive breakdown of the barrier between the mental hospital and the community and a redefinition of roles of patients and treatment staff within the hospital walls.[5] These changes are closely related to a change in the psychiatric image of the mental patient. Instead of being viewed as an irresponsible person whose sole task is to submit passively to the ministrations of the staff, he is coming to be regarded as an individual capable of exerting some degree of self-control and participating responsibly in decisions about his welfare.

This change has been accompanied by a corresponding change in the concept of mental illnesses. Instead of being seen as caused primarily by hereditary biological defects, they are now viewed as forms of maladaptation to stress. Although organically based deficiencies are recognized as contributing to failure to deal adequately with the stresses of life, disturbing experiences leading to faulty assumptive worlds and correspondingly inadequate behavior patterns are also believed to play a significant role. The final clinical picture reflects the cumulative effects of severe failures and frustrations in relationships with others. It follows that the mental patient is not merely a helpless victim of obscure, impersonal pathological processes, which can be treated only by physical and chemical agents, if at all, but a person in distress who might be helped to rebuild his self-confidence and correct some of his distorted perceptions and maladaptive behavior by suitable experiences with other persons.

The advent of psychopharmacological agents has paradoxically enhanced interest in psychotherapeutic approaches and increased their usefulness. Tranquilizers, by diminishing patients' overactivity, have made them less anxiety-producing to each other and to the treatment staff. Furthermore, behavioral changes induced by tranquilizers or antidepressants are demonstrations that the patients can be helped. As a result, these drugs have revived therapeutic optimism in the staff and enabled them more easily to deal with patients as individuals. These improvements in staff attitudes, in turn, enable patients to interact more usefully with them, further reinforcing the new attitudes in both staff and patients. That some of the therapeutic benefit of these drugs lies in the changes they produce in the staff is suggested by the observation that their effects seem to be more striking in public than private mental hospitals. In the latter, they cannot produce as great a change in the attitudes of treatment personnel because the attitudes were already good before the drugs were introduced.

The activities of the therapeutic community center on the extensive use of group methods involving patients, patients and staff, and staff alone. The principles of group therapy with hospitalized patients do not differ from those with outpatients, but differences in type of patient and in the setting have led to certain modifications. For maximal value, groups within the hospital are tailored to the degree of illness of the patients and also are closely integrated with the general program of the hospital. In general, since inpatients tend to be sicker than outpatients, their groups for the most part use directive methods which make less demand on the participant than evocative ones.[6]

The most withdrawn patients may benefit from simple group activities such as rhythm bands, which break the monotony of their lives and help to enhance their capacity for sensory discrimination and ability to co-operate with others at the simplest level. Patients who are in better contact may benefit from didactic groups in which the therapist assumes major responsibility for the group's functioning. The therapist assigns topics for reading at a level of difficulty within the limits of the patients' capabilities and actively guides the discussion. The material affords intellectual stimulation and, because it is emotionally neutral, enables the patients to discuss it without more emotional involvement than they are able to handle.[7]

Free-interaction groups are useful for convalescent patients and even for ones who are quite sick, but for the latter they may be overstimulating. Schizophrenics have great difficulties in communicating with others, and groups who do not offer direct guidance may become quite stormy. The introduction of a group therapy program using free interaction methods into one ward of a hospital led to an increase in combative and destructive behavior on the ward, as compared with a similar ward in which patients did not receive group therapy. These and other signs of disturbance, however, fell off more sharply in the therapy than in the control ward with the passage of time. More importantly, they were accompanied by a drop in nighttime sedation to about half the previous level, suggesting that patients may have gained increased inner calmness through expressing their feelings more freely. The group patients also showed a prompt and striking improvement in control of bladder functions, which seems to be related to an increase in self-respect.[8]

Psychodramatic methods in hospitals can be used in a wide variety of ways, from helping patients to solve deep-seated personal problems to simple behavioral training. At one extreme they have been used, for example, to free a schizophrenic patient from her attachment to an imaginary lover, by having a therapist play the role of an intimate friend of the lover in such a way as to bring about a resolution of the relationship.[9] At the other end of the spectrum, psychodramatic techniques have been found especially helpful in enabling patients to confront and master practical problems they will meet on return to community life, such as how to shop and how to answer questions about where they have been.[10]

The transition back to the community can also be facilitated by therapeutic social clubs, conducted by the patients under staff supervision. These clubs elect their own officers and plan social and recreational activities. Through these activities, members strengthen their capacities to handle themselves in social situations.[11]

Therapeutic social clubs represent one means of helping patients to assume limited responsibilities. Many groups go further, enabling patients to share some responsibility for the hospital program, within the limits set by their disability. One ward administrator, for example held weekly group meetings of his most disturbed patients. Under his guidance they elected officers, ran the sessions along parliamentary lines, and held to an agenda consisting of administrative problems of the ward that they wished to consider. On the basis of their discussion they made recommendations that he always took seriously, accepting some and explaining to the group why he could not accept others. In addition to helping the patients by giving them a sense of responsibility for their own care, this type of group enabled the psychiatrist to learn of conditions requiring modification that would otherwise have escaped his attention.[12]

In one private hospital the least disturbed patients assumed responsibility for organizing their own activities and making suggestions for the over-all hospital program. It is reported that patients in these groups lost their originally indifferent attitude about the hospital. Instead, "They had begun to think of the hospital as something in which they had a share, and they tried to make it something of which they could be proud."[13] An ingenious example of co-ordination of group therapy with the over-all hospital program is so-called "round table psychotherapy."[14] Six patients, initially elected by an entire ward, form the round table, which meets for an hour not oftener than three times a week. The rest of the ward is the audience. For the first half hour the round table listens to a recording of the last meeting—an effective means of bringing home to each patient how he sounds to others. During the next half hour they discuss one another's symptoms and try to help each other to find better solutions to their difficulties in living. Before each meeting the therapist, who, with the patient's knowledge, listens to the meetings behind a one-way screen, has a ten-minute interview with each member. This includes a friendly critique of what he did at the last group session, an opportunity for him to explain what he would do at the next session, and encouragement to take an active interest in the other patients. Each patient is told that when he is considered for parole, the advice he has given to others will be used as evidence in determining the soundness of his judgment.

The round table is responsible for maintaining order during the meeting. It is empowered to eject unruly members of the audience and can also, by majority vote, expel those of its own members who are not ready for it and elect replacements. Its most important administrative function is to recommend its members for parole. This recommendation is usually followed, but if not, the reasons are fully explained to the round table. Thus, the round table technique seeks to modify patients' behavior by encouraging them to overcome their self-centeredness and to strengthen their self-esteem by permitting them to assume responsibilities.

Group methods with inpatients, as with outpatients, have beneficial emotional, cognitive, and behavioral effects. Their most important over-all beneficial effect is probably to restore to patients a sense of individuality and of some control over their own destinies. The expectation that they are capable of self-control and of assuming some degree of responsibility for themselves and others, which is implicit in all forms of group therapy, bolsters their self-respect and stimulates their hopes.

From a more specific emotional standpoint, group methods can be used to stimulate apathetic patients and to control overanxious or overexcitable ones. The control is exerted through overcoming the members' isolation and subjecting them to group standards. In contrast to impersonal mechanical restraints or seclusion rooms, which implicitly encourage patients to abandon all self-control by terrifying them and conveying the staff's conviction that they cannot manage themselves, group standards tend to become internalized as "self-control." The remarkable effectiveness of group controls is illustrated by an experience in the admission ward of a naval hospital, where unruly patients had traditionally been controlled by sedation, seclusion, and restraints. A new ward administrator was determined to establish powerful group expectations, shared by patients and staff, that patients could control their own behavior and that restraints would not be used. He achieved this through daily community meetings of patients and staff followed by a meeting of the staff alone. In the course of ten months, during which close to a thousand patients were admitted to the service, he did not have to put one in restraint or seclusion.[15]

Groups help hospitalized patients to clarify and correct their perceptions of others and to practice improved ways of behaving through guiding their interactions in modified social situations.

Since patients cannot collaborate in their own treatment without actively involving the staff, it follows naturally that they should meet together to discuss issues of common concern. Thus the program of the therapeutic community includes groups attended by patients and treatment staff. Usually regular patient-staff group meetings are confined to hospital units, such as wards. In an English hospital that has been a trailbreaker in developing the therapeutic community, all the patients and staff meet together daily to discuss personal problems of patients and disciplinary questions.[16] The procedure is highly informal, staff members as well as patients being addressed by their first names, and most decisions as to policy matters or how to deal with patients' infractions of rules are made by the entire group.

The introduction of a group therapy program inevitably changes the whole social structure of the hospital. Patients participating in these groups can no longer be expected to follow the staff's orders blindly. They expect to have a say in planning hospital programs, demand explanations, and, with the support of the group, may talk back. This change in the patients requires corresponding changes in the attitudes of the staff. They do not in any sense abdicate their authority or responsibility, but they must discharge their functions in a democratic rather than authoritarian manner. This may arouse considerable anxiety in those who were trained to perform in the latter way. Thus to operate successfully a therapeutic community must include a training program for the staff that also makes full use of group methods in which they have a chance to express and discuss their own feelings and that builds up group standards supporting them in their new roles. As the patients become persons instead of anonymous objects, the staff members also become persons instead of functionaries.

In short, the introduction of group methods tends to improve the entire communication network of the hospital. Patients come to communicate more successfully with each other as they discover that their opinions and feelings count. They also become a major means of conveying the group standards of the hospital to each other. In the conventional hospital, patients also influence each other greatly, but their communications occur largely outside of the staff's awareness and control. Through group methods the staff is able to impart their standards effectively and also to keep better informed of the patient's attitudes towards the hospital program. Group methods enhance patient-staff communication in several ways. They increase the actual amount of therapeutically oriented contact between them and make it easier for patients to express their real feelings. They also enable patients and staff to discuss common institutional problems and to participate jointly in decision-making. These experiences impel staff members to communicate more fully with each other as they seek to modify their own behavior along lines required by the new program and help each other work through the feelings aroused by their more personalized contacts with patients.

The gradual change in mental hospitals from custodial institutions to therapeutic communities has been manifested in a variety of other ways. At the simplest level, it is reflected in the changed decor of hospital wards. From bleak, bare barracks, most have become tastefully furnished with draperies, lamps, tables, chairs, and the ubiquitous television set. The concept of treatment as the responsibility of all members of the treatment staff has led to the increasing use of nonmedical therapists such as psychologists, social workers, nurses, and aides as group leaders and to increased democratization and flexibility of the hierarchical staff organization.

As patients demonstrate their capacities for responsibility and self-control the barriers between the mental hospital and the surrounding community lose their justification, so changes within the hospital have been paralleled by their increasing integration with the world outside. This has been symbolized by the unlocking of doors, which now open in both directions for patients. It is becoming easier both to enter mental hospitals and to leave them. The doors also open to admit the public, as evidenced by the growth of all sorts of volunteer programs.

As aspects of the same trend, programs are being developed in which psychiatric treatment teams are used to forestall hospitalization by visiting patients in their homes,[17] and programs of systematic after-care of discharged hospital patients are rapidly expanding. Another sign of hospital-community integration is that most new units for mental patients are being attached to general hospitals. Thus mental hospitals are becoming links in a therapeutic chain rather than end stations. Ever-growing community understanding and support is reflected in increased budgets for mental health as well as active participation by many community groups in planning and carrying out hospital programs.

All these changes have combined significantly to enhance

the therapeutic success of mental hospitals, as shown by a steadily rising discharge rate. This has been so marked that despite increasing admissions to mental hospitals, their resident population has progressively declined for the last few years. This gratifying development is in part attributable to the new tranquilizing drugs. As indicated earlier, however, much of their efficacy may lie in their ability to facilitate application of the principles of the therapeutic community.

SUMMARY

Traditional mental hospital programs are based on the assumption that mental patients are irresponsible and potentially dangerous to themselves and others. Hence they must be removed from the community into a protective environment, where all decisions as to their care must be made by the treatment staff. These hospitals exert pressures on patients in many ways analogous to those used by thought reform. Experiences culminating in admission often stir the patient emotionally. Once in the hospital he perceives himself as entirely dependent on the treatment staff for release. He is completely immersed in the hospital world, his communication with the outer world is severely restricted, and his sense of personal identity is weakened through the hospital routines. These are based on an unshakable assumptive system according to which everything that happens to him is treatment. His behavior is guided primarily by the hospital privilege system, which rewards conformity and passivity. The isolation, highly simplified life, authoritarian atmosphere, and impersonality of the hospital enable certain patients to mobilize their recuperative forces, but for many who do not respond promptly, these features may retard recovery.

Recognition of the antitherapeutic aspects of conventional hospitals has led to the development of the concept of the therapeutic community, based on a view of mental patients as capable of exerting self-control and assuming some degree of responsibility. These qualities are cultivated by group methods involving both staff and patients, fitted to the degree of illness of the patients and integrated closely into the over-all program. Groups, in which staff members may participate, stimulate apathetic patients and control overexcitable ones through group standards that are readily internalized, rather than through mechanical restraints that foster loss of control.

These methods also bolster patients' self-respect and enable them to share in decision-making about aspects of their lives in the hospital. They afford opportunities to correct cognitive distortions and faulty behavior patterns. They improve communication throughout the hospital community and change the social structure of the hospital from an authoritarian to a democratic one. The changes within the hospital are paralleled by breakdown of the barrier between it and the community, signalized by unlocking of doors, and growing participation of community members in hospital programs. Therapeutic communities thus become links in a treatment chain rather than end stations. The development of the concepts of the therapeutic community, facilitated by tranquilizers, which help patients to be more accessible to interpersonal influences, has led to progressive improvement in treatment results.

... the croquet balls were live hedgehogs, and the mallets live flamingoes, and the soldiers had to double themselves up and stand on their hands and feet, to make the arches .... Alice soon came to the conclusion that it was a very difficult game indeed. (*Alice's Adventures in Wonderland,* Chapter 8)

11 Symptom Relief and Attitude Change— Report of a Research Study of Psychotherapy

All the forms of interpersonal healing and influence reviewed in this book seem to involve both relief of distress and attitude change, though their relative importance differs with different procedures. In primitive and religious healing improvement in health is accompanied by the overcoming of feelings of alienation and despair and improvement in the patient's relations with his group. Religious conversion experiences, though primarily changes of attitude, are typically accompanied by an enhanced sense of well-being. Changes of attitude induced by thought reform are automatically accompanied by surcease from the distress that is part of the process. Individual, group, and milieu psychotherapies, when successful, produce improvement in patient's symptoms and their ability to live more comfortably with themselves and others. Symptomatic improvement and attitude change are obviously related. The better a person feels, the more he will be able to

mobilize the courage required to modify the attitudes contributing to his symptoms, and these modifications, in turn,
should lead to more success and satisfaction in his interactions
with others, thereby reducing his distress.

On the other hand, there is no reason to think that distress
reduction and attitude change are identical. Experimental
studies of the placebo effect on the one hand and of persuasion on the other suggest that different processes are probably involved. For example, symptom relief as seen in the placebo effect seems primarily due to mobilization of the patient's
expectation of help, whereas attitude changes may be related
to the prestige and power of the persuader and the specific
influencing techniques he uses.

Thus a major goal of research in psychotherapy is more precise specification of conditions producing symptom relief and
attitude change, and of the relationship between them.

As suggested in Chapter 1, another important problem with
respect to different forms of interpersonal healing is whether
their effects really differ from each other and if so, in what
respects. This involves the question of comparison of immediate and long-term effects, for it is theoretically quite possible that different psychotherapies might differ in their short-
term but not their long-term results, or vice versa.

These are vast and complex problems, which will require
many years and much research to unravel. The purpose of this
chapter is to report a small contribution to their solution,
which may also serve to tease out and tie together the threads
of symptom relief, attitude change, and duration of psychotherapeutic effect, which have run through the tangled skein
of this book.

The study, to which reference has already been made,[1] was
a preliminary effort to identify some of the short- and long-
term similarities and differences between the effects of different
forms of psychotherapy. To this end three different methods
were selected: individual therapy, in which patients were seen
one hour once a week; group therapy, in which groups of five

to seven patients were seen one and a half hours a week; and minimal contact therapy, in which they were seen not more than a half hour once every two weeks. The first two therapies differed from the third in amount of treatment contact. They differed from each other in that patients were treated singly in one therapy and in a group in the other.

The patients were all outpatients in the Phipps Clinic of The Johns Hopkins Hospital, diagnosed as having a psychoneurosis or personality disorder. They were all white, from eighteen to fifty-five years old, and about two-thirds were women. They were assigned at random to the three types of treatment, conducted by three psychiatrists in the second year of residency training. Each had six patients in each form of treatment. The design called for each patient to receive six months of treatment. Although this goal was not quite achieved, it was reasonably approximated. By starting with 91 patients we finally finished with the required 54, of whom 37 (66 per cent) had six months and 48 (89 per cent) had at least four months of treatment.

The patients were evaluated at the end of the experimental period of treatment and six months, eighteen months, and five years later. It was possible to examine 30 of the 54 treated patients at all three re-evaluations. No effort was made to control patients' treatment experiences during the follow-up period, but they were watched carefully. In line with our thinking about the effects of psychotherapy, we chose as measures of improvement criteria that are used by all the healing arts—increased comfort and increased efficiency.[2] Changes in discomfort were measured by a simple scale of symptoms on which the patient indicated which ones he had and how much they distressed him. Measurement of change in efficiency was more difficult, since efficiency in personal functioning cannot be determined simply by what a person does. The meanings of his actions to himself and others must also be taken into account. Our solution was to devise a social ineffectiveness scale, consisting of items such as overdependence, overinde-

210 PERSUASION AND HEALING

pendence, officiousness, isolation, impulsiveness, and caution.[3]
The patient was rated on each of these categories on the basis
of two observed interviews, one with him and one with a relative. By using two informants and four raters, we hoped to
minimize bias.

In analyzing our results, we were struck by the amount of
formal help these patients continued to receive even while in
treatment at the Clinic and during the follow-up period. During the six-month period of the experiment, about one-fourth
of the patients were simultaneously getting some other form
of medical help, and less than half (45 per cent) reported that
they had received no additional help whatsoever. During the
first eighteen months two-thirds had at least six months of
medical or psychiatric treatment. Of the 30 whom we were
able to interview three and a half years later, 15 reported at
least one contact during this period with a professional medical
or non-medical help-giving person that was more than casual
and lasted some time.

The results with respect to lessening of discomfort are summarized graphically in Chart 1.[4] In this chart, as in Chart 2,
decreases in score indicated improvement. Since initial discomfort scores and changes in discomfort did not differ significantly with the type of treatment, results for all three forms
of treatment are combined. It will be seen from Chart 1 that
average improvement is marked by the first evaluation at six
months. As discussed in Chapter 4, it probably occurs more
rapidly than this.[5] Although the average score is somewhat
lower at five years than at six months, it does not show a progressive trend during the intervening time. Of considerable
interest, in view of the widely held belief that symptom relief
is transient, is the finding that the average discomfort score
remains low throughout the follow-up period. This means that
for many of the patients the relief of discomfort produced
during the first six months is persistent.

The findings with regard to improvement in social effectiveness, graphically summarized in Chart 2, show some interesting

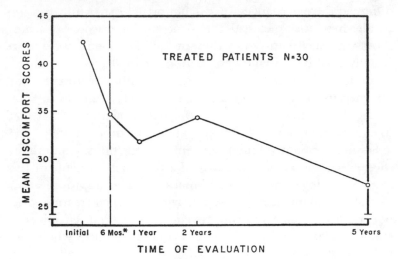

Chart 1. Mean Scores on Discomfort Scale

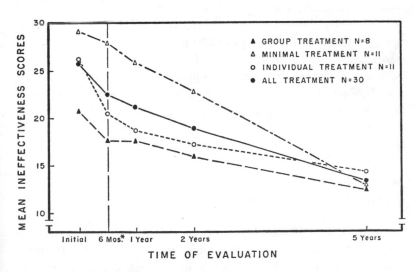

Chart 2. Mean Scores on Social Ineffectiveness Scale

differences from changes in discomfort. First, while patients in all three therapies had the same initial discomfort scores, those who stayed in group therapy for six months were more socially effective initially (i.e., had lower ineffectiveness scores) than those who stayed in individual or minimal treatment. This was probably due to the greater strenuousness of group therapy, under the adverse conditions of this experiment, which tended to cause the more socially inept patients to drop out.[6]

Second, amount of improvement during the six months of the experiment seems related to the type of treatment, in that those receiving group or individual treatment improved about the same amount, while those receiving minimal treatment did not improve. That is, improvement in social effectiveness seemed related to amount of treatment contact, which was not true of discomfort relief.[7]

Finally, during the follow-up period patients continued to improve progressively in social effectiveness, so that the average improvement between six months and five years is about twice as great as during the initial six-month period. By the end of five years, however, the difference in favor of individual and group therapies as opposed to minimal therapy, which was pronounced at six months, has disappeared.

These results suggest certain highly tentative but interesting conclusions. First, it would seem that "spontaneous recovery" is a misnomer. In light of the help-seeking activities of the patients in this study, their progressive improvement in social effectiveness probably represents the average effect of non-specific help.[8]

Second, improvement in comfort and improvement in social effectiveness are indeed largely different processes.[9] The former appears to be produced by the patients' expectation of help, in that it occurs promptly and to the same degree on the average no matter what is done for the patient. Improvement in social effectiveness, in contrast, seems to be related to the amount of contact with a helping person, suggesting that some sort of influencing or learning process is involved.

Third, the fact that the group of patients functions more effectively some years after treatment than immediately at its close raises the intriguing possibility that the function of psychotherapy may be primarily to speed up a process that would go on in any case with most patients. Therapies may differ primarily in the speed with which they enable patients to achieve their full potential for recovery.[10]

Of the many questions raised by these findings, one may be singled out because its implications involve some crucial issues in the study of psychotherapy. If the patients stayed so well, on the average, for five years following treatment, what is the explanation for their initial high levels of discomfort and ineffectiveness? There are several possibilities, all compatible with each other and all deserving further exploration. One is that some patients and their families may exaggerate their complaints initially in order to convince the psychiatrist of their need for help and minimize them subsequently so as not to disappoint him. Another possibility is that patients come to the clinic when they are in some sort of crisis situation. When this is resolved—and perhaps psychotherapy facilitates it's resolution—they return to their previous level of well-being and social effectiveness.

Another area of investigation suggested by our findings is the effect on the patient and those about him of his coming to the clinic. This may, for example, change his family's perception of him from a bad person to a sick one, with corresponding changes in their behavior that might reinforce the benefits of therapy. From the patient's standpoint knowing that the clinic is behind him may give him more leverage in his dealings with others. Moreover, having taken the plunge and sought help at the clinic, he may thereafter find it easier to seek help from others. This is suggested by the high proportion of patients seeking help during the follow-up period. Unfortunately, information is lacking on the amount of help they sought during an equivalent interval before coming to the clinic, which might cast light on this question.

In short, the findings of the study raise questions about many aspects of psychotherapy. Among these are the meanings of patients' complaints, the circumstances leading them to seek psychiatric help, the effects of this on their life patterns, and the kinds of life experience related to "spontaneous improvement."

SUMMARY

This chapter reports a research study of psychotherapy with psychiatric outpatients, using group and individual forms of evocative therapy and minimal treatment. The results add some confirmation to the supposition that psychotherapy produces two distinguishable but related types of effect—relief of distress and improvement in personal functioning. Symptom relief results primarily from the patient's expectation of help, so that it occurs rapidly, is independent of the particular type of therapy, and can be duplicated in some patients by administration of a placebo. Improvement in personal functioning occurs more gradually and seems to be related to the kind of therapeutic experience, suggesting that it may be the result of a learning process. In this study, the beneficial effects on behavior of six months of psychotherapy were less than those observed several years later, suggesting that the function of psychotherapy may be to accelerate a process that would occur in any case as the result of a patient's interactions with help-givers. The study raises many questions as to the conditions leading patients to seek treatment, the meanings of their reports, and the factors causing both initial and sustained improvement, which require further investigation.

"Impenetrability! That's what I say!"

"Would you tell me, please," said Alice, "what that means?"

"I meant by 'impenetrability,' " said Humpty Dumpty, "that we've had enough of that subject and it would be just as well if you'd mention what you mean to do next, as I suppose you don't mean to stop here all the rest of your life." (*Through the Looking Glass,* Chapter 6)

12 | American Psychotherapy in Perspective

Human beings spend most of their lives interacting with each other. In the process they influence each other powerfully for good or ill. This book has singled out for study one particular class of influencing procedures—the psychotherapy of adults. This is a help-giving process in which a professionally trained person, sometimes with the aid of a group, tries to relieve certain types of distress by facilitating changes in attitudes. As a relationship in which one person tries to induce changes in another, psychotherapy has much in common with child-rearing, education, and various forms of leadership. Its closest affinities, however, are with time-limited interactions between a sufferer and specially trained persons that stress either healing or attitude change. The former include therapeutic rituals in primitive societies and healing religious shrines in our own, the latter religious revivalism and Communist thought reform.

This chapter attempts to recapitulate the main points emerging from our survey, with special reference to their implications for psychotherapy in America today. Features that American psychotherapies share with other forms of interpersonal healing and influence are stressed. The justification for relative neglect of characteristics that might distinguish them from each other and from other healing methods is that such characteristics would gain significance only to the extent that the results produced by them cannot be accounted for by their common features. Despite the voluminous literature delineating differences between schools of psychotherapy, convincing evidence is lacking that these correspond to any important differences in the immediate or long-term results. Perhaps when common features of different psychotherapies and their effects are better understood, certain of their divergencies will become important.[1]

PSYCHIATRIC ILLNESS AND PSYCHOTHERAPY

Psychiatric illnesses and psychotherapies are intimately interwoven with their sociocultural settings. The illnesses are the results or expressions of disharmonies within a person and between him and his society. Because a person's patterns of perceiving and relating to others reflect his internal psychic state, and affect it in turn, these are two sides of the same coin. Moreover, the cause-effect sequence runs both ways. A person's internal harmony or conflict affects his relationships with others, and his interpersonal experiences influence his internal state. They may disorganize him, as seen in the primitive who dies from a witch's curse, or help him to reintegrate himself, as in religious conversion.

Cultural factors determine to a large extent which conditions are singled out as targets of the influencing process, and how they manifest themselves. The same phenomena may be viewed as signs of mental illness in one society, of demoniacal possession in another, and as eccentricities to be ignored in a third. Moreover, the behavior of the afflicted person is greatly influenced by culturally determined expectations as to how persons so defined should behave.

Since the distress is related to the behavior of the person in his totality, it involves all levels of his functioning. Purely psychic and purely bodily disorders exist only as logical extremes of a continuum. Although the locus of the major disturbance may differ considerably in the different types of distress with which we have been concerned, the biological, psychological, and social components are always all involved to some degree.

The aim of psychotherapy is to relieve distress by encouraging beneficial changes in all aspects of personal functioning. Emotionally it tries to produce an optimal level of excitation to facilitate change, quieting the overexcited patient and stimulating the apathetic or complacent one. At a combined cognitive-emotional level it tries to engender his hopes and strengthen his self-esteem. In the cognitive realm it attempts to supply him with new information and new ways of perceiving what he already knows, to enable him to straighten out his assumptive systems concerning himself and persons close to him. Socially, it tries to foster improvement in his interpersonal behavior, so that he gains more satisfaction and suffers less frustration in his interactions with others.

Attainment of these goals is sought through the performance of certain prescribed activities in the context of a particular relationship between the healer (often assisted by a group) and the patient. Both activities and relationship are determined in part by aspects of the culture, especially its assumptive world and the culturally sanctioned training of the healer.

In all cultures, however, the relationship seems to have three features. First, the influencer (and group) genuinely care about the sufferer's welfare. They are deeply committed to bringing about the kind of change they deem desirable and expend considerable effort in the attempt. Second, the influencing figures have a certain ascendancy or power, which may rest on a variety of interrelated attributes. These may include their socially determined role and status, their ability to inspire the sufferer's expectation of relief, and their control of means of coercion. Their ascendancy enables them to exert more or less direct pressure on him and sometimes encourages him to imitate or emulate them. Third, the influencer mediates between the person being influenced, the influencing group (if there is one), and the larger society. In many cases he also represents suprapersonal—often supernatural—forces that are postulated by the group's world view and that the sufferer must appease or win over.

The specific means of guidance is a ritual or task that is viewed as the way by which the sufferer is brought to see the errors of his ways and correct them, thereby gaining relief. The task requires the active participation of all involved and is typically repetitive. Some therapeutic or influencing tasks closely prescribe the sufferer's activities; others impel him to take the initiative and the influencing figures reward statements that accord with the requirements of the treatment scheme and discourage those that do not.

The influencing process expresses and is guided by a conceptual system that includes illness and health, the deviant and the normal. It explains the cause of the sufferer's distress and specifies desirable goals for him. It cannot be shaken by him or by his failure to gain relief. Acceptance of it gives him a means for understanding his distress and of regaining a sense of unity with his fellows, so that it becomes a way of promoting both internal and external harmony.

American psychotherapy is colored by certain interrelated features of American society, notably its diversity, the high value it places on democracy and science, and the methods of training psychotherapists. The diversity of American society permits the co-existence of various therapies based on differing conceptual schemes representing the value systems of different subcultures. This may have certain virtues. A patient whose outlook is at variance with one group may find acceptance in another, that is, he need not conform to one particular life style in order to gain healing group support. Moreover, variations among different groups enable the psychiatrist to represent attitudes and values differing from those of the patient. If the differences are not too great, they may help the latter to gain some new and useful perspectives on his problems. On the other hand, differences in world view of psychiatrist and patient, based on differences in their backgrounds, may more or less seriously impede communication between them. In addition, the absence of a single, all-embracing world view shared by the patient, the therapist, and the larger society limits the amount of pressure the therapist can mobilize to help the patient change his attitudes. No form of American psychotherapy can approximate the influencing power of primitive healing or thought reform in this respect, though perhaps an ideal therapeutic community, which completely immerses the patient in a culture expressing a self-consistent assumptive world, could approach it.

Despite the variety of American culture, almost all segments place a high value on democracy and science. The democratic ideal assigns a high worth to individual self-fulfillment. It regards behavior that is apparently self-directed as more admirable than behavior apparently caused by external pressures. Thus it values independence of thought and action, within limits, and the rebel or deviate, if not too extreme, may continue to count on group tolerance and even respect. The whole concept of the therapeutic community, with its view of the hospital inmate as a responsible person entitled to kindness, understanding, and respect, is an expression of the democratic world view.

The scientific ideal reinforces the democratic one by valuing lack of dogmatism. It also values objectivity and intellectual comprehension, and these features may not be entirely advantageous for psychotherapy. They tend to result in an overevaluation of its cognitive aspects. From the patient's standpoint, "insight" in the sense of ability to verbalize self-understanding may be mistaken for genuine attitude change. From the therapist's standpoint, the scientific attitude may lead to undue stress on the niceties of interpretation and avoidance of frankly emotion-arousing techniques such as group rituals and dramatic activities, even though there is universal agreement that in order to succeed psychotherapy must involve the patient's emotions.

Both democratic and scientific ideals tend to cause many American therapists to underestimate the extent to which psychotherapy is an influencing process. Members of a democracy do not like to see themselves as exercising power over someone else, and the scientist observes—he does not influence. So the most prestigious forms of psychotherapy in America are termed scientific and permissive though in many respects they are neither.

Within the broad framework of the democratic, scientific world view, American psychotherapy embodies the values of the medical tradition on the one hand and psychoanalysis on the other. Since psychoanalysis was founded by a physician, it shares some aspects of the medical orientation, but also differs in certain respects.

The physician's role is an exception to the over-all democratic pattern of relationships in America. He is expected to be authoritarian with his patients. Psychoanalysis rejects this aspect of the medical orientation and also diverges from it in stressing psychological rather than bodily causes of distress. It shares the medical viewpoint that the physician's primary obligation is to his patient, with its corollary insistence on the privacy of the doctor-patient relationship. In this regard it also accepts, though with reservations, the medical conceptualization of illness as residing primarily in the patient.

Actually, psychiatric illness often seems to be the expression of a disturbed interactional system involving several persons. The one who comes to treatment becomes labeled as the patient by this act, but the major locus of the disturbance may well lie elsewhere.[2] Acceptance of the medical view of mental illness has led to neglect of group and community forces in production and relief of distress and maintenance of beneficial changes. Although theories of psychotherapy increasingly recognize that disturbed interpersonal relationships in childhood are related to maladaptations of adult life, they regard the causal sequence as running primarily from the adult patient's internal disharmonies to his external ones. This results in an undue emphasis on helping him to resolve his internal conflicts in the belief that resolution of the external difficulties will necessarily follow. Exploration of the potentialities of the reverse procedure, namely trying to resolve external conflicts as a means of facilitating resolution of inner ones, or working at both levels simultaneously, has received considerable impetus from group therapy and the therapeutic community, so this one-sidedness may soon be rectified.

The divergent views of medicine and psychoanalysis with regard to the major etiological factors in illness may have contributed not only to the relative neglect of bodily factors in mental illness and of physical and pharmacological remedies by psychologically oriented psychiatrists, but also to their overemphasis by medically oriented ones. This split bids fair to be resolved by advances in neurophysiology and psychopharmacology, which should eventually make it possible to trace out in some detail the interplay between bodily and mental states.

Differences between medical and psychoanalytic conceptualizations of the role of the therapist are reflected in the division of American psychotherapies into directive and evocative approaches. The former, favored by psychiatrists who have maintained their primary identification as physicians, use the conventional authoritarian physician-patient relationship to instigate behaviors that will expose the patient to corrective experiences. As in the rest of medical practice, treatment is directed towards alleviation of a particular symptom or symptom-complex. Evocative therapies, used by psychiatrists who see themselves primarily as psychotherapists, are modeled on a democratic pattern of relationship and try to evoke a wide range of the patient's attitudes in the treatment situation. The therapist guides the course of therapy to some extent by subtle cues of approval or disapproval.

Long-term evocative therapy involves detailed scrutiny of many aspects of the patient's present and past life, including his reactions to the therapist himself. This may mobilize a variety of emotions, such as resentment, anxiety, and guilt, which may supply incentives for change. The therapist tries to guide the process at a cognitive level by his interpretations.

It is interesting that evocative therapies are usually termed "permissive," which reflects the adherence of therapists using this method to the democratic world view and their corresponding reluctance to recognize the extent to which they influence their patients. A further incentive to overlook the persuasive aspects of this type of treatment lies in the therapist's natural desire to use the patient's productions as independent confirmation of his theories. It is easy to do this because the influencing cues are often so subtle as to escape awareness of both therapist and patient.

In short, American psychotherapy, when viewed against the background of other methods of persuasion and healing, appears to embody certain biases related to the scientific, democratic values of society and to its own medical and psychoanalytic ancestry. These biases have virtues and disadvantages. They imply respect for the patient's individuality, which strengthens his self-esteem, and emphasis on self-understanding, which helps most persons to deal more effectively with the problems of life. On the other hand, they may result in inadequate attention to emotional aspects of the therapeutic process, the role of group forces, and the influencing power of the therapist.

The popularity of religious healing and healing cults in America may be related to the fact that they stress the very areas in which conventional forms of psychotherapy are deficient. Their therapeutic procedures operate in the framework of an infallible theory that explains the patient's troubles and prescribes the methods of cure. The healer glories in his claimed powers and exerts them unabashedly. His own attitudes, in many cases shared and reinforced by a group of believers, strongly mobilize the patient's hopes, and the group helps to sustain any beneficial changes.

Mention of beneficial changes leads to the knotty question of the effectiveness of psychotherapy. This is extraordinarily difficult to evaluate. Nevertheless, a few very tentative generalizations may be ventured. Since the forms of suffering treated by psychotherapy involve all levels of a person's functioning as well as his relations to his group, the effectiveness of these methods is limited by externally and internally fixed boundaries to the patient's adaptive capacities. Externally the benefits of treatment may be limited by unmodifiable environmental stresses, such as serious illness in a family member. Limits to therapeutic benefit are also set by stresses induced by the assumptive systems of the patient's society or by conflicting assumptive systems of the groups to which he belongs. No amount of psychotherapy, for example, can abolish certain stresses confronting a Negro in parts of the South, or those impinging on a child one of whose parents is a militant atheist and the other a devout Catholic.

Resolution of culturally induced stresses lies beyond the psychiatrist's powers. The best he can do is improve the patient's ability to deal with them; their correction lies in the hands of political, social, and religious leaders. He may be able to affect social stresses indirectly by offering insights that help shape the aims and guide the activities of these leaders, but this becomes preventive psychiatry rather than psychotherapy.[3] Internally set limitations to psychotherapeutic effectiveness include biological deficiencies and very deeply ingrained maladaptive patterns resulting from severely damaging life experiences.

To be a good prospect for psychotherapy, a person must have a certain adaptive capacity and flexibility, often referred

to as "ego-strength." Qualities like verbal facility and intelligence seem related to ability to profit from most forms of
American psychotherapy, partly because these qualities make
it easier to play the psychotherapeutic game and also because
they go with assumptive systems valuing self-knowledge. Other
personal attributes that make persons good candidates for psychotherapy are similar to those related to general accessibility to influence—a high degree of distress, anxiety, self-
dissatisfaction, and feelings of social or personal insecurity.

There is a bit of evidence that methods of psychological
healing have nonspecific and specific effects. The former are
of the nature of symptom relief and seem to result from mobilization of the patient's expectation of help. They therefore
usually appear fairly promptly and are unrelated to the type
of therapy. The specific effects lie in the realm of changes in
attitudes and behavior, and these presumably would differ to
some extent depending on the conceptual scheme and method
underlying the type of therapy used.

The long-term effects of psychotherapy are especially hard
to evaluate because of the fact that the patient continues to be
exposed to a bombardment of experiences with beneficial or
noxious potentialities during and after treatment.

Whether or not the changes initiated by psychotherapy are
sustained depends on the nature of these new stresses and
whether the gains achieved through psychotherapy enable the
patient to cope with them more successfully than before. Moreover, the extent to which he receives group support for his
new attitudes and behavior is probably crucial. Here the existence of many groups with a wide range of ideologies may be
an advantage, for if the patient after therapy can no longer
find support from his former group, he may be able to get it
from a new one. Group support need not be expressed as increased liking. What really counts is whether his new self
achieves recognition and respect. He may gain this through
being able to embody the group's values more successfully, or,
on the contrary, in line with our democratic values he may

win increased respect for being able to think and act more independently. In any case, he can more readily maintain changes induced by therapy to the extent that they enable him to feel less derogated and isolated.

Every experienced psychotherapist has treated cases in which therapy seemed to have far-reaching and permanent effects, enabling the patient to reach a level of comfort and effectiveness that he would have been most unlikely to attain without treatment. By and large, however, the effect of successful psychotherapy seems to be to accelerate or facilitate healing processes that would have gone on more slowly in its absence. This is, of course, the function of most medical treatment. If psychotherapists did no more than reduce duration of suffering and disability, this would be well worth their efforts.

It seems that patients come to psychotherapy when they are under internal or external pressures to modify their feelings and behavior, and the psychotherapist assists in the process much as a midwife might at the birth of a baby. What he does may make a lot of difference in how smoothly or rapidly the process occurs, but the extent to which he causes it is uncertain.

IMPLICATIONS FOR RESEARCH

As this survey has made evident, though there is an abundance of clinical lore, the amount of experimentally verified knowledge about psychotherapeutic processes is disappointingly meager. This is not through want of trying, as psychotherapy has absorbed the attention of many able investigators and been amply supported financially during the past decade.[4] Though this is not the place for detailed consideration of research aspects of psychotherapy, a brief attempt to make explicit some of the major areas of difficulty and the most promising directions of progress seems appropriate.[5]

One set of problems arises from the conditions of psychotherapeutic practice. Most experienced psychiatrists have a considerable emotional involvement in the efficacy of their methods. Each has become expert in a particular mode of psychotherapy as the result of long and arduous training. His self-esteem, status, and financial security are linked to its effectiveness. Under these circumstances he can hardly be expected to be an impartial student of his own method, and any data he reports cannot escape the suspicion of bias. Theoretically there is an easy solution to this dilemma, which is to separate the roles of researcher and therapist. The psychiatrist would permit himself to be observed by trained researchers through a one-way vision screen or by means of sound films and tape recordings of interviews. Unfortunately, many of the most sophisticated and experienced psychotherapists are unwilling to submit their work to this sort of systematic impartial scrutiny.

The obvious objection that such an examination would constitute an unacceptable infringement of the psychiatrists' confidential relationships with their patients is reinforced by other less clearly articulated misgivings. Objective study of psychiatrists' methods entails certain risks. It might turn out that what they actually do differs from what they say they do, that changes in the patients are not caused by the maneuvers to which they attribute them, and that their results are no better than those obtained by practitioners of other methods. All in all, they can hardly be blamed for subscribing to a bit of wisdom attributed to Confucius, "A wise man does not examine the source of his well being." But the effect of his prudence is to force researchers in psychotherapy to study treatment as carried out by younger therapists who are often still in training, and the results obtained are always open to question on the grounds that the therapists were insufficiently experienced.[6] Although reluctance of experienced psychiatrists to participate in research has been a serious obstacle, it is gradually yielding to the persistent blandishments of researchers.

A similar type of superficial but troublesome hindrance to psychotherapy research arises from the fact that its subjects are human beings who can be disciplined only up to a point.

Therapists chafe at the restrictions imposed by research requirements and are tempted to circumvent them when they believe that they interfere with treatment. Captive patients in hospitals can be fairly easily controlled, but outpatients are another matter. They break appointments, drop out of treatment without warning, and take vacations at the wrong times. Another practical obstacle lies in the fact that certain forms of psychotherapy involve prolonged, frequent contacts with the patient, so no one practitioner can accumulate an adequate sample for study in a reasonable period of time. This consideration tends to cause researchers to stick to the study of short-term psychotherapy to increase the available sample of patients, with inevitable neglect of long-term methods of equal theoretical interest.

Difficulties for research presented by personal qualities of therapists and patients and aspects of the methods are surmountable in principle. Another type of obstacle presents a more serious problem because it is inherent in the very nature of psychotherapy. Being concerned with all levels of human functioning from the biological to the social, psychotherapy raises all the issues concerned with human nature and the communication process. The range and complexity of this subject matter create difficulties of conceptualization. Some formulations try to encompass all its aspects. Many of these have been immensely insightful and stimulating and have illuminated many fields of knowledge. To achieve all-inclusiveness, however, they have resorted to metaphor, have left major ambiguities unresolved, and have formulated their hypotheses in terms that cannot be subjected to experimental test.

The opposite approach has been to try to conceptualize small segments of the field with sufficient precision to permit experimental test of the hypotheses, but these formulations run the risk of achieving rigor at the expense of significance. The researcher is faced with the problem of delimiting an aspect of psychotherapy that is amenable to experimental study and at the same time includes the major determinants of the problem under consideration. He finds himself in the predicament of the Norse god Thor who tried to drain a small goblet only to discover that it was connected with the sea. Under these circumstances there is an inevitable tendency to guide the choice of research problems more by the ease with which they can be investigated than by their importance. One is reminded of the familiar story of the drunkard who lost his keys in a dark alley but looked for them under the lamp post because the light was better there. This has led to a considerable amount of precise but trivial research.

In spite of these obstacles, certain areas of research in psychotherapy are beginning to look promising. Individual and group sessions afford excellent opportunities to study human communication systems. The most basic questions in this area, such as the effect of the bodily presence or absence of the therapist on the productions of the patient, require elucidation.[7] Interesting research is being done on the formal properties of the interaction system formed by therapist and patient, such as how much each speaks, how this changes over time, and how changes in the speech patterns of one participant affect the patterns of the other.[8]

Especially pertinent to psychiatry are studies of the means by which therapist and patient can influence the content of each other's productions through subtle, nonverbal, cues. Experimental studies of verbal conditioning have demonstrated that if a person cares what another thinks of him, his verbalizations are readily influenced by cues of approval or disapproval. Therefore if the therapist has an hypothesis in mind—and he could not do reasearch without one—he might well unwittingly convey it to the patient, who might oblige by producing supportive material. Obviously, this type of confirmation is of dubious value. Until the personal and situational conditions determining the influence of the therapist's expectancies on the patient's productions, and the kinds of material most susceptible and most resistant to this type of influence are better understood, hypotheses about human nature supported solely by patients' productions in psychotherapy must be considered to be unproven.

The demonstration of the conditionability of patients' verbalizations leads directly to a fundamental question about which very little is known—the relationship between what a person says and what he actually feels. An experimental approach to this problem is afforded by a study of patients' emotional responses to what transpires in the interview, as revealed through various physiological measures.[9] These methods may help to define the personal and situational factors arousing patients' anxieties on the one hand and hopes on the other, as well as personal differences in emotional responsivity, which have formed the basis of personality classifications since the days of Hippocrates. Some patients are too phlegmatic, others too excitable, and the optimal degrees of therapeutically useful tension for them may be quite different.

Better understanding of the types of therapy that most effectively mobilize patients' favorable expectations is especially needed. One promising experimental approach has been the investigation of conditions determining responses of psychiatric patients to inert medications whose therapeutic properties lie in their symbolization of the physician's role. This proves to be quite a complex matter involving the interaction of personality characteristics, attitudes towards physicians and medication, and properties of the therapeutic situation.

Studies of the effects of patients' emotional states on their progress must include the question of the definition of improvement. Although investigation of the therapeutic process can illumine many theoretical issues of human interaction, their practical value depends on solution of this question. For without adequate criteria of improvement there is no way of deciding which of the processes in psychotherapy are relevant to its goal and which are not. Decision as to what type of change constitutes improvement rests on considerations of value rather than scientific pertinence, and this has tended to confuse the issue. It seems possible to approach the problem from a research standpoint by using the same criteria of improvement as do all healing arts—reduction of distress and improvement of functioning. Since symptoms of distress are subjective, one must rely on the patient's report, which may be strongly colored by the impression he may wish to make on the researcher. Physiological measures offer hope of gaining more objective criteria of distress. Successful functioning is not merely a matter of behavior but of attitudes, so evaluation of this criterion must take into account not only the patient's behavior, but its meanings for himself and those who are important to him. Despite these and other methodological problems, the question of the effects of psychotherapy proves to be researchable and is leading to the accumulation of interesting data on the effects of duration of treatment, amount of therapeutic contact, and presence or absence of other patients in the treatment situation.[10]

A special problem in the evaluation of psychotherapy lies in the fact that the psychotherapeutic interview is only a tiny fraction of the patient's encounters with others, and it is therefore hard to disentangle its effects from those of other personal contacts. Therapy may be given credit for improvement really due to a change in the patient's living pattern such as getting married or, conversely, its potentially beneficial effects may be wiped out by a personal catastrophe. To complicate matters further, because of the reciprocal nature of human behavior, improvement in the patient started by therapy may lead to favorable changes in the attitudes of others. Therapy may have given him the courage to ask his girl to marry him. Questions of this type loom especially large with respect to long-term treatment, which requires some way of determining whether the patient handles stress he meets subsequent to undergoing therapy more comfortably and effectively than before.

Ultimate elucidation of the effects of psychotherapy thus depends on success in conceptualizing human interactions, at both personal and social levels. For the sociocultural determinants of mental illness and its treatment must also be taken into account. All in all, considering the theoretical and practical problems involved, it is easy to see why research on psychotherapy has not yet registered any major triumphs. Many hopeful leads are now appearing, however, so that significant progress along many fronts may be confidently anticipated.

IMPLICATIONS FOR PRACTICE

The practice of psychotherapy cannot wait until research has yielded a solid basis for it. In the meanwhile, this survey has suggested certain implications for practice that may be worth explicit mention. The pattern of psychotherapeutic practice in America is seriously imbalanced in that too many of the ablest, most experienced psychiatrists spend most of their time with patients who need them least. This has been the unfortunate, though probably inevitable, consequence of the concept of mental illness as personal malfunctioning, which in itself represents a great gain in understanding. The trouble is that this view makes it impossible to draw the line, so that many persons who are showing essentially normal responses to the wear and tear of life or who are unhappy for reasons other than personal malfunctioning see themselves—and are seen by others—as proper candidates for psychotherapy.

Those candidates for psychotherapy who have education and money naturally seek out psychiatrists with the most prestige. Since in our society the highest prestige attaches to psychoanalytic training in its broadest sense, candidates gravitate towards the best practitioners of evocative therapy. Because analytic training has the highest prestige, it attracts the ablest young psychiatrists, who, having completed it settle down in the largest cities and devote themselves largely to the long-term treatment of the patients just described. They would have to be superhuman to resist this temptation. They cannot very well turn away persons who come to them for help, especially when they are personally congenial (being on the whole of the same intellectual and social level as themselves), pay their bills, are seldom worrisome during the course of treatment, and show a gratifying response.

In the meantime, there are not nearly enough trained psychiatrists to care for the less attractive lower class, seriously ill patients who crowd outpatient clinics and state hospitals and who, from both a medical and a social standpoint, present by far the greater challenge.

Obviously there is no easy remedy for this state of affairs, for which no one can be blamed. Trends that may gradually rectify it are the steady increase in trained nonmedical psychotherapists on the one hand, and the elucidation of the biological components of mental illness on the other. These trends will in time modify the public image of both mental illness and psychotherapy. It may be hoped eventually that the situationally distressed or morally perturbed will come to seek sources of help other than psychiatrists, who then will be free to devote themselves to the treatment of the severely mentally ill, for which their medical training uniquely qualifies them.

Our survey has suggested that much, if not all, of the effectiveness of different forms of psychotherapy may be due to those features that all have in common rather than to those that distinguish them from each other. This does not necessarily mean that all therapies are interchangeable. It may well turn out, when types of patients and effects of therapy are better understood, that certain approaches are better for some types of patients than for others and that they differ in certain of their effects, which have not as yet been specified. Until these questions are clarified, the advance of both knowledge and practice is probably better served by members of different schools defending their own positions, while being tolerant of other schools, than by being uncritically eclectic. For the therapist's ability to help his patient depends partly on his self-confidence, and this in turn depends on mastery of a particular conceptual scheme and its accompanying techniques. Since the leading theories of psychotherapy represent alternative rather than incompatible formulations, it is unlikely that any one of them is completely wrong. As an eminent philosopher has wisely said: "A clash of doctrines is not a disaster—it is an opportunity."[11] The activity stimulated by the clash of psychotherapeutic doctrines will eventually yield sufficient information either to prove that they are to all practical purposes identical or to clarify and substantiate differences between them.[12]

A further implication of this survey for psychotherapy is that the emotional components of the process deserve more attention. At a physiological level, certain drugs seem to have promise as the means of producing optimal emotional excitation. It may be possible through their use to stir up over-apathetic patients, relax overinhibited ones, and dampen those who are too excited, in each case improving their accessibility to the therapist and creating a favorable state for the production of change.

At a symbolic level, it is important to mobilize the patient's expectancy for help, or at least to do nothing to counteract it. The psychiatrist should therefore be prepared to modify his approach, within limits possible for him, to meet his patients' conceptions of therapy, insofar as he can discern them. For patients who cannot conceive of a treatment that does not involve getting a pill or injection, it may be advisable to offer a prescription as a means of establishing and solidifying a therapeutic relationship. Once this has occurred, it is often possible to help the patient modify his expectations and the medication is dispensed with.[13]

The question of how far a physician should go to meet a patient's expectations is a thorny one. Obviously he cannot use methods in which he himself does not believe. Moreover, reliance on the healing powers of faith, if it led to neglect of proper diagnostic or treatment procedures, would clearly be irresponsible. On the other hand, faith may be a specific antidote for certain emotions such as fear or discouragement, which may constitute the essence of a patient's illness. For such patients, the mobilization of expectant trust by whatever means may be as much an etiological remedy as penicillin for pneumonia.

It is important for the psychiatrist to accept the fact that he inevitably exerts a strong influence on his patients. He cannot avoid doing so; therefore it is better that he exert his influence consciously than unconsciously. It has been said that "in all therapy trouble is apt to follow the ignorant application of important forces,"[14] and this applies particularly when the important force is the therapist himself. This leaves open, of course, the question of how the therapist should best use his influence—for example, whether with a particular patient he should ostensibly be directive or permissive. But he will be better able to reach the correct decision if he remembers that in either case he significantly affects what transpires.

Finally, this review emphasizes the desirability of exploiting group forces more fully to produce and sustain therapeutic change. This means not only the use of group therapeutic methods, but the inclusion of persons important to the patient in his treatment. For hospitalized patients it means full use of the potentialities of the "therapeutic community." For out-patients it implies more attention to the resources in the patient's environment that might be mobilized to facilitate and perpetuate his improvement. "No man is an island," and the degree and permanence of change in any individual will depend in part on corresponding changes in those close to him and on support from his wider milieu.

Notes

CHAPTER 1: PSYCHOTHERAPY IN AMERICA TODAY

1. A good summary of psychoanalytic theory is Brenner (1954); of conditioned reflex theory, Pavlov (1941); and of learning theories, Hilgard (1948).

2. For an excellent concise statement of the interplay of social and personal factors in the causes, manifestations, and treatment of mental illness, see Clausen (1959). Freedman and Hollingshead (1957) present interesting data demonstrating that the diagnosis of psychoneurosis is the result of an interaction process involving the patient, the physician, and the social group.

3. Clausen and Yarrow (1955).

4. For an account of contemporary German and Russian psychotherapy, see Winkler (1956) and Guilyarovsky (1958), respectively.

5. This issue is interestingly discussed by Skinner (1956) and C. R. Rogers (1956).

6. Hollingshead and Redlich (1958) thoroughly document this point.

7. See, for example, the work of Rood (1958) with sex offenders.

8. The figure for psychiatrists represents approximately the membership of the American Psychiatric Association in 1959. Figures for clinical psychologists and psychiatric social workers were obtained from the *Health Manpower Chart Book* (1955).

9. This figure is also obtained from the *Health Manpower Chart Book* (1955).

10. Healing cults are astonishingly popular. A survey (Reed, 1932) found some 36,000 sectarian medical practitioners, exclusive of esoteric and local cults, which equalled almost one-fourth of the total number of medical practitioners at that time, to whom people paid at least $125,000,000 annually. One physician found that 43 per cent of his private patients and 26 per cent of his clinic patients had patronized a cult during the three months preceding their visits to him. Although one reason for the continuing popularity of these cults is that most persons recover from acute illnesses regardless of what is done or not done to them, it seems likely that the adherents of cults also derive more specific benefits, such as increased peace of mind and sense of well-being.

11. Steiner (1945).

12. In 1958 the United States Public Health Service alone spent about two million dollars for research in psychotherapy.

13. Good reviews and discussions of improvement data are found in Appel *et al.* (1953), Teuber (1953), and Eysenck (1952). Recently Wolpe (1958) and Ellis (1957) have claimed that their methods produce an improvement rate of over 90 per cent in neurotics, and Whitehorn and Betz (1954) have found that certain physicians obtain an improvement rate of about 80 per cent with groups of hospitalized schizophrenics, but these results have not yet been duplicated by others.

14. Characteristic follow-up studies are those of Hastings (1958) and Levitt (1957). See also Chapter 11.

15. Zubin (1959).

16. Thompson (1950), p. 235. Of course, treatment contact cannot be attenuated indefinitely without reducing its effectiveness, but the lower limit of effective contact has yet to be determined. Imber *et al.* (1957) present experimental evidence indicating that treatment limited to not more than half an hour every two weeks is less effective in producing certain types of immediate improvement than treatment consisting of an hour once a week. See Chapter 11.

17. Conn (1949, 1953), Ellis (1957), Wolpe (1958). It is instructive in this regard to compare two reports of group therapy with peptic ulcer patients, one of which was limited to six weeks (Chappell *et al.*, 1936), the other unlimited in time (Fortin and Abse, 1956). Though the studies, unfortunately, are not strictly comparable, both seemed to obtain about the same results. Especially interesting is Shlien's experiment (1957) indicating that, with the identical type of therapy, patients improve more promptly if they know in advance that therapy will last only ten weeks than if no time limit is set.

18. J. Seeman, quoted in Shlien (1957).

19. The role of therapists' attitudes is considered in Chapter 7.

20. Regardless of theoretical orientation, observers show a high degree of agreement with respect to patients who are greatly improved or apparently cured. Agreement drops sharply, however, with respect to lesser degrees of improvement, suggesting that the criteria underlying these judgments need greater explication than has yet been achieved. Conceptual and methodological questions involved in the evaluation of improvement are discussed in Parloff *et al.* (1954) and Frank (1959a).

21. Barron and Leary (1955).

CHAPTER 2: A CONCEPTUAL FRAMEWORK FOR PSYCHOTHERAPY

1. A manful attempt to construct such a scheme has been made by Kardiner *et al.* (1945). A brilliant, if less inclusive, scheme for relating personality to culture is offered by Spiro (in press). See also Kluckhohn *et al.* (1953).

2. Glass (1957) reports that both the intensity and the duration of combat are related to the rate of neuropsychiatric breakdown.

3. Pasamanick and Lilienfeld (1955), for example, report a statistically significant association between mental retardation and damaging prenatal experiences.

4. This term has been borrowed from Cantril, but it is given a much wider meaning here. He confines it to the sphere of perceptions only, but his discussion of the "assumptive form world" seems to justify the broader use. For example, he says: "The net result of our purposive actions is that we create for ourselves a set of assumptions which serve as guides and bases for future actions." (Cantril, 1950, p. 87.)

Kelly (1955, p. 561) has developed an elaborate theory of psychological functioning and a psychotherapeutic method based on the "fundamental postulate" that a "person's processes are psychologically channelized by the ways in which he anticipates events."

5. This is the "double-bind" hypothesis of the etiology of schizophrenia (Bateson *et al.*, 1956).

6. Housman (1922).

7. This psychoanalytic term refers to more-or-less automatic and unconscious ways of protecting the self against unpleasant emotions, especially anxiety. See Fenichel (1945), Chapter IX, pp. 141-167.

8. The example is from Cantril (1957).

9. The example is from Frank (1946a).

10. See discussion by Leary (1957), pp. 91-131, of the interpersonal reflex for a good account of this process.

11. The concept of the self-fulfilling prophecy is developed by Merton (1957), pp. 421-436.

12. Another important source of the influence of one's peers may lie in a postulated drive to evaluate one's opinions and abilities by comparison with others. This tendency is stronger, the greater the perceived similarity between the opinions and abilities of others and one's own (Festinger, 1954).

CHAPTER 3: RELIGIOUS HEALING

1. For examples see Webster (1942).

2. Elspeth Huxley (1959), p. 19. Presumably Njombo was aware of the ministrations of the shaman (see note 10 of this chapter), although he appeared comatose to his employers.

3. Warner (1941). The quotes are from pages 241 and 242.

4. Cannon (1957).

5. Richter (1957).

6. Will (1959) cites two examples of deaths of schizophrenics possibly precipitated by their sense of "unrelatedness." Adland (1947) reviews the literature on "acute exhaustive psychoses" up to that time and cites a case in which the process was successfully interrupted when the psychiatrist succeeded in making contact with the patient. Rosen (1946) describes his successful interruption of three acute catatonic excitements by playing the role of the patient's protector, in terms of the patient's delusional system. The less dramatic but careful studies of Lesse (1958) demonstrate that anxiety is a forerunner of many psychopathological symptoms and parallels them in severity.

7. Nardini (1952). The quotes are from pages 244 and 245.

8. Major Clarence L. Anderson, quoted in Kinkead (1959), p. 149. Strassman et al. (1956) present an interesting discussion of apathy as a reaction to severe stress in war prisoners. Schmale (1958, p. 271) concludes from a careful study of forty-two hospitalized medical patients that "psychic states of helplessness or hopelessness may be related to increased biological vulnerability." Although containing serious methodological flaws, the study gains plausibility from accounts of a similar relationship of illness to noxious emotional states in primitives and prisoners.

9. The discussion of primitive healing is based primarily on the following sources: Deren (1953); Gillin (1948), reprinted in Lessa and Vogt (1958); Leighton and Leighton (1941); Opler (1936); Lévi-Strauss (1958); and Sachs (1947).

10. Although anthropologists draw distinctions between terms such as "shaman," "witch doctor," and "medicine man," "shaman" seems to be gaining acceptance as the generic designation for primitive healers of all types and is so used in the text.

11. See Field (1955). Still another way of acquiring shamanistic powers is through inheritance (Sachs, 1947).

12. This account is taken from Lévi-Strauss (1958). Quotations are from pages 193, 194, and 196. Translation is by Elizabeth K. Frank.

13. See p. 44; also see Sachs (1947).

14. Field (1955) gives sketchy examples of long-term individual therapy in the African Gold Coast, and Lederer (1959) adds a consideration of exorcism in the Middle Ages and in Zen Buddhism. Both writers discuss parallels with Western psychotherapy.

15. The account is condensed from Gillin (1948). Quotes are from pages 389, 391, and 394.

16. The altars are Christian. In Christianized societies embarrassing problems may be created by incompatibilities between the assumptive systems underlying healing rituals and Christian beliefs. As a result, a considerable part of the healing rite may be devoted to arranging a truce between them. In the example, much time was spent in prayers to Christian saints, explaining to them why it was necessary to traffic with non-Christian spirits.

17. Lévi-Strauss (1958), p. 217.

18. As in Western medicine, the criterion of the success of a healing procedure is not always the patient's recovery. The old surgical quip comes to mind: "The operation was successful but the patient died."

19. Lévi-Strauss (1958), p. 219.

20. Rasmussen (1929), reprinted in Lessa and Vogt (1958), pp. 362-367, offers an excellent account of a confessional ritual.

21. "There can be no doubt that for the primitive thought confession acts as a real purgation, an elimination of evil matter in the patient's body . . . naming a sin is to recall it, to give it form and substance, so that the officiating medicine man can deal with it in the prescribed manner. No vague announcement of sinfulness suffices; each sin that has been committed must be specified. Sometimes when the patient can think of nothing serious done by him he will confess imaginary sins." (Webster, 1942, p. 311.)

22. Deren (1953) gives a fascinating account of the emotional exaltation of a Haitian voodoo ceremony as experienced by herself.

23. The account of Lourdes is drawn mainly from Cranston (1957). The quotes are from pages 31, 35, 37, and 127, respectively. See also Janet (1925), Volume 1, Chapter 1.

24. Weatherhead (1951), p. 153.

25. Everson (1958).

26. Cranston (1957), p. 125.

27. Unfortunately, reports of similar cures in medical settings contain no information on the patients' emotional states, so it is impossible to determine whether or not the same psychological factors may be involved.

28. Salzman (1957) distinguishes between spiritual healing attributed to spiritual forces and faith healing based on faith in the healer. He gives interesting examples of the methods and theories of faith healers (among whom he includes the charlatans) in America today.

29. Reed (1932), pp. 109 f.

30. Rehder (1955).

31. The phrase is from Weatherhead (1951), p. 26, and is his characterization of religious faith as it refers to healing.

32. The striking similarity between religious healing in primitive groups and in the Christian world with respect to the interplay of patient, healer, group, and the supernatural world is highlighted by the two following quotations. The first (Ackerknecht, 1942, p. 514) sums up primitive healing. The second (Weatherhead, 1951, p. 486) summarizes Christian spiritual healing, in which the author firmly believes.

"The medicine man is a soul doctor . . . . He gives peace by confessing his patient. His rigid system, which ignores doubt, dispels fear, restores confidence, and inspires hope . . . the primitive psychotherapist works not only with the strength of his own personality. His rite is part of the common faith of the whole community which not seldom assists *in corpore* at his healing act . . . . The whole weight of the tribe's religion, myths, and community spirit enters into the treatment."

"The intercession of people united in love for Christ . . . and the laying on of hands . . . by a priest or minister or other person who is the *contact-point . . . of a beloved, believing and united community standing behind him and supporting his ministration to a patient who has been taught to understand the true nature of Christian faith* . . . is the true ministry of the Church. (Author's italics.)

CHAPTER 4: THE PLACEBO EFFECT IN MEDICAL
AND PSYCHOLOGICAL TREATMENT

1. Shapiro (1959), p. 303.
2. Webster's New Collegiate Dictionary, 1957 edition.
3. Wolf (1950).
4. Bloch (1927).
5. Volgyesi (1954).
6. Wolf and Pinsky (1954).
7. Frank (1952).
8. Gliedman et al. (1958).
9. Hampson et al. (1954).
10. Beecher (1955).
11. Lasagna et al. (1954). It should be added that occasionally a patient
who expresses strong distrust of doctors reacts positively to a placebo. A diabetic
who was a trained nurse, for example, was the despair of her physicians because of her refusal to take her medicines and her constant diatribes against
them. Yet in the very midst of her rebelliousness she showed a striking relief
of abdominal pain following an injection of distilled water by a physician. This
suggested that her attitude might have been an overcompensation for strong
feelings of dependency, as if she were longing to accept help but could not
admit it. The analogy to "skeptics" who benefit from a pilgrimage to Lourdes
(Chapter 3) is obvious.
12. Hankoff et al. (1958).
13. Rosenthal and Frank (1956).
14. Frank et al. (1959). This study is described more fully in Chapter 11.
15. Gliedman et al. (1958).
16. Kraines (1943), p. 135. Author's italics.

CHAPTER 5: RELIGIOUS REVIVALISM
AND THOUGHT REFORM

1. James (1936) offers a classic account of these experiences. Argyle (1958)
estimates that between 10 per cent and 30 per cent of religious people have
undergone a more-or-less violent conversion experience.
2. Clark (1929) found that 57 per cent of a group of sudden converts experienced subsequent joy. Quoted by Argyle (1958), p. 160.
3. Weininger (1955).
4. James (1936), p. 34.
5. Sargant (1957) discusses the part played by excessive emotional excitation
in facilitating attitude change in religious revivals, brain-washing and similar
phenomena. The material on John Wesley's methods is taken from this source.
6. The source of the material on Billy Graham's revivals is Argyle (1958).

7. "It is the rejoicing, singing, irrepressible happiness of the Salvationist which often makes him such a powerful savior of other men." (Begbie, 1909, p. 19.) This book contains nine vivid vignettes of London slum dwellers who were converted by the Salvation Army.

8. Argyle (1958), pp. 54 f.

9. Sargant (1957), p. 220.

10. Deren (1953), p. 165. A. Huxley (1959) speculates interestingly on how the physiological disorders created by starvation and disease might predispose to hallucinatory religious experiences.

11. Sargant (1957), p. 99. He comments (p. 109): "The best way to avoid possession, conversion, and all similar conditions is to avoid getting emotionally involved in the proceedings."

12. Hoffer (1958) offers a brilliant if somewhat uneven discussion of mass movements, much of which is directly pertinent to religious revivalism.

13. This statement may require qualification on two counts. Members of some primitive societies may have just as little individual freedom of action and live in as completely determined a social environment as Communist prisoners, though the forms of restriction differ. To speak of the goal of revivalist religion as circumscribed is only partly true, for the assumption is that being saved will bring far-reaching changes in its train. Nevertheless, the immediate goal is to bring about a clearly defined inner experience signalized by a particular act. Thought reform lacks such a definite end point.

14. See pp. 117 ff.

15. See Chapter 10.

16. The interrogator's zeal is enhanced by the fact that he wishes to believe in the genuineness of the patient's confession. According to his ideology, the prisoner would not have been arrested if he had not been guilty. Therefore, the prisoner's admission would tend to confirm and support the interrogator's world view. It also would help him justify to himself the suffering he had inflicted on the prisoner and would relieve his own anxiety about not having obtained a confession. Thus both prisoner and interrogator might collaborate in erecting a shared delusional system, each confirming the other in the false belief.

The collaboration of interrogators and accused to produce a confession that confirms the assumptive world of a society is fascinatingly portrayed in the following example from Lévi-Strauss (1958): An adolescent was accused of witchcraft, a capital crime, because a girl had a convulsion just after he touched her. Brought before the priests, he first tried vainly to deny his guilt. He then changed his tactics and made up a long account of his initiation into witchcraft, including how he had been taught the use of two drugs, one of which made girls mad and the other cured them. Ordered to produce the drugs, he got two roots, ate one, feigned a trance, and brought himself out of it with the other. He then gave the second to the girl and declared her cured. This still did not satisfy the family of the girl, so he invented a more dramatic story, telling how all his ancestors were sorcerers and how he could change into a cat and do other wonderful things by means of magic feathers. Then he was ordered to produce one of the feathers. After tearing down several walls in his home he finally found an old feather in the mud, which he presented to his prosecutors with a long explanation of how it was used. Then he had to repeat the whole story in the public square, adding new embellishments all the time and ending with a touching lamentation over the loss of his super-natural powers. After this he was freed.

Thus the boy acquits himself not by proving his innocence, but by producing evidence confirming his guilt. It seems obvious that the judges want to believe that he is a sorcerer, for they do not suggest tests that would be impossible for him to pass, such as changing himself into a cat, but ask him only to find a feather. Lévi-Strauss sums up (p. 191): "The judges require [the accused] to corroborate a system to which they hold only a fragmentary clue and which they want him to reconstitute in an appropriate way . . . . The confession, strengthened by the participation, even the complicity of the judges, turns the accused from culprit into a collaborator in the charge . . . the youth succeeded in transforming himself from a menace to the physical security of the group into proof of its mental coherence." Lévi-Strauss adds that the boy, too, be-came convinced (p. 192): "Since [sorcerers] exist, he may well be one. And how was he to know in advance the signs that would reveal his vocation to him? Perhaps they are to be found in this ordeal . . . . For him too, the coherence of the system and the role assigned to him to prove it have a value no less essential than the personal safety he risks in the exploit."

To what extent the effort to confirm their world view may have contributed to the enormous effort made by the Chinese Communists to obtain confessions is an open question, but unless something like this was at work it is hard to explain why they went to such lengths to convert not only influential per-sons such as intellectuals and foreigners who would serve propaganda purposes, but even lowly merchants and artisans, whom they could just as easily have summarily shot. In any case, one would expect those groups who are least sure of their world view to be the most fervent proselytizers, other things being equal. Thus it has been shown that if a religious sect makes a prophecy, it starts to proselytize only after the prophecy fails (Festinger *et al.*, 1956). These considerations may have some pertinence for some current American psychotherapeutic training programs (see pp. 125 f.).

17. Hinkle and Wolff (1956) present an excellent description of both Chinese and Russian procedures and a consideration of their relevance for psychotherapy. Kinkead (1959) is the chief source for Korean prisoners, and Lifton (1957a) for the revolutionary colleges and (1956) for American civilian prisoners. Rickett and Rickett (1957) and Rigney (1956) offer contrasting first-hand accounts of thought reform—the former through the eyes of a convert, the latter through those of an implacable foe. Beck and Godin (1951) are the source of first-hand material on Russian techniques.

18. Chapter 10.

19. Rigney's (1956) description of this experience is worth quoting (p. 23):

As time went on, I was more and more avoided by those I knew, until finally, I was practically deserted by all.

No one visited me.

Hardly anyone recognized me on the street.

Usually, if a Chinese who knew me, saw me coming, he or she turned and went in the opposite direction, or simply refused to look at me, in passing.

Friends and acquaintances destroyed all their photographs that featured me—destroyed all evidences, as letters, recommendations, books, indications of ever having known me, spoken to me or received any benefit from me.

I was abandoned.

Staff members and students of Fu Jen, many of whom I had helped, now turned against me, accused me to the police, requesting my arrest, in order to save themselves.

20. Kinkead (1959), p. 155.

21. See Rigney (1956), p. 36, and Beck and Godin (1951), p. 185, for vivid accounts of the disorganizing effects of sleep deprivation.

22. Lifton (1957a), p. 14.

23. Bettelheim's discussion of his concentration camp experiences (1943) and of the effects of having to say "Heil Hitler" in Nazi Germany (1952) is pertinent in this connection, as is Festinger's (1957) theory of cognitive dissonance.

24. In Russian prisons, "No prisoner was ever allowed to see any prisoner confined in any cell but his own . . . . Prisoners were conducted along the corridors by warders . . . [who by tapping metal parts of their uniforms] gave audible warning that they had a prisoner with them and thus avoided meeting others. If an encounter occurred, however, the prisoner had to face the wall . . . ." Beck and Godin (1951), pp. 61 f.

25. Schein (1957), p. 25.

26. Kinkead (1959), p. 137. Asch (1952) in a classic experiment demonstrated that a single person had great difficulty in maintaining a perceptual judgment when opposed by a unanimous group and that the support of even one person who agreed with him greatly increased his ability to withstand the group pressure. Hardy (1957) has duplicated this finding with respect to statements of attitudes about divorce.

The contrast between the way ex-prisoners behaved in a hospital ward, as compared with other American soldiers, bore striking witness to the effectiveness of the Communist isolation procedures. Most of the ex-prisoners stayed on the wards—less than 5 per cent asked for passes to go to town, and those who did go went alone. They formed no groups, did not play cards, and stayed as much by themselves as they could. But they talked compulsively and incessantly to the treatment personnel and seemed unable to evaluate whether the things they said about each other might be harmful or not (Mayer, 1956).

The clinical impression of apathy and personal isolation in most of the prisoners was borne out by their performance on psychological tests. The outstanding characteristic of the stories they made up to explain neutral pictures that they were shown was the rarity of interaction and feeling. Their interpretations of ink blots, which often reveal hidden attitudes and feelings, were described as showing varying degrees of apathy coupled with strong pent-up aggressive-destructive feelings (Singer and Schein, 1958).

27. Schein (1957), p. 23.

28. Rigney (1956), p. 31.

29. Rigney (1956), p. 51.

30. Rickett and Rickett (1957), p. 114.

31. Beck and Godin (1951), pp. 45 f.

32. The free-association technique of psychoanalysis has a similar effect, partly also attributable to the mobilization of guilt. Cf. p. 160.

33. That producing a state of distressing confusion in a person is an effective means of increasing his susceptibility to influence is suggested by the fact that giving a patient contradictory commands may be an effective way of rapidly inducing a hypnotic trance. The technique of Zen Buddhism that involves forcing a novitiate to meditate endlessly on insoluble problems, such as "clapping with one hand," also comes to mind in this connection (Stunkard, 1951).

34. Beck and Godin (1951), p. 44.

35. Lifton (1957a), p. 9.

36. Schein (1956), p. 163.

37. Schein (1956), p. 163.

38. Lifton (1957b), p. 269. Similar confabulations are known to occur in intensive long-term psychotherapy. See pp. 122 f.

39. Rigney (1956), p. 51.

40. Rickett and Rickett (1957), p. 207.

41. John Wesley's Methodist classes (p. 78) come to mind in this connection.

42. Segal (1957), p. 37.

43. Singer and Schein (1958).

CHAPTER 6: EXPERIMENTAL STUDIES OF PERSUASION

1. Rosenberg (1956).

2. Kelman (1953). Summarized in Hovland *et al.* (1953), pp. 226 f.

3. Kelman (1953) attributes the greater opinion change in the low incentive group to the fact that implicit verbal responses (i.e., thoughts) accompanying the writing of essays under this condition were more supportive and less interfering than those of the high incentive group because the former had to make a choice, had to put out more effort in competing for the prize, and had no conflicting thoughts aroused by overt pressure to conform. Janis and King (1954) explain their results (discussed on pp. 100 f.) in the same way. Festinger (1957) can account for these and many other findings by his ingenious theory of "cognitive dissonance." According to this theory, there is a strong drive to resolve internal conflict. The low incentive group felt more conflict when they conformed than the high incentive one, since they had a less valid reason to do so. The easiest way to resolve this conflict was to decide that they really preferred jungle comics after all.

4. King and Janis (1956).

5. Hovland *et al.* (1953), p. 237. Festinger (1957) explains these results by the assumption that improvising arguments in favor of a view with which one disagrees creates internal dissonance, whereas reading someone else's arguments aloud does not, because the goal is simply to read convincingly. Only in the first condition, therefore, would there be incentive to reduce dissonance by changing one's opinion to conform with one's statements.

6. Mouton *et al.* (1955-56). See also Helson *et al.* (1956).

7. Janis and King (1954).

8. Hovland *et al.* (1953), pp. 174-214; Janis (1954).

9. See pp. 134-140.

10. Hilgard (1948), pp. 82-120.

11. Greenspoon (1955).

12. Krasner (1958) has written a detailed critical review of studies of the conditioning of verbal behavior through 1957.

13. Krasner *et al.* (1959). Still other attributes of the experimenter may affect the kind of influence he exerts. For example, a slight soft-spoken woman was more successful than a big, athletic man in conditioning male students to express moderately hostile words (Binder *et al.,* 1957).

14. Taffel (1955), Sarason (1958). This result was not confirmed in one study of graduate students (J. M. Rogers, 1960). A possible explanation of the discrepancy may be that a patient with high anxiety, interviewed by a member of the hospital staff, would be hoping for relief from him, whereas a graduate student in a laboratory would be unlikely to expect this from another. That is, the difference in findings is consistent with the view that a major determinant of the success of operant conditioning is the subject's feeling of dependency on the interviewer. Anxiety would play a part only as it affected this dependency.

15. Sarason (1958). In psychotherapy a patient may appear to comply with the therapist as a way of avoiding actual change of attitude. Too ready agreement is a well recognized form of defense against personal pressure. In this sense compliance may express a high degree of defensiveness. This is a good example of the need to exercise caution in attempting to generalize from the laboratory to the clinic.

16. Cairns and Bandura (unpublished).

17. Greenspoon (1954).

18. Taffel (1955).

19. Hildum and Brown (1956).

20. Krasner (1958).

21. Mandler and Kaplan (1956). In contrast to these findings, an experiment completed after this chapter was written found a positive correlation between degree of the subjects' expressed awareness and degree of their conditioning, but, as in other studies, conditioning occurred even when the subject failed consciously to connect the experimenter's behavior with what he was saying (G. Saslow, personal communication).

22. Krasner and Ullmann (unpublished). In a later experiment (Krasner *et al.,* 1959) undergraduate psychology students who did not spontaneously indicate awareness of the experimenter's clues right after the experiment later claimed that they had been at least partly aware but had "forgotten" to mention it. Apparently the subject's attitude to the experimenter influences not only the extent to which he can be conditioned but also his report of awareness.

23. Bandura *et al.* (1960).

24. Murray (1956). The protocol is in C. R. Rogers (1942), pp. 261-437. C. R. Rogers (1951) states that since then "we have gradually dropped the vestiges of subtle directiveness" evident in that case (p. 30).

25. See also the discussion of the fabrications of infantile memories by Freud's patients to fit his theories, under a therapeutic technique in which the analyst was supposed to function only as a mirror in which the patient could see himself reflected (pp. 122 f.).

26. A recent experiment with college students, however, demonstrated that verbal reinforcement significantly increased the proportion of early childhood memories connected with the family as compared to nonfamily memories. This comes close to the type of content of psychotherapeutic interviews (Quay, 1959).

27. Parloff *et al.* (1960).

28. Kelman (1958) offers an illuminating discussion of this distinction.

29. See especially the experiments of Janis and King (1954), and King and Janis (1956), discussed on pp. 100 f., and the discussion of control of "output" (p. 87) and insistence that the prisoners participate actively in the discussion of thought reform (p. 92).

30. See pp. 156 ff.

31. Bauer (1958).

32. Schramm and Danielson (1958).

CHAPTER 7: THE PSYCHIATRIST AND THE PATIENT

1. See pp. 2 f.

2. The type of relationship offered by therapists seems to be determined more by levels of experience than by their theories. One experimental study found that therapists of different schools agreed highly as to the nature of the therapeutic relationship, and that experienced practitioners of different schools agreed more highly than did junior and senior members of the same persuasion. Furthermore, study of taped interviews showed that experts of different schools created relationships more similar to each other than experts and novices of the same school (Fiedler, 1950). Apparently experience in actual practice overcomes doctrinaire differences. This finding was confirmed from the standpoint of the patient, in that patients treated by therapists of different schools attributed their improvement to different therapeutic methods, but described their relationship with the therapist similarly (Heine, 1953). See also the discussion of personal qualities of the therapist, pp. 129-133.

3. See pp. 46, 50, 54, 70.

4. In emphasizing the close relationship between personal integration and group integration, I do not wish to exclude the possibility that an individual may sustain his integration largely by adherence to the values of internalized reference groups. The brilliant but socially isolated scientist, for example, may maintain his self-esteem through his dedication to the pursuit of truth, which enables him to view himself as a member of the "scientific community," a group existing only as an abstract embodiment of certain values.

5. The problem of divergencies in assumptive worlds between psychiatrist and patient is thrown into sharp relief when the psychiatrist tries to practice in a totally different culture. Thus a Sudanese Western-trained psychiatrist,

Dr. Tigani El Mahi, found that he obtained much better results with his African patients by collaborating with local witch doctors than by ignoring them.

A less striking demonstration of the importance of congruence or lack of it between therapist's and patient's world views is suggested by the finding that clients at a university counseling center who shared the therapist's permissive tolerant attitudes and were willing to explore their personal problems were more apt to benefit from counseling than those with a punitive morality or a "fundamentalist" or mystical religious orientation (C. R. Rogers and Dymond, 1954, Chapters 11 and 12).

6. This point is well developed by Ruesch (1953).

7. Robinson et al. (1954).

8. Factors causing clinic patients to leave treatment are considered at length by Frank et al. (1957). The text may give the erroneous impression that attitudes of psychiatrists and the nature of psychotherapy are the only reasons for the greater tendency of lower-class patients to drop out. Probably of at least equal importance is the fact that they face greater practical obstacles to repeated clinic visits. Even if the clinic fee is remitted, the cost of transportation or of lost wages due to missed time at work may be a real financial strain. A mother must impose on the good nature of family members or neighbors to mind the children, or pay someone to act as baby-sitter. These difficulties mount with increasing duration of treatment—the financial drain becomes more burdensome, the patience of relatives thinner. Because obstacles to continuance of treatment are greater for lower-class than for middle- or upper-class patients, lower-class ones who stay are probably more highly motivated, on the whole. This may account for the fact that they improve at least as much as upper-class patients.

9. Since all training institutes referred to in the text teach Freudian psychoanalysis or one of its offshoots, for simplicity's sake they are referred to by the generic term "analytic institute," and the terms "psychoanalytic" and "analytic" are used interchangeably. This should not be taken to imply that doctrinal differences among different schools are unimportant, but only that they are not relevant for this discussion.

10. The characterization of directive-organic and analytic-psychological psychiatrists is taken from Hollingshead and Redlich (1958).

11. Potter et al. (1957).

12. Since this statement may be surprising to some readers, it may be supported by the following quotations from leading contemporary psychoanalysts: ". . . I once regarded it [psychoanalysis] . . . as also a therapeutic program par excellence. True, Freud warned us against the emphasis on the therapeutic effect. Now I know he was right; therapeutic effect it does have, but, in my opinion, were this its chief or only value, psychoanalysis would be doomed." (Menninger, 1958, p. xi.)

Dr. Harry I. Weinstock, when chairman of a fact-gathering committee of the American Psychoanalytic Association, stated: "No claims regarding the therapeutic usefulness of analytic treatment are made by the American Psychoanalytic Association." (Quoted in Eysenck, 1960, p. 40.)

13. See pp. 133 f.

14. Winokur (1955), Wyatt (1956).

15. Freud (1920), p. 321. Italics are Freud's.

16. See pp. 154-167.

17. Chapter 5.

18. Glover (1952), p. 403.

19. Chapter 6.

20. See pp. 134-137.

21. In a questionnaire study of a large number of psychiatrists treating patients in outpatient clinics (Board, 1959, p. 188), 82 per cent thought the "outstanding difficulty" with unsuccessfully treated patients was "the patient's incapacity for treatment," indicating that this way of explaining failures is not confined to psychoanalysts.

22. See p. 15.

23. Responses of Freudian, Adlerian, and Jungian psychiatrists to a questionnaire afford some measure of the success of the training programs of analytic institutes as methods of indoctrination (Wolff, 1954). Seventy per cent stated that they believed their form of therapy to be the best, a high figure in the absence of evidence that one therapy is more effective than another. Only 25 per cent professed themselves satisfied with their theoretical orientation. It is interesting that these consisted mostly of adherents of Adler and Jung. Wolff comments (p. 470): "The degree of identification of each member with the leader of the group is greater in minority groups, which defend their new system against the system of the majority group." A little calculation reveals that 52 per cent (75 per cent of 70 per cent) believed their therapy to be best not only in the absence of objective evidence but also without being sure of the soundness of the theory on which it was based.

The marked discrepancy between professed faith in the treatment method and in the theory behind it is interesting. That most practitioners of a treatment method would believe in it is hardly unexpected since their livelihood and professional status depend on it. Also, psychiatrists of every persuasion can find support for their doctrines in the productions of their patients, but in view of the potency of psychotherapy as an influencing situation, the validity of this material is open to considerable question (see pp. 108 ff., 155 f.).

The relatively great reluctance of the questionnaire responders to express complete satisfaction with the underlying conceptual scheme is probably based on the fact that, both as Americans and as physicians, psychiatrists attach a high value to the scientific attitude, which is opposed to dogmatism. In the institutes, doctrines are presented as incomplete in some respects and subject to modification in the light of new data. Furthermore, even if the psychiatrist were completely satisfied with the conceptual framework, he might be inhibited from saying so publicly because this would be incompatible with a scientific attitude. In the light of these considerations, that even one-fourth of the respondents would affirm publicly that they believe their theory to be the best is striking.

Wheelis (1958) offers a brilliant discussion of the institutionalization of psychoanalysis as hampering its development as a science, and he describes the plight of the analyst when he becomes disillusioned about the efficacy of the technique (p. 231): "Of those courses open to him the least painful is a retreat into dogma. If he takes this path, the cancerous doubts which threaten his vested professional interest are abolished by fiat . . . . Henceforth the criterion of truth is not experience, but the book. The sanctity of psycho-analytic theory and technique is maintained, but at the cost of severing its connection with clinically observed events."

24. Festinger (1954) offers an interesting theoretical exposition of this phenomenon in terms of the need to validate the correctness of one's own feelings and ideas against the experiences of other persons and shows how this is related to the tendency of prophetic religious sects to start proselytizing only after their prophecy has failed (Festinger *et al.*, 1956).

25. Freud's handling of the discovery that traumatic experiences in infancy, which formed a cornerstone of psychoanalytic theory, were often fabrications, illustrates this point.

26. Bruner (1956).

27. In the early days of psychoanalysis, before the setting and procedures had achieved their culturally induced symbolic power, the analyst might find it necessary to impress the patient by other means. This is illustrated by Freud's example of the patient who fails to shut the door to the waiting room when the waiting room is empty. He points out that this omission "throws light upon the relation of this patient to the physician. He is one of the great number of those who seek authority, who want to be dazzled, intimidated. Perhaps he had inquired by telephone as to what time he had best call, he had prepared himself to come on a crowd of suppliants . . . . He now enters an empty waiting room which is, moreover, most modestly furnished, and he is dis-appointed. He must demand reparation from the physician for the wasted respect that he has tendered him, and so he omits to close the door between the reception room and the office . . . . He would also be quite unmannerly and supercilious during the consultation if his presumption were not at once restrained by a sharp reminder." In terms of this discussion, Freud interprets the patient's behavior as expressing a lack of confidence in him as a successful healer and seeks to restore this confidence by a brusque command (Freud, 1920), pp. 212 ff.

28. Reider (1953).

29. Berman (1949) speaks of the importance of the therapist's "dedication." One influential psychiatrist goes so far as to say that the psychiatrist should "risk committing his own existence in the struggle for the freedom of his partner's." (Binswanger, 1956, p. 148.)

Though few Western psychiatrists would go this far, as mentioned on p. 52, in at least one primitive society the shaman acts out a dramatic struggle between his own spirits and the demons possessing the patient, in which his defeat would supposedly result in his death (personal communication from Professor George P. Murdock).

In connection with the importance of the therapist's concern for the patient and his own emotional involvement, it is worth mentioning the tentative find-ing that medical students obtained at least as good therapeutic results as part-time senior psychiatrists in a large, public mental hygiene clinic (Ginsburg and Arrington, 1948). Since the measure of improvement was very crude, this finding must be viewed with caution, but it does suggest that the value of experience and training may perhaps be counteracted in part by other factors. It is probable that most of the senior psychiatrists were putting in a little time at the clinic while in transition to private practice, so that their interest in the patients may have been rather perfunctory. Medical students, on the other hand, are emotionally aroused in many ways by their first encounters with patients. Uncertainty and apprehensiveness mingle with zeal and enthusiasm. Not having been disillusioned by experience, they are apt to be more optimistic than their seniors (Strupp, 1958). Thus they may well have shown greater emotional interest in their patients, which compensated for their lack of professional experience. See also the studies of Whitehorn and Betz described on pp. 132 f.

30. Breuer and Freud (1955), p. 265. See also Ginsburg (1950).

31. Holt and Luborsky (1958).

32. Caudill (1957).

33. Parloff (1956).

34. Bandura (1956).

35. Knupfer *et al.* (1959) present data suggesting that some supervisors tend to rate residents in terms of their therapeutic skill, others in terms of their ability to fit into an organization. Their conclusion is worth quoting (p. 384): "We wish to emphasize that *almost nothing is known about who gets the best results in psychotherapy* and that this question cannot appropriately be studied without studying the changes in patients. If we study supervisors' opinions, or even styles of performance, we are studying stereotypes of the Good Therapist, the Correct Therapy and the Ideal Person." (Author's italics.)

36. Polansky and Kounin (1956), p. 262. Along the same lines, a survey of medical patients showed that the patients' feeling that the doctor took a personal interest in them was the main determinant of whether they liked him or not. When the patients were asked what they liked most about their doctors, 70 per cent of the answers could be classed under this heading, whereas the lack of personal interest accounted for 63 per cent of the aspects of their doctors they did not like so well. Their perception of his competence carried much less weight. Only 31 per cent of the answers mentioned competence as the quality they liked most, and only 5 per cent mentioned lack of it as the major source of dislike (American Medical Association, undated).

Another straw showing the wind blowing in the same direction comes from an experiment in group therapy using three different therapists, each treating a different group. There were many patients who dropped out prematurely in two of the groups, but only one left the third. Patients who dropped out were more likely than those who stayed to complain that the therapist was an enigma, that they did not know him, and that he did nothing for them. Furthermore, the therapist who lost only one patient was observed to interact more freely with his patients than the other two (Nash *et al.*, 1957).

37. Blaine and McArthur (1958).

38. Whitehorn and Betz (1954, 1957), Betz (1958).

39. Clinical impressions of personal attributes related to treatability by psychotherapy are excellently summarized by Wolberg (1954), pp. 230-243, and Cameron (1950), pp. 50-62. In recent years increasing numbers of statistical evaluations of treatability have been appearing. Although their findings are in general agreement, the extent to which they can be generalized is uncertain

because most have been made in the same type of treatment setting—the publicly supported psychiatric clinic—and have used very crude measures of improvement.

Most of these studies have been made in clinics of the United States Veterans Administration. The major reasons for this are that they have trained research persons on their staffs, they have a sufficiently large number of patients to make statistical studies possible, and they are under continuous pressure to evaluate their programs so as to learn how to increase their efficiency. Since patients in these settings have to be veterans, this limits the range of the patient population chiefly to young males. Moreover, most of the therapy is conducted by relatively untrained psychiatrists, since these clinics are way stations en route to private practice for men starting their careers. Finally, the treatment, by and large, is in the analytic tradition, emphasizing insight, and the usual frequency of interviews is only once a week, although a few patients may be seen more often. Treatment seldom lasts more than a few months. The criterion of treatability in the great majority of these studies has been whether the patient remains in treatment, not whether he profits from it. It is not necessary to look far for the reasons for this. The length of time a patient stays in treatment is easy to measure, whereas evaluation of improvement bristles with difficult theoretical and methodological problems (see pp. 15 f., 229 f.). From the practical side, mental hygiene clinics would like to be able to predict whether or not a different group of patients will remain in treatment, since the chief wastage in these clinics is caused by the large proportion of patients—ranging from 30 per cent to 65 per cent of those seen initially—who leave treatment prematurely. These studies have been critically reviewed and additional data presented by Frank *et al.* (1957) and Rosenthal and Frank (1958). See also Lorr *et al.* (1958) and Katz *et al.* (1958).

40. The qualities considered favorable for psychoanalysis are closely related to educational level. Gibson *et al.* (1959) report that 60 per cent of patients in psychoanalysis are college graduates, as contrasted with 6 per cent of the general population.

41. Barron (1953a, 1953b) presents psychological test data supporting the proposition that patients whose distress is related to environmental pressures have greater adaptive capacity or "ego-strength" and do better in treatment than those who show no such relationship.

In this connection, one might think that patients whose illnesses fluctuate in severity would be better candidates for psychotherapy than those with stationary or slowly progressive conditions, on the ground that fluctuations were evidence of emotional responsiveness to environmental pressures. Actually, in one study (Frank *et al.*, 1957) patients with fluctuating illnesses seemed more likely to remain in treatment, but showed no greater tendency to improve than those with stationary conditions. This suggests that most fluctuations were caused by internal rhythms rather than by outer stresses. Perhaps patients with fluctuating illnesses stayed in treatment longer because a steady state of misery is apt to produce eventual adaptation to it with resignation. Continual fluctuations in severity, on the other hand, cause recurrent exacerbations of misery followed by hope of relief. On both counts, patients with these conditions might be predisposed to seek therapy and remain in it.

42. Tyhurst (1957).

43. A bit of experimental evidence that emotional reactivity is related to treatability is the finding reported by Lunde *et al.* (1958) that patients with a good prognosis show a drop in blood pressure to an injection of a substance similar to that produced by a person's own body when he is under stress.

44. See p. 22.

45. See p. 10.

46. Kubie (1936), p. 140.

47. See pp. 78, 84-87.

48. Kaufman and Beaton (1947). Also pertinent to this point are the findings that persons who are socially insecure tend to be persuasible (p. 103) and that anxiety is positively related to conditionability (p. 106).

49. Kirtner and Cartwright (1958) in a careful comparison of patients who succeeded with those who failed in psychotherapy found that the former, among other attributes, had a strong need for people to relate to in order to feel worthwhile and a tendency to berate or disvalue themselves.

50. Schachter (1959).

51. Sears (1950), cited by Schachter (1959).

CHAPTER 8: INDIVIDUAL PSYCHOTHERAPY

1. For an excellent theoretical discussion of central excitation and learning, see Hebb (1955).

2. See, for example, Dollard and Miller (1950) and Shoben (1953) for explanations of psychotherapy in terms of learning theory.

3. Sargant (1957) regards the production of strong emotional excitation as the core of many methods of psychological influence and healing.

4. Quoted in Zilboorg (1941), p. 70.

5. Until recent years psychiatrists relied almost entirely on electroconvulsive therapy as a method of excitation, but modern pharmacological agents can also be used for this purpose. For example, Mead *et al.* (1958) suggest that pretreatment of chronic schizophrenics with ephedrine to induce physiological tension may increase their responsiveness to chlorpromazine. Edwards (1958) discusses the possible beneficial effects on the same group of patients of heavy dosages of chlorpromazine followed by abrupt withdrawal, which may be expected to produce strong emotional reactions. Savage (1957) discusses the use of LSD (lysergic acid diethylamide) to overcome resistance in schizophrenics by bringing painful and repressed effects to the fore.

A modern exponent of Zen draws an explicit parallel between Western shock treatments and the "inducement of shock by blows with a stick or a thundering cry . . . . We can see a good example in the case of a student who attempted suicide several times, and was awakened and cured by a thundering cry of a master . . . ." (Sato, 1958, p. 214.)

6. Rothman and Sward (1956, 1957) describe an interesting use of relaxing agents as an adjunct to the psychotherapy of certain refractory neurotics.

7. Whitehorn and Betz (1957). See p. 132.

8. French (1952) places great emphasis on the personally disintegrating effects of frustration and the integrating power of hope. See also Rado (1956) on the "welfare emotions."

9. Chapter 4.

10. "Client-centered therapy" is the phrase used by C. R. Rogers (1951) to describe his type of psychotherapy. The increasing length of treatment has been discussed on p. 15.

11. The term is borrowed from Lewin's trail-breaking paper (1947), p. 34.

12. Jackson (1959).

13. The term "permissive," which is generally used in contrast to "directive," implies that the former therapies exert less influence on the patient than the latter. As this chapter attempts to show, this is probably not the case (see Finesinger and Kellam, 1959); therefore the term "evocative," suggested by Whitehorn (1959), has been used instead because I believe it more accurately describes what occurs.

14. Certain directive techniques disregard insight into the nature of the patient's specific problem or distress and try to train him in a particular set of exercises that will enable him to function more effectively in all situations. These exercises involve relaxation techniques, often coupled with the development of conscious control over visceral functions. In the Western world the most notable examples are progressive relaxation (Jacobson, 1929) and autogenous training (Schultz and Luthe, 1959). The latter, especially, is in many ways similar to yoga. Consideration of these methods lies beyond the scope of this book.

15. For accounts of directive psychotherapies, see Salter (1958), Wolpe (1958), and Ellis (1958). Stevenson (1959) describes a form of psychotherapy that seems midway between evocative and directive and may prove to combine the best features of both. The example is from Ellis (1959). The quotations are from pages 341 and 342 (italics are the author's).

16. See pp. 13-17.

17. Wolpe (1958).

18. Freud initially viewed psychoanalysis not as an evocative method in the sense used here, but as a specific technique for exposing the causes of the patient's symptoms—his repressed memories of emotionally traumatic early experiences—and removing them through interpretation of their relationship to his symptomatology. (See Whitehorn, 1947.) Fenichel (1941) is an influential modern exponent of this position.

The psychoanalytic method of free association, however, evokes not only the patient's repressed memories, but a very wide range of his thoughts and feelings, including his values, ideals, and attitudes towards the analyst. Thus the process activates not only his pathogenic attitudes but also his healthy adaptive potentialities. In this sense, the term "evocative" seems appropriately descriptive.

Colby (1951) and Menninger (1958) present two good recent conceptualizations of psychoanalysis. Ingham and Love (1954) present an excellent simple account of evocative psychotherapy. Wolberg (1954) is a compendious survey of all forms of psychotherapy, emphasizing evocative varieties. Both books contain verbatim protocols, as does C. R. Rogers (1942). This note may serve as a blanket acknowledgment of indebtedness to these sources and others cited elsewhere for ideas in the text whose specific origins I can no longer identify.

19. Hypnotic methods can be used primarily for evocative as well as directive purposes. See Wolberg (1945) for an extended description and discussion of "hypnoanalysis."

20. C. R. Rogers (1957).

21. Macalpine (1950) and Nunberg (1951) discuss how transference reactions give the analyst power over the patient. Fisher (1953, p. 253) found that he could suggest dreams to persons in psychoanalysis, indicating "a high degree of suggestibility in patients under analysis." DeGrazia (1952) offers a brilliant, if polemical, account of the influencing power of the therapist in all "permissive" therapies.

22. W. Stekel, quoted in Wolff (1954).

23. C. R. Rogers (1953).

24. Murray (1956).

25. Rosenthal (1955); see also Ehrenwald (1957).

26. Heine (1953).

27. The analyst's belief in the objectivity of his procedures may be so strong that he may fail to recognize their indoctrinating effect even when it is blatant. The following example is offered with some hesitancy, since it may appear to be a *reductio ad absurdum,* yet it is reported by a highly competent analyst. The fact that it is from group rather than individual therapy may partly account for the bluntness of the indoctrination, as the group situation militates against subtlety:

". . . the group were discussing subjects which suggested that they were concerned about my announcement in the preceding session that I would be away for four weeks." (Note that an interpretation is already implied—the topics discussed might have suggested something else to a therapist with a different orientation.) "In my interpretation I put it to them that such an imposed break aroused fantasies in them of my going off with a woman in order to have sexual pleasures with her and that this aroused their jealousy and aggressive impulses, the consequences of which they feared and which, as I pointed out to them in turn, each tried to cope with in his own particular way." Later in the same session the therapist (Dr. E.) said he represented to them "the 'ideal' man with the 'perfect' penis who can even stand up to whatever Mrs. X or Miss R. wants to do to that penis in their masturbation phantasies and doesn't persecute them." Soon after this, the following exchange took place:

Mrs. X: "I also had a horror—not a horror but rather a surprised feeling —that Dr. E's desk could stand up . . . . At this point it might easily fall down in the middle."

Dr. E.: "This penis! (Laughter) You know, it is not very difficult—"

Mrs. X: "No, it is not very difficult. (All laugh.)

Dr. E.: "The desk that stands up and falls down . . . ."

Mrs. X: "I know."

The quotations are from pages 42 and 44 of Ezriel (1956). Ezriel nowhere considers the probability that Mrs. X's associations might have been suggested by his interpretations.

28. Janis and King (1954), described on pp. 100 f.

29. As Menninger (1958) says: ". . . the essence of psychoanalytic treatment is intellectual honesty, and no one in honesty can predict with definiteness what the future will bring. Yet if the analyst did not *expect* to see improvement, he would not start—and so taking the case *is* an implied prediction." "The patient who submits himself for psychoanalytic therapy begins with a certain blind faith in the psychoanalyst, regardless of the disclaimers he may profess. He begins, too, with various hopes and expectations, regardless of the skepticism he may express . . . ." (Pp. 31 and 42, author's italics.)

30. See pp. 128 f.

31. Alexander and French (1946).

32. Sherif and Harvey (1952).

33. Cantril (1941).

34. Dibner (1958), Bordin (1955). For the relation of anxiety to dependence and influencibility, see pp. 106, 137 f.

35. The quote is from Menninger (1958, p. 55) who adds: "This is not quite right, of course, because there have been some responses . . . on the part of the therapist. *But they have not been what the patient expected.*" (Italics added.)

According to analytic theory, the continuation of the frustration causes the patient to regress to earlier ways of dealing with it, thereby re-experiencing emotionally some of the frustrations of his childhood. By re-experiencing them in a new setting he is enabled to work them through to more satisfactory solutions, appropriate to adulthood. In any case there is no question but that an ambiguous therapeutic situation not only elicits appropriate feelings of anxiety and frustration, but also tends to revive those originally felt in the patient's childhood towards significant family figures, the so-called transference reactions, and these contribute importantly to the patient's emotional arousal.

36. Rickett and Rickett (1957), p. 114, quoted on pp. 90 f.

37. Menninger (1958), pp. 100-101.

38. Goffman (1959), p. 133.

39. Lidz (1956).

40. See Kubie (1936), Chapter 7.

41. Breuer and Freud (1955), p. 295.

42. Glover (1931, 1952). The quotation is from the second paper, p. 405.

43. The example of Mr. Angelo (pp. 178 f.), though taken from group therapy, illustrates this point.

44. Fenichel (1941, p. 20) for example, while recognizing that other modes of influence may be involved in psychoanalysis, places the greatest stress on cognitive restructuring through interpretations. For Fenichel, elimination of the patient's "resistance" enables him to abandon his neurotic solutions of his problems: ". . . we obtain the desired effect upon the patient all the more lastingly and efficaciously if we succeed in using no other means of eliminating resistances than the confrontation of his reasonable ego with the fact of his resistance and the history of its origin. This confrontation bringing him as it does recognition of the unconscious part of his resistance, also renders the resistance itself superfluous."

45. Cameron (1950) lays special emphasis on the importance of helping the patient to reconceptualize his experiences.

CHAPTER 9: GROUP PSYCHOTHERAPY

1. For a brief, popularly written overview of group therapies, see Frank (1959b).

2. See, for example, Harris (1939).

3. J. Alexander (1952).

4. Low (1950), Wechsler (1960)

5. Moreno is a prolific writer, and no single publication encompasses all aspects of psychodrama. A representative statement is Moreno (1958).

6. For detailed descriptions of evocative or free-interaction group therapies, see Powdermaker and Frank (1953), Slavson (1943, 1956), and Foulkes and Anthony (1957).

7. The example is modified from Frank and Ascher (1956).

8. The phrase is used by C. A. Mace in his introduction to Foulkes and Anthony (1957).

9. This point is well discussed by Dreikurs (1951).

10. This example has been reported previously in Frank (1959b).

11. See p. 165.

12. See p. 9.

13. The term was introduced by Foulkes (1948). The examples of mirror and transference reactions are described more fully and discussed in Powdermaker and Frank (1953), pages 237-239 and 245-248 respectively.

14. Frank (1957b).

15. Nash *et al.* (1957).

16. This point is especially stressed by McCann (1953).

17. See Bach (1954) for an illuminating discussion of the "peer court" that may develop in early group meetings, in which everyone judges everyone else.

18. Frank (1957b).

19. Newcomb (1947).

20. Frank (1957a).

21. Foulkes (1948, p. 29) surmizes: "The deepest reason why these patients . . . can reinforce each other's normal reactions and wear down and correct each other's neurotic reactions, is that *collectively they constitute the very Norm, from which, individually, they deviate.*" (Author's italics and capitalization.)

22. See Wolf and Schwartz (1959). The interplay between group and individual sessions is also well discussed by Bach (1954), Chapter 5, pp. 50-66.

23. As in the example cited on pp. 46-49.

CHAPTER 10: INSTITUTIONAL GROUP INFLUENCES—
THE TRADITIONAL MENTAL HOSPITAL AND
THE THERAPEUTIC COMMUNITY

1. Recent studies of hospitals as social systems are Belknap (1956), Caudill (1958), and Stanton and Schwartz (1954).

2. Administrative problems created by the "multiple subordination" principle of hospital organization are excellently discussed by Henry (1954).

3. The comparison of the traditional mental hospital with thought reform leans heavily on Goffman's papers (1957a, 1957b, 1959), and the quoted phrases are his.

4. See p. 42.

5. The development of the concept of the therapeutic community probably was initiated by efforts to rehabilitate repatriated British prisoners of war who were emotionally disturbed. See, for example, Bion and Rickman (1943) and Foulkes (1948). Good descriptions of therapeutic communities are given by Baker *et al.* (1953), Jones (1958), and Wilmer (1958). See also Greenblatt *et al.* (1955) and Bettelheim (1950).

6. See Frank (1955).

7. Klapman has a good description and discussion of directive group methods in institutions (1959, Chapter 12).

8. Frank (1952). Stanton and Schwartz (1954, Chapter 16) offer an interesting discussion of the psychological and social meanings of incontinence in hospitalized mental patients.

9. Moreno (1958).

10. Overholser and Enneis (1959).

11. Blair (1955).

12. Cruvant (1953).

13. Wender and Stein (1953). The quotation is from page 213.

14. McCann (1953).

15. Wilmer (1958).

16. Baker *et al.* (1953).

17. Friedman *et al.* (1960).

CHAPTER 11: SYMPTOM RELIEF AND ATTITUDE CHANGE—
REPORT OF A RESEARCH STUDY OF PSYCHOTHERAPY

1. See p. 71. The project is described most fully from a methodological standpoint in Frank (1959a).

2. The thinking that led to this decision is fully discussed by Parloff *et al.* (1954).

3. It will be noted that the scales are couched in negative terms—relief of discomfort rather than improvement in comfort, and decrease of social ineffectiveness rather than increase in effectiveness. This was necessitated by the difficulty in establishing an end point for health. The absence of symptoms is determinable, but the scaling of degrees of positive well-being presented insuperable technical problems.

4. Charts 1 and 2 include only the thirty patients who were evaluated at every follow-up visit. That they are a representative sample is indicated by the fact that the average of their discomfort and ineffectiveness scores initially and at six months do not differ significantly from the averages of the total sample. This also holds true for patients receiving group, individual, and minimal contact therapy considered separately.

5. See p. 71.

6. The experimental design made group therapy more stressful than the usual group therapy program by assigning patients to groups without selection and without opportunity to meet their group therapists in advance. In groups organized for strictly therapeutic purposes some principle of selection is regularly employed, and patients have at least one individual interview with the therapist before joining his group.

7. For the total sample, average changes between initial and six-month scores were statistically significant for both group and individual therapy, and at six months the changes differed significantly from those produced by minimal therapy (p <.01).

8. Goldstein (1960) offers an excellent review and critique of the concept of "spontaneous recovery."

9. Further evidence that improvement in comfort and social effectiveness represents different processes is suggested by the finding that changes in them are only slightly correlated at different evaluations. The correlations, using all the patients available at each evaluation, range from +.23 to +.37.

10. This result is in keeping with Zubin's finding that no specialized form of psychiatric treatment exceeds the five-year recovery rate from routine hospital care (1959). It also accords wth a finding by Whitehorn and Betz with schizophrenics at a teaching psychiatric hospital. They found that at the close of treatment patients of one type of doctors had an 80 per cent improvement rate and patients of another type a 31 per cent improvement rate. Five years later the figures were 77 per cent and 65 per cent respectively. That is, apparently the greater therapeutic success of the first type of doctors lay in their ability to mobilize the recovery potential of their patients more promptly (Whitehorn, 1960).

CHAPTER 12: AMERICAN PSYCHOTHERAPY IN PERSPECTIVE

1. Masserman (1957) offers an interesting, broadly conceived consideration of psychotherapy from historical and comparative standpoints.

2. This point has been elaborated by Bateson and his coworkers (1956) and Haley (1959), and also by Lidz et al. (1957).

3. An excellent example of a socially effective psychiatric document is Group for the Advancement of Psychiatry (1957). See also Frank (1958, 1960).

4. See footnote 12, Chapter 1.

5. An excellent discussion of research problems in psychotherapy is to be found in Group for the Advancement of Psychiatry (1959). See also Frank (1959a).

6. The contributions of Carl Rogers and his group (C. R. Rogers and Dymond, 1954), based mainly on studies of therapy conducted by experienced psychologists represent an important exception to this statement. Strupp (1960) has devised ingenious indirect methods for studying attitudes and techniques of experienced medical and nonmedical psychotherapists.

7. Dr. K. M. Colby is currently experimenting with this (personal communication).

8. See, for example, Lennard and Bernstein (1960) and Saslow (1959).

9. The literature on measurement of human autonomic functioning, with special reference to psychotherapy, is superbly summarized by Lacey (1959).

10. See, for example, Shlien (1957); also see Chapter 11.

11. Whitehead (1925), p. 266.

12. Dreikurs (1960).

13. Frank (1946b).

14. Modell (1955), p. 56.

Acknowledgments

The writing of this book was made possible by a fellowship at the Center for Advanced Study in the Behavioral Sciences, for 1958-1959. I am deeply grateful to Ralph Tyler, the Director of the Center, and to its staff, for giving me this opportunity and affording ideal conditions for its fulfillment. The research studies reported in Chapters 4 and 11 have been financed in part by the United States Public Health Service and the Ford Foundation. Their generous support is gratefully acknowledged. My thinking has been greatly influenced by the late Lester H. Gliedman. I wish further to express my great debt to John Whitehorn for his guidance and encouragement over many years.

These acknowledgments would be incomplete without an expression of gratitude to Miss Frances Partlow for her invaluable help with all technical aspects of the manuscript and to Mrs. Helen Nash for preparing the index. Finally, my wife, Elizabeth K. Frank, deserves a special word of appreciation for supplying patient, loving support during the prolonged birth pangs of this volume.

JEROME D. FRANK

Bibliography

Ackerknecht, E. H. (1942). Problems of primitive medicine. *Bull. History Med.*, 11, 503-521.

Adland, M. L. (1947). Review, case studies, therapy, and interpretation of the acute exhaustive psychoses. *Psychiat. Quart.*, 21, 38-69.

Alexander, F., and French, T. M. (1946). *Psychoanalytic therapy: principles and application.* New York: Ronald Press.

Alexander, J. (1952). They 'doctor' one another. *Saturday Evening Post*, Dec. 6, 1952, p. 31.

American Medical Association (undated). *What Americans think of the medical profession, report on a public opinion survey.* Chicago: American Medical Association.

Appel, K. E., Lhamon, W. T., Myers, J. M., and Harvey, W. A. (1953). Long term psychotherapy. *In*: Association for Research in Nervous and Mental Disease, *Psychiatric treatment* (Research Publication 31), 21-34. Baltimore: Williams and Wilkins.

Argyle, M. (1958). *Religious behavior.* London: Routledge and Kegan Paul.

Asch, S. E. (1952). *Social psychology.* New York: Prentice-Hall.

Bach, G. (1954). *Intensive group psychotherapy.* New York: Ronald Press.

Baker, A. A., Jones, M., Merry, J., and Pomryn, B. A. (1953). A community method of psychotherapy. *Brit. J. med. Psychol.*, 26, 222-244.

Bandura, A. (1956). Psychotherapist's anxiety level, self-insight, and psycho-therapeutic competence. *J. abnorm. soc. Psychol.*, 52, 333-337.

——, Lipsher, D. H., and Miller, Paula E. (1960). Psychotherapists' approach-avoidance reactions to patients' expressions of hostility. *J. consult. Psychol.*, 24, 1-8.

Barron, F. (1953a). Some test correlates of response to psychotherapy. *J. consult. Psychol.*, 17, 235-241.

—— (1953b). An ego-strength scale which predicts response to psychotherapy. *J. consult. Psychol.*, 17, 327-333.

——, and Leary, T. F. (1955). Changes in psychoneurotic patients with and without psychotherapy. *J. consult. Psychol.*, 19, 239-245.

Bateson, G., Jackson, D. D., Haley, J., and Weakland, J. (1956). Toward a theory of schizophrenia. *Behavioral Science*, 1, 251-264.

Bauer, R. A. (1958). The communicator and the audience. *J. Conflict Resolution*, 2, 67-77.

Beck, F., and Godin, W. (1951). *Russian purge and the extraction of confessions.* New York: Viking Press.

Beecher, H. K. (1955). The powerful placebo. *J. Amer. Med. Assoc.*, 159, 1602-1606.

Begbie, H. (1909). *Twice-born men: a study in regeneration.* New York: Fleming H. Revell.

Belknap, I. (1956). *Human problems of a state mental hospital.* New York: McGraw-Hill.

Berman, L. (1949). Countertransferences and attitudes of the analyst in the therapeutic process. *Psychiatry*, 12, 159-166.

Bettelheim, B. (1943). Individual and mass behavior in extreme situations. *J. abnorm. soc. Psychol.*, 38, 417-452.

—— (1950). *Love is not enough.* Glencoe, Ill.: Free Press.

—— (1952). Remarks on the psychological appeal of totalitarianism. *Amer. J. Econ. and Soc.*, 12, 89-96.

Betz, Barbara J. (1958). How do personal attitudes and interests influence psy-chotherapeutic effectiveness? *In: Proceedings of the Sixth Annual Psychiatric Institute*, 14-28. Princeton: New Jersey Neuro-Psychiatric Institute.

Binder, A., McConnell, D., and Sjoholm, Nancy A. (1957). Verbal conditioning as a function of experimenter characteristics. *J. abnorm. soc. Psychol.*, 55, 309-314.

Binswanger, L. (1956). Existential analysis and psychotherapy. *In*: Fromm-Reichmann, Frieda, and Moreno, J. L., eds., *Progress in psychotherapy*, 144-148. New York: Grune and Stratton.

Bion, W. R., and Rickman, J. (1943). Intra-group tensions in therapy: their study as the task of the group. *Lancet*, 245, 678-681.

Blaine, G. B., and McArthur, C. C. (1958). What happened in therapy as seen by the patient and his psychiatrist. *J. nerv. ment. Dis.*, 127, 344-350.

Blair, D. A. S. (1955). The therapeutic social club. *Ment. Hyg.*, 39, 54-62.

Bloch, B. (1927). Ueber die Heilung der Warzen durch Suggestion. *Klin. Wochenschr.*, 6, 2271-2325.

Board, F. A. (1959). Patients' and physicians' judgments of outcome of psy-chotherapy in an outpatient clinic. *A.M.A. Arch. gen. Psychiat.*, 1, 185-196.

Bordin, E. S. (1955). Ambiguity as a therapeutic variable. *J. consult. Psychol.*, 19, 9-15.

Brenner, C. (1954). *An elementary textbook of psychoanalysis.* New York: International Universities Press.

Breuer, J., and Freud, S. (1955). Studies on hysteria. *In: The complete psychological works,* Vol. 2, 3-305. London: Hogarth.

Bruner, J. (1956). Freud and the image of man. *Amer. Psychologist,* 11, 463-466.

Cairns, R. B., and Bandura, A. (unpublished). The influence of dependency-anxiety on the effectiveness of social reinforcers.

Cameron, D. E. (1950). *General psychotherapy: dynamics and procedures.* New York: Grune and Stratton.

Cannon, W. B. (1957). 'Voodoo' death. *Psychosom. Med.,* 19, 182-190.

Cantril, H. (1941). *The psychology of social movements.* New York: John Wiley.

——— (1950). *The 'why' of man's experience.* New York: Macmillan.

——— (1957). Perception and interpersonal relations. *Amer. J. Psychiat.,* 114, 119-126.

Caudill, W. A. (1957). Problems of leadership in the overt and covert social structure of psychiatric hospitals. *In: Symposium on preventive and social psychiatry,* 345-363. Washington, D. C.: Walter Reed Army Institute of Research.

——— (1958). *The psychiatric hospital as a small society.* Cambridge: Harvard Univer. Press.

Chappell, M. N., Stefano, J. J., Rogerson, J. S., and Pike, F. H. (1936). The value of group psychological procedures in the treatment of peptic ulcer. *Amer. J. Diges. Diseases and Nutrition,* 3, 813-817.

Clark, E. T. (1929). *The psychology of religious awakening.* New York: Macmillan.

Clausen, J. A. (1959). The sociology of mental illness. *In:* Merton, R. K., Broom, L., and Cottrell, L. S., eds., *Sociology today,* 485-508. New York: Basic Books.

———, and Yarrow, M. R. (1955). Paths to the mental hospital. *J. soc. Issues,* 11, 25-32.

Colby, K. M. (1951). *A primer for psychotherapists.* New York: Ronald Press.

Conn, J. H. (1949). Brief psychotherapy of the sex offender: a report of a liaison service between a court and a private psychiatrist. *J. clin. Psychopath.,* 10, 1-26.

——— (1953). Hypnosynthesis III. hypnotherapy of chronic war neuroses with a discussion of the value of abreaction, regression, and revivication. *J. clin. exp. Hypnosis,* 1, 29-43.

Cranston, Ruth (1955). *The miracle of Lourdes.* New York: McGraw-Hill. Also New York: Popular Library, 1957.

Cruvant, B. A. (1953). The function of the 'administrative group' in a mental hospital group therapy program. *Amer. J. Psychiat.,* 110, 342-346.

DeGrazia, S. (1952). *Errors of psychotherapy.* New York: Doubleday. Especially Chapter 4, 42-65, and Chapter 5, 66-102.

Deren, Maya (1953). *Divine horsemen: the living gods of Haiti.* London: Thames and Hudson.

Dibner, A. S. (1958). Ambiguity and anxiety. *J. abnorm. soc. Psychol.,* 56, 165-174.

Dollard, J., and Miller, N. E. (1950). *Personality and psychotherapy: an analysis in terms of learning, thinking, and culture.* New York: McGraw-Hill.

Dreikurs, R. (1951). The unique social climate experienced in group psychotherapy. *Group Psychother.*, 3, 292-299.

—— (1960). Are psychological schools of thought outdated? *J. ind. Psychol.*,
16, 3-10.

Edwards, R. V. (1958). Clinical confirmation of Heistad's predictions. *Amer. J.
Psychiat.*, 115, 363.

Ehrenwald, J. (1957). The telepathy hypothesis and doctrinal compliance in
psychotherapy. *Amer. J. Psychother.*, 11, 359-379.

Ellis, A. (1957). Outcome of employing three techniques of psychotherapy. *J.
clin. Psychol.*, 13, 344-350.

—— (1958). Rational psychotherapy. *J. gen. Psychol.*, 59, 35-49.

—— (1959). A homosexual treated with rational psychotherapy. *J. clin.
Psychol.*, 15, 338-343.

Everson, T. C. (1958). Spontaneous regression of cancer. *Connecticut med. J.*,
22, 637-643.

Eysenck, H. J. (1952). The effects of psychotherapy: an evaluation. *J. consult.
Psychol.*, 16, 319-323.

—— (1960). What's the truth about psychoanalysis? *Reader's Digest*, 76,
38-43.

Ezriel, H. (1956). Experimentation within the psycho-analytic session. *Brit. J.
Phil. Sci.*, 7, 29-48.

Fenichel, O. (1941). *Problems of psychoanalytic technique.* Translated by D.
Brunswick. Albany: Psychoanal. Quart.

—— (1945). *The psychoanalytic theory of neurosis.* New York: W. W. Norton.

Festinger, L. (1954). A theory of social comparison processes. *Hum. Relat.*, 7,
117-140. Reprinted in Hare, A. P., Borgatta, E. F., and Bales, R. F., eds.,
Small groups: studies in social interaction, 163-187. New York: Knopf, 1955.

—— (1957). *A theory of cognitive dissonance.* Evanston, Ill.: Row, Peterson.

——, Riecken, H. W., and Schacter, S. (1956). *When prophecy fails*, Min-
neapolis: Univer. Minnesota Press.

Fiedler, F. E. (1950). A comparison of therapeutic relationships in psychoanalytic, nondirective and Adlerian therapy. *J. consult. Psychol.*, 14, 436-445.

Field, M. J. (1955). Witchcraft as a primitive interpretation of mental disorder.
J. ment. Science, 101, 826-833.

Finesinger, J. E., and Kellam, S. G. (1959). Permissiveness—its definition, usefulness and application in psychotherapy. *Amer. J. Psychiat.*, 115, 992-996.

Fisher, C. (1953). Studies on the nature of suggestion: Part I. Experimental
induction of dreams by direct suggestion. *J. Amer. Psychoanalyt. Assoc.*, 1,
222-255.

Fortin, J. N., and Abse, D. W. (1956). Group psychotherapy with peptic ulcer.
Int. J. Group Psychother., 6, 383-391.

Foulkes, S. H. (1948). *Introduction to group analytic psychotherapy.* London:
Heinemann.

——, and Anthony, E. J. (1957). *Group psychotherapy: the psycho-analytic
approach.* Baltimore: Penguin Books.

Frank, J. D. (1946a). Emotional reactions of American soldiers to an unfamiliar
disease. *Amer. J. Psychiat.*, 102, 631-640.

—— (1946b). Psychotherapeutic aspects of symptomatic treatment. *Amer. J.
Psychiat.*, 103, 21-25.

Frank, J. D. (1952). Group therapy with schizophrenics. *In*: Brody, E. B., and Redlich, F. C., eds., *Psychotherapy with schizophrenics*, 216-230. New York: International Universities Press.

—— (1955). *Group therapy in the mental hospital.* Washington, D. C.: American Psychiatric Association, Mental Hospital Service (Monograph series No. 1), December, 1955.

—— (1957a). Some determinants, manifestations, and effects of cohesiveness in therapy groups. *Int. J. Group Psychother.*, **7**, 53-63.

—— (1957b). Some aspects of cohesiveness and conflict in psychiatric outpatient groups. *Bull. Johns Hopkins Hosp.*, **101**, 224-231.

—— (1958). The great antagonism. *Atlantic Monthly*, **202**, 58-62.

—— (1959a). Problems of controls in psychotherapy as exemplified by the Psychotherapy Research Project of the Phipps Psychiatric Clinic. *In*: Rubinstein, E. A., and Parloff, M. B., eds., *Research in psychotherapy*, 10-26. Washington, D. C.: American Psychological Association.

—— (1959b). *Group methods in therapy.* New York: Public Affairs Pamphlets (No. 284).

—— (1960). Breaking the thought barrier: psychological challenges of the nuclear age. *Psychiatry*, **23**, 245-266.

——, and Ascher, E. (1956). Therapeutic emotional interactions in group treatment. *Postgrad. Med.*, **19**, 36-40.

——, Gliedman, L. H., Imber, S. D., Nash, E. H., and Stone, A. R. (1957). Why patients leave psychotherapy. *A.M.A. Arch. Neurol. and Psychiat.*, **77**, 283-299.

——, ——, ——, Stone, A. R., and Nash, E. H. (1959). Patients' expectancies and relearning as factors determining improvement in psychotherapy. *Amer. J. Psychiat.*, **115**, 961-968.

Freedman, L. Z., and Hollingshead, A. B. (1957). Neurosis and social class: I. Social interaction. *Amer. J. Psychiat.*, **113**, 769-775.

French, T. M. (1952). *The integration of behavior.* Vol. 1, *Basic postulates.* Chicago: Univer. Chicago Press.

Freud, S. (1920). *A general introduction to psychoanalysis.* New York: Liveright.

Friedman, T. T., Rolfe, Phyllis, and Stewart, S. E. (1960). Home treatment of psychiatric patients. *Amer. J. Psychiat.*, **116**, 807-809.

Gibson, R. W., Cohen, Mabel B., and Cohen, R. A. (1959). On the dynamics of the manic-depressive personality. *Amer. J. Psychiat.*, **115**, 1101-1107.

Gillin, J. (1948). Magical fright. *Psychiatry*, **11**, 387-400.

Ginsburg, S. W. (1950). Values and the psychiatrist. *Amer. J. Orthopsychiat.*, **20**, 466-478.

——, and Arrington, W. (1948). Aspects of psychiatric clinic practice. *Amer. J. Orthopsychiat.*, **18**, 322-333.

Glass, A. J. (1957). Observations upon the epidemiology of mental illness in troops during warfare. *In*: *Symposium on preventive and social psychiatry*, 185-198. Washington, D. C.: Walter Reed Army Institute of Research.

Gliedman, L. H., Nash, E. H., Imber, S. D., Stone, A. R., and Frank, J. D. (1958). Reduction of symptoms by pharmacologically inert substances and by short-term psychotherapy. *A.M.A. Arch. Neurol, and Psychiat.*, **79**, 345-351.

Glover, E. (1931). The therapeutic effect of inexact interpretation: a contribution to the theory of suggestion. *Int. J. Psycho-anal.*, **12**, 397-411.

Glover, E. (1952). Research methods in psychoanalysis. *Int. J. Psycho-anal.*, 33, 403-409.

Goffman, E. (1957a). Characteristics of total institutions. *In: Symposium on preventive and social psychiatry*, 43-84. Washington, D. C.: Walter Reed Army Institute of Research.

—— (1957b). Interpersonal persuasion. *In: Group processes: transactions of the third conference*, 117-193. New York: Josiah Macy, Jr. Foundation.

—— (1959). The moral career of the mental patient. *Psychiatry*, 22, 123-142.

Goldstein, A. P. (1960). Patient's expectancies and non-specific therapy as a basis for (un)spontaneous remission. *J. clin. Psychol.*, 16, 399-403.

Greenblatt, M., York, R. H., and Brown, E. L. (1955). *From custodial to therapeutic patient care in mental hospitals*. New York: Russell Sage Foundation.

Greenspoon, J. (1954). The effect of two nonverbal stimuli on the frequency of members of two verbal response classes. *Amer. Psychol.*, 9, 384.

—— (1955). The reinforcing effect of two spoken sounds on the frequency of two responses. *Amer. J. Psychol.*, 68, 409-416.

Group for the Advancement of Psychiatry (1957). *Psychiatric aspects of school desegregation*. New York: Group for the Advancement of Psychiatry (Report No. 37).

—— (1959). *Some observations on controls in psychiatric research*. New York: Group for the Advancement of Psychiatry (Report No. 42).

Guilyarovsky, V. (1958). The contemporary situation in Soviet psychiatry. *In:* Masserman, J. H., and Moreno, J. L., *Progress in Psychotherapy*, Vol. 3, 270-274. New York: Grune and Stratton.

Haley, J. (1959). The family of the schizophrenic: a model system. *J. nerv. ment. Dis.*, 129, 357-374.

Hampson, J. L., Rosenthal, D., and Frank, J. D. (1954). A comparative study of the effects of mephenesin and placebo on the symptomatology of a mixed group of psychiatric outpatients. *Bull. Johns Hopkins Hosp.*, 95, 170-177.

Hankoff, L. D., Freedman, N., and Engelhardt, D. M. (1958). The prognostic value of placebo response. *Amer. J. Psychiat.*, 115, 549-550.

Hardy, K. R. (1957). Determinants of conformity and attitude change. *J. abnorm. soc. Psychol.*, 54, 289-294.

Harris, H. I. (1939). Efficient psychotherapy for a large outpatient clinic. *New England J. Med.*, 221, 1-5.

Hastings, D. W. (1958). Follow-up results in psychiatric illness. *Amer. J. Psychiat.*, 114, 1057-1066.

Health manpower chart book (1955). Washington, D. C.: U. S. Department of Health, Education, and Welfare (Public Health Service publication No. 511).

Hebb, D. O. (1955). Drives and the C.N.S. (conceptual nervous system). *Psycholog. Rev.*, 62, 243-254.

Heine, R. W. (1953). A comparison of patients' reports on psychotherapeutic experience with psychoanalytic, nondirective and Adlerian therapists. *Amer. J. Psychother.*, 7, 16-23.

Helson, H., Blake, R. R., Mouton, Jane S., and Olmstead, J. A. (1956). Attitudes as adjustments to stimulus, background, and residual factors. *J. abnorm. soc. Psychol.*, 52, 314-322.

Henry, J. (1954). The formal structure of a psychiatric hospital. *Psychiatry*, 17, 139-151.

Hildum, D. C., and Brown, R. W. (1956). Verbal reinforcement and interviewer bias. *J. abnorm. soc. Psychol.*, 53, 108-111.

Hilgard, E. R. (1948). *Theories of learning.* New York: Appleton-Century-Crofts.

Hinkle, L. E., Jr., and Wolff, H. G. (1956). Communist interrogation and indoctrination of 'enemies of the state.' *A.M.A. Arch. Neurol. and Psychiat.*, 76, 115-174.

Hoffer, E. (1958). *The true believer.* New York: New American Library of World Literature.

Hollingshead, A. B., and Redlich, F. C. (1958). *Social class and mental illness.* New York: John Wiley.

Holt, R. R., and Luborsky, L. (1958). *Personality patterns of psychiatrists,* Vol. 1. New York: Basic Books.

Housman, A. E. (1922). *Last poems.* London: Richards Press Ltd.

Hovland, C. I., Janis, I. L., and Kelley, H. H. (1953). *Communication and persuasion: psychological studies of opinion change,* New Haven: Yale Univer. Press.

Huxley, A. (1959). *Heaven and hell.* Baltimore: Penguin Books.

Huxley, Elspeth (1959). Science, psychiatry—or witchery? *New York Times Magazine,* May 31, 1959, 17-19.

Imber, S. D., Frank, J. D., Nash, E. H., Stone, A. R., and Gliedman, L. H. (1957). Improvement and amount of therapeutic contact: an alternative to the use of no-treatment controls in psychotherapy. *J. consult. Psychol.*, 21, 309-315.

Ingham, H. V., and Love, L. R. (1954). *The process of psychotherapy.* New York: McGraw-Hill.

Jackson, D. D. (1959). Family interaction, family homeostasis and some implications for conjoint family psychotherapy. *In:* Masserman, J. H., ed., *Individual and familial dynamics,* 122-141. New York: Grune and Stratton.

Jacobson, E. (1929). *Progressive relaxation.* Chicago: Univer. Chicago Press.

James, W. (1936). *The varieties of religious experience.* New York: Modern Library.

Janet, P. (1925). *Psychological healing,* Vol. 1. New York: Macmillan, Chapter 1, Miraculous healings, 21-53.

Janis, I. L. (1954). Personality correlates of susceptibility to persuasion. *J. Personality,* 22, 504-518.

———, and King, B. (1954). The influence of role-playing on opinion change. *J. abnorm. soc. Psychol.*, 49, 211-218.

Jones, M. (1953). *The therapeutic community.* New York: Basic Books.

Kardiner, A., Linton, R., DuBois, C., and West, J. (1945). *The psychological frontiers of society.* New York: Columbia Univer. Press.

Katz, M. M., Lorr, M., and Rubinstein, E. A. (1958). Remainer patient attributes and their relation to subsequent improvement in psychotherapy. *J. consult. Psychol.*, 22, 411-413.

Kaufman, M. R., and Beaton, L. E. (1947). A psychiatric treatment program in combat. *Bull. Menninger Clinic,* 11, 1-14.

Kelly, G. A. (1955). *The psychology of personal constructs.* Vol. 2, *Clinical diagnosis and psychotherapy.* New York: W. W. Norton.

Kelman, H. C. (1953). Attitude change as a function of response restriction. *Hum. Relat.*, 6, 185-214.

Kelman, H. C. (1958). Compliance, identification and internalization: three processes of attitude change. *J. Conflict Resolution,* 2, 51-60.

King, B., and Janis, I. (1956). Comparison of the effectiveness of improvised versus non-improvised role-playing in producing opinion changes. *Hum. Relat.,* 9, 177-186.

Kinkead, E. (1959). *In every war but one.* New York: W. W. Norton.

Kirtner, W. L., and Cartwright, D. S. (1958). Success and failure in client-centered therapy as a function of in-therapy behavior. *J. consult. Psychol.,* 22, 329-333.

Klapman, J. W. (1959). *Group psychotherapy: theory and practice.* New York: Grune and Stratton.

Kluckhohn, C., Murray, H. A., and Schneider, D. M. (1953). *Personality in nature, society and culture.* New York: Knopf.

Knupfer, Genevieve, Jackson, D. D., and Kireger, G. (1959). Personality differences between more and less competent psychotherapists as a function of criteria of competence. *J. nerv. ment. Dis.,* 129, 375-384.

Kraines, S. H. (1943). *The therapy of neuroses and psychoses.* Philadelphia: Lea and Febiger.

Krasner, L. (1958). Studies of the conditioning of verbal behavior. *Psychol. Bull.,* 55, 148-170.

——, and Ullmann, L. (unpublished). Variables in the verbal conditioning of schizophrenic subjects.

——, Weiss, R. L., and Ullmann, L. P. (1959). Responsivity to verbal conditioning as a function of two different measures of 'awareness.' *Amer. Psychologist,* 14, 388.

Kubie, L. (1936). *Practical aspects of psychoanalysis.* New York: W. W. Norton.

Lacey, J. I. (1959). Psychophysiological approaches to the evaluation of psychotherapeutic process and outcome. *In*: Rubinstein, E. A., and Parloff, M. B., eds., *Research in psychotherapy,* 160-208. Washington, D. C.: American Psychological Association.

Lasagna, L., Mosteller, F., von Felsinger, J. M., and Beecher, H. K. (1954). A study of the placebo response. *Amer. J. Med.,* 16, 770-779.

Leary, T. F. (1957). *Interpersonal diagnosis of personality.* New York: Ronald Press.

Lederer, W. (1959). Primitive psychotherapy. *Psychiatry,* 22, 255-263.

Leighton, A. H., and Leighton, Dorothy C. (1941). Elements of psychotherapy in Navaho religion. *Psychiatry,* 4, 515-523.

Lennard, H. L., and Bernstein, A. (1960). *The anatomy of psychotherapy.* New York: Columbia Univer. Press.

Lessa, W. A., and Vogt, E. Z. (1958). *Reader in comparative religion.* Evanston, Ill.: Row, Peterson.

Lesse, S. (1958). Psychodynamic relationships between the degree of anxiety and other clinical symptoms. *J. nerv. ment. Dis.,* 127, 125-130.

Lévi-Strauss, C. (1958). *Anthropologie structurale.* Paris: Librairie Plon.

Levitt, E. E. (1957). The results of psychotherapy with children. *J. consult. Psychol.,* 21, 189-196.

Lewin, K. (1947). Frontiers in group dynamics: concept, method and reality in social science, social equilibria and social change. *Hum. Relat.,* 1, 5-41.

Lidz, T. (1956). Some unsolved problems of psychoanalytic psychotherapy. Discussion. *In*: Fromm-Reichmann, Frieda, and Moreno, J. L., eds., *Progress in psychotherapy*, 102-107. New York: Grune and Stratton.

———, Cornelison, Alice R., Fleck, S., and Terry, Dorothy (1957). The intrafamilial environment of schizophrenic patients: 2. marital schism and marital skew. *Amer. J. Psychiat.*, 114, 241-248.

Lifton, R. J. (1956). 'Thought reform' of Western civilians in Chinese Communist prisons. *Psychiatry*, 19, 173-195.

——— (1957a). Thought reform of Chinese intellectuals: a psychiatric evaluation. *J. soc. Issues*, 13, 5-20.

——— (1957b). Chinese Communist thought reform. *In: Group processes: transactions of the third conference*, 219-312. New York: Josiah Macy, Jr. Foundation.

Lorr, M., Katz, M. M., and Rubinstein, E. A. (1958). The prediction of length of stay in psychotherapy. *J. consult. Psychol.*, 22, 321-327.

Low, A. (1950). *Mental health through will-training*. Boston: Christopher Pub. House.

Lunde, F., Mansfield, Elaine, and Smith, J. A. (1958). Mecholyl chloride as a prognostic test in psychiatric patients. *J. nerv. ment. Dis.*, 127, 430-436.

Macalpine, Ida (1950). The development of the transference. *Psychoanal. Quart.*, 19, 501-539.

Mandler, G., and Kaplan, W. K. (1956). Subjective evaluation and reinforcing effect of verbal stimulus. *Science*, 124, 582-583.

Masserman, J. H. (1957). Evolution vs. 'revolution' in psychotherapy: a biodynamic integration. *Behavioral Science*, 2, 89-100.

Mayer, Maj. W. E. (1956). The evaluation of the American soldier in combat. Paper presented to Conference of Air Science, Maxwell Air Force Base, November, 1956.

McCann, W. H. (1953). The round-table technique in group psychotherapy. *Group Psychother.*, 5, 233-239.

Mead, Beverley T., Ellsworth, R. B., and Grimmett, J. O. (1958). The treatment of drug-resistive chronic schizophrenics. *J. nerv. ment. Dis.*, 127, 351-358.

Menninger, K. (1958). *Theory of psychoanalytic technique*. New York: Basic Books.

Merton, R. K. (1957). *Social theory and social structure*. Glencoe, Ill.: Free Press.

Modell, W. (1955). *The relief of symptoms*. Philadelphia: Saunders.

Moreno, J. L. (1958). Fundamental rules and techniques of psychodrama. *In*: Masserman, J. H., and Moreno, J. L., eds., *Progress in psychotherapy*, Vol. 3. New York: Grune and Stratton.

Mouton, Jane S., Blake, R., and Olmstead, J. A. (1955-56). The relationship between frequency of yielding and the disclosure of personal identity. *J. Personality*, 24, 339-347.

Murray, E. J. (1956). A content-analysis method for studying psychotherapy. *Psychol. Monogr.*, 70, 420.

Nardini, J. E. (1952). Survival factors in American prisoners of war of the Japanese. *Amer. J. Psychiat.*, 109, 241-247.

Nash, E. H., Frank, J. D., Gliedman, L. H., Imber, S. D., and Stone, A. R. (1957). Some factors related to patients' remaining in group psychotherapy. *Int. J. Group Psychother.*, 7, 264-274.

Newcomb, T. M. (1947). Autistic hostility and social reality. *Hum. Relat.*, 1, 69-86.

Nunberg, H. (1951). Transference and reality. *Int. J. Psycho-anal.*, 32, 1-9.

Opler, M. E. (1936). Some points of comparison and contrast between the treatment of functional disorders by Apache shamans and modern psychiatric practice. *Amer. J. Psychiat.*, 92, 1371-1387.

Overholser, Winfred, and Enneis, J. M. (1959). Twenty years of psychodrama at Saint Elizabeths Hospital. *Group. Psychother.*, 12, 283-292.

Parloff, M. B. (1956). Some factors affecting the quality of therapeutic relationships. *J. abnorm. soc. Psychol.*, 52, 5-10.

———, Goldstein, N., and Iflund, B. (1960). Communication of values and therapeutic change. *A.M.A. Arch. of gen. Psychiat.*, 2, 300-304.

———, Kelman, H. C., and Frank, J. D. (1954). Comfort, effectiveness, and self-awareness as criteria of improvement in psychotherapy. *Amer. J. Psychiat.*, III, 343-351.

Pasamanick, B., and Lilienfeld, A. M. (1955). Association of maternal and fetal factors with development of mental deficiency: 1. abnormalities in the prenatal and paranatal periods. *J. Amer. Med. Assoc.*, 159, 155-160.

Pavlov, I. P. (1941). *Lectures on conditioned reflexes.* Vol. 2, *Conditioned reflexes and psychiatry*, Translated and edited by W. H. Gantt, New York: International Universities Press.

Polansky, N., and Kounin, J. (1956). Clients' reactions to initial interviews. *Hum. Relat.*, 9, 237-264.

Potter, H. W., Klein, Henriette R., and Goodenough, D. R. (1957). Problems related to the personal costs of psychiatric and psychoanalytic training. *Amer. J. Psychiat.*, 113, 1013-1019.

Powdermaker, Florence B., and Frank, J. D. (1953). *Group psychotherapy: studies in methodology of research and therapy.* Cambridge: Harvard Univer. Press.

Quay, H. (1959). The effect of verbal reinforcement on the recall of early memories. *J. abnorm. soc. Psychol.*, 59, 254-257.

Rado, S. (1956). *Psychoanalysis of behavior.* New York: Grune and Stratton.

Rasmussen, K. (1929). An Eskimo shaman purifies a sick person. *In: Report of the Fifth Thule Expedition, 1921-24, Intellectual Culture of the Igluik Eskimos.* Vol. 7, 133-141. Copenhagen: Gyldendalske Boghandel, Nordisk Forlag.

Reed, L. S. (1932). *The healing cults; a study of sectarian medical practice: its extent, causes and control.* Chicago: University of Chicago Press.

Rehder, H. (1955). Wunderheilungen, ein experiment. *Hippokrates*, 26, 577-580.

Reider, N. (1953). A type of transference to institutions. *J. Hillside Hosp.*, 2, 23-29.

Richter, C. P. (1957). On the phenomenon of sudden death in animals and man. *Psychosom. Med.*, 19, 191-198.

Rickett, A., and Rickett, Adele (1957). *Prisoners of liberation.* New York: Cameron Associates.

Rigney, H. W. (1956). *Four years in a Red hell.* Chicago: Henry Regnery.

Robinson, H. A., Redlich, F. C., and Myers, J. K. (1954). Social structure and psychiatric treatment. *Amer. J. Orthopsychiat.*, 24, 307-316.

Rogers, C. R. (1942). *Counseling and psychotherapy*. New York: Houghton Mifflin.

—— (1951). *Client-centered therapy: its current practice, implications and theory*. Boston: Houghton Mifflin.

—— (1953). A research program in client-centered therapy. *In*: Association for Research in Nervous and Mental Disease, *Psychiatric treatment* (Research publication 31), 106-113. Baltimore: Williams and Wilkins.

—— (1956). Part II of: Rogers, C. R., and Skinner, B. F. Some issues concerning the control of human behavior: a symposium. *Science*, 124, 1060-1066.

—— (1957). A therapist's view of the good life. *Humanist*, 17, 291-300.

——, and Dymond, Rosalind, eds. (1954). *Psychotherapy and personality change*. Chicago: Univer. Chicago Press.

Rogers, J. M. (1960). Operant conditioning in a quasi-therapy setting. *J. abnorm. soc. Psychol.*, 60, 247-252.

Rood, R. (1958). The nonpsychotic offender and the state hospital. *Amer. J. Psychiat.*, 115, 512-513.

Rosen, J. N. (1946). A method of resolving acute catatonic excitement. *Psychiat. Quart.*, 20, 183-198.

Rosenberg, Pearl P. (1952). An experimental analysis of psychodrama. Ph.D. thesis, Radcliffe College. Summarized in Mann, J. H., Experimental evaluations of role playing. *Psychol. Bull.*, 53 (1956), 227-234.

Rosenthal, D. (1955). Changes in some moral values following psychotherapy. *J. consult. Psychol.*, 19, 431-436.

——, and Frank, J. D. (1956). Psychotherapy and the placebo effect. *Psychol. Bull.*, 53, 294-302.

——, —— (1958). The fate of psychiatric clinic outpatients assigned to psychotherapy. *J. nerv. ment. Dis.*, 127, 330-343.

Rothman, T., and Sward, K. (1956). Studies in pharmacological psychotherapy: 1. treatment of refractory psychoneuroses and personality disorders with thiopental (pentothal) sodium and methamphetamine (desoxyn). *A.M.A. Arch. Neurol. and Psychiat.*, 75, 95-105.

——, —— (1957). Studies in pharmacologic psychotherapy: 3. effective psychotherapy during drug-induced states. *A.M.A. Arch. Neurol. and Psychiat.*, 78, 628-642.

Ruesch, J. (1953). Social factors in therapy. *In*: Association for Research in Nervous and Mental Disease, *Psychiatric treatment* (Research publication 31), 59-93. Baltimore: Williams and Wilkins.

Sachs, W. (1947). *Black anger*. New York: Grove Press.

Salter, A. (1958). *Conditioned reflex therapy*. New York: Farrar, Straus.

Salzman, L. (1957). Spiritual and faith healing. *J. Pastoral Care*, 11, 146-155.

Sarason, I. G. (1958). Interrelationships among individual difference variables, behavior in psychotherapy and verbal conditioning. *J. abnorm. soc. Psychol.*, 56, 339-344.

Sargant, W. (1957). *Battle for the mind: a physiology of conversion and brainwashing*. Garden City, New York: Doubleday.

Saslow, G., and Matarazzo, J. D. (1959). A technique for studying changes in interview behavior. *In*: Rubinstein, E. A., and Parloff, M. B., eds., *Research in psychotherapy*, 125-157. Washington, D. C.: American Psychological Assoc.

Sato, K. (1958). Psychotherapeutic implications of Zen. *Psychologia*, 1, 213-218.

Savage, C. (1957). The resolution and subsequent remobilization of resistance by LSD in psychotherapy. *J. nerv. ment. Dis.*, 125, 434-437.

Schachter, S. (1959). *The psychology of affiliation: experimental studies of the sources of gregariousness.* Stanford: Stanford Univer. Press.

Schein, E. H. (1956). The Chinese indoctrination program for prisoners of war. *Psychiatry*, 19, 149-172.

———— (1957). Reaction patterns to severe chronic stress in American army prisoners of war of the Chinese. *J. soc. Issues*, 13, 21-30.

Schmale, A. H. (1958). Relationship of separation and depression to disease. *Psychosom. Med.*, 20, 259-277.

Schramm, W., and Danielson, W. (1958). Anticipated audiences as determinants of recall. *J. abnorm. soc. Psychol.*, 56, 282-283.

Schultz, J. H., and Luthe, W. (1959). *Autogenic training: a psychophysiologic approach in psychotherapy.* New York: Grune and Stratton.

Sears, R. R. (1950). Ordinal position in the family as a psychological variable. *Amer. sociol. Rev.*, 15, 397-401.

Seeman, J. (1957). Quoted in Shlien, J. M., Time-limited psychotherapy: an experimental investigation of practical values and theoretical implications. *J. counsel. Psychol.*, 4, 318-322.

Segal, J. (1957). Correlates of collaboration and resistance behavior among U.S. Army POW's in Korea. *J. soc. Issues*, 13, 31-40.

Shapiro, A. K. (1959). The placebo effect in the history of medical treatment: implications for psychiatry. *Amer. J. Psychiat.*, 116, 298-304.

Sherif, M., and Harvey, O. J. (1952). A study in ego functioning: elimination of stable anchorages in individual and group situations. *Sociometry*, 15, 272-305.

Shlien, J. M. (1957). Time-limited psychotherapy: an experimental investigation of practical values and theoretical implications. *J. counsel. Psychol.*, 4, 318-322.

Shoben, E. J. (1953). A theoretical approach to psychotherapy as personality modification. *Harvard educ. Rev.*, 23, 128-142.

Singer, Margaret T., and Schein, E. H. (1958). Projective test responses of prisoners of war following repatriation. *Psychiatry*, 21, 375-385.

Skinner, B. F. (1956). Part I of: Rogers, C. R., and Skinner, B. F. Some issues concerning the control of human behavior: a symposium. *Science*, 124, 1057-1060.

Slavson, S. R. (1943). *An introduction to group therapy.* New York: Commonwealth Fund.

————, ed. (1956). *The fields of group psychotherapy.* New York: International Universities Press.

Spiro, M. E. (in press). Social system, personality, and functional analysis. In: Kaplan, B., ed., *Studying personality cross-culturally.* Evanston, Ill.: Row, Peterson.

Stanton, A. H., and Schwartz, M. (1954). *The mental hospital.* New York: Basic Books.

Steiner, L. (1945). *Where do people take their troubles?* New York: International Universities Press.

Stekel, W. (1943). *Interpretation of dreams.* New York: Liveright.

Stevenson, I. (1959). Direct instigation of behavioral changes in psychotherapy. *A.M.A. Arch. gen. Psychiat.*, 1, 99-107.

Strassman, H. D., Thaler, M. B., and Schein, E. H. (1956). A prisoner of war syndrome: apathy as a reaction to severe stress. *Amer. J. Psychiat.*, 112, 998-1003.

Strupp, H. H. (1958). The psychotherapists' contribution to the treatment process. *Behavioral Science*, 3, 34-67.

——— (1960). *Psychotherapists in action.* New York: Grune and Stratton.

Stunkard, A. (1951). Some interpersonal aspects of an Oriental religion. *Psychiatry*, 14, 419-431.

Taffel, C. (1955). Anxiety and the conditioning of verbal behavior. *J. abnorm. soc. Psychol.*, 51, 496-501.

Teuber, H.-L., and Powers, E. (1953). Evaluating therapy in a delinquency prevention program. *In*: Association for Research in Nervous and Mental Disease, *Psychiatric Treatment* (Research publication 31), 138-147. Baltimore: Williams and Wilkins.

Thompson, Clara (1950). *Psychoanalysis: evolution and development.* New York: Hermitage House.

Tyhurst, J. S. (1957). The role of transition states—including disasters—in mental illness. *In: Symposium on preventive and social psychiatry*, 149-172. Washington, D. C.: Walter Reed Army Institute of Research.

Volgyesi, F. A. (1954). 'School for patients,' hypnosis-therapy and psychoprophylaxis. *Brit. J. med. Hypnotism*, 5, 8-17.

Warner, W. L. (1941). *A black civilization: a social study of an Australian tribe.* New York: Harpers.

Weatherhead, L. D. (1951). *Psychology, religion, and healing.* New York: Abingdon-Cokesbury Press.

Webster, H. (1942). *Taboo: a sociological study.* Stanford: Stanford Univer. Press.

Wechsler, H. (1960). The self-help organization in the mental health field: Recovery, Inc., a case study. *J. nerv. ment. Dis.*, 130, 297-314.

Weininger, B. (1955). The interpersonal factor in the religious experience. *Psychoanal.*, 3, 27-44.

Wender, L., and Stein, A. (1953). The utilization of group psychotherapy in the social integration of patients: an extension of the method to self-governing patient groups. *Int. J. Group Psychother.*, 3, 210-218.

Wheelis, A. (1958). *The quest for identity.* New York: W. W. Norton.

Whitehead, A. N. (1925). *Science and the modern world.* New York: Macmillan.

Whitehorn, J. C. (1947). The concepts of 'meaning' and 'cause' in psychodynamics. *Amer. J. Psychiat.*, 104, 289-292.

——— (1959). Goals of psychotherapy. *In*: Rubinstein, E. A., and Parloff, M. B., eds., *Research in psychotherapy*, 1-9. Washington, D. C.: American Psychological Association.

——— (1960). Studies of the doctor as a crucial factor for the prognosis of schizophrenic patients. *Internat. J. Soc. Psychiat.*, 6, 71-77.

———, and Betz, Barbara J. (1954). A study of psychotherapeutic relationships between physicians and schizophrenic patients. *Amer. J. Psychiat.*, 111, 321-331.

———, ——— (1957). A comparison of psychotherapeutic relationships between physicians and schizophrenic patients when insulin is combined with psychotherapy and when psychotherapy is used alone. *Amer. J. Psychiat.*, **113**, 901-910.

Will, O. A. (1959). Human relatedness and the schizophrenic reaction. *Psychiatry*, **22**, 205-223.

Wilmer, H. (1958). *Social psychiatry in action: a therapeutic community.* Springfield, Ill.: Thomas.

Winkler, W. T. (1956). The present status of psychotherapy in Germany. *In:* Fromm-Reichmann, Frieda, and Moreno, J. L., eds., *Progress in psychotherapy*, 288-305. New York: Grune and Stratton.

Winokur, G. (1955). 'Brainwashing'—a social phenomenon of our time. *Hum. Organization*, **13**, 16-18.

Wolberg, L. R. (1945). *Hypnoanalysis.* New York: Grune and Stratton.

—— (1954). *The technique of psychotherapy.* New York: Grune and Stratton.

Wolf, A., and Schwartz, E. K. (1959). Psychoanalysis in groups: clinical and theoretic implications of the alternate meeting. *Acta psychotherapeutica psychosomatica et orthopaedagogica*, **7** (supp.), 404-437.

Wolf, S. (1950). Effects of suggestion and conditioning on the action of chemical agents in human subjects—the pharmacology of placebos. *J. clin. Invest.*, **29**, 100-109.

——, and Pinsky, R. H. (1954). Effects of placebo administration and occurrence of toxic reactions. *J. Amer. Med. Assoc.*, **155**, 339-341.

Wolff, W. (1954). Fact and value in psychotherapy. *Amer. J. Psychother.*, **8**, 466-486.

Wolpe, J. (1958). *Psychotherapy by reciprocal inhibition.* Stanford: Stanford Univer. Press.

Wyatt, F. (1956). Climate of opinion and methods of readjustment. *Amer. Psychologist*, **11**, 537-542.

Zilboorg, G. (1941). *A history of medical psychology.* New York: W. W. Norton.

Zubin, J. (1959). Role of prognostic indicators in the evaluation of therapy. *In:* Cole, J. O., and Gerard, R. W., eds., *Psychopharmacology: problems in evaluation*, 343-355. Washington, D. C.: National Academy of Sciences—National Research Council (Publication 583).

Index

Academy of Religion and Mental Health, 13
Adaptation: failure of, 19-20
Adler, Alfred, 248n*23*
Aesthetic appeal: of healing rituals, 53; at Lourdes, 55-56
Alcoholics: regarded as mentally ill in America, 6; as recipients of psychotherapy, 9-10
Alcoholics Anonymous: discussion of, 172, 173
Altruism: in healing rituals, 51, 56, 63; at Lourdes, 56, 63; in therapy groups, 183
Ambiguity: of assumptive world, 28-29; and thought reform, 89; of evocative therapy, 158, 168
American society: and psychotherapy, 116-18; 218-19
Analytic institutes, 119, 121-27. *See also* Psychoanalysis
Analytic schools, 154-55. *See also* Psychoanalysis
Anxiety: effect on assumptive world,

32-33; as cause of death, 41, 61; combatted by religious rituals, 52; combatted by placebos, 69-70; relief of by psychotherapy, 72; related to conditioning, 106, 245n*14*; in psychotherapist, 131; related to dependency, 137, 137-38, 139; influenced by ambiguity, 159; influence on pathological symptoms, 238n6
Apologia and self-image, 161
Assumptive systems: characteristics of 20-21; and emotional states, 21-22, 26; and behavior, 22-23; validation of, 23-24, 30-31, 156; diversity in America, 117-18, 140, 218-19; of mental hospitals, 205; and improvement, 223, 224. *See also* Assumptive world
Assumptive world: and childhood experiences, 24-26; cultural influences on, 27; related to convalescence, 27-30; changes in, 31-33, 146, 178-80; and primitive healing, 43-44, 49-50;

and Lourdes, 54; related to religious conversion, 76, 78; in thought reform, 82, 88; relation to psychotherapy, 82, 145; of children, 171; defines healer's role, 217; term initiated by Cantril, 237n4; need to validate, 241-42n16; in psychiatrist and patient, 246-47n5. *See also* Assumptive systems

Attitude change: and relief of suffering, 64; permanence of, 76, 78, 93, 146; and emotional excitation, 96, 143; experiments on, 98-113; participation and, 98, 112; mechanisms of, 244n3, 244n4. *See also* Religious revivalism; Thought reform

Awareness: and persuasion, 104, 112-13; and conditioning, 104-05, 106-09

Behavioral aspects: of psychotherapy, 145, 151, 167; of group therapies, 185-87, 190, 206; of mental hospital, 195-96, 205; of therapeutic community, 202-03

Brain-washing. *See* Thought reform

Breuer, Joseph: use of hypnosis, 4

Celsus, 143

Child-rearing, 215

Childhood experiences: and deviant behavior, 9-10; in formation of assumptive world, 24-26

Children: formation of neurosis in, 25-26; attitude change in, 99-100; ordinal position, 138-39, 140; identification of with parents, 166; assumptive world of, 171

Christian Science, 13, 53

Chronic disease: emotional stress in, 9, 178-80

Class. *See* Social class

Clergymen: as psychotherapists, 12-13

Client-centered therapy, 145. *See also* Evocative therapies

Cognitive aspects: of all psychotherapy, 145, 167; of directive psychotherapy, 151, 162, 168; of evocative psychotherapy, 161-62, 168-69; and interpretation, 165-66; of group therapies, 185, 190, 206; of mental hospital, 195. *See also* Conceptual schemes

Cohesiveness: breakdown of, 85, 87; in therapy groups, 182-83, 188, 190

College students: role-playing by, 98-99, evaluation of psychotherapy by, 131-32; anxiety in, 138

Communication: in thought reform, 87; in evocative psychotherapy, 153-54; in group therapy, 187, 190; in therapeutic community, 203-04, 206; research in, 228. *See also* Operant conditioning

Compliance: in thought reform, 93; in operant conditioning, 110; as defense mechanism, 245n15. *See also* Conformity

Comprehensiveness of conceptual schemes: of healing rituals, 49-50, 117; of Lourdes, 54; of thought reform, 81, 87, 94-95; of religious revivalism, 81, 94-95; of psychoanalysis, 121, 141; discussed, 218

Conceptual schemes: in religious healing, 50-51, 62-63; of healing sects, 60; of psychoanalysis, 122-25, 127-28; of directive psychotherapy, 150, 168; of evocative psychotherapies, 156-57, 165, 168, 233; of mental hospital, 195, 205; diversity of, 233. *See also* Comprehensiveness of conceptual schemes; Irrefutability of conceptual schemes; Cognitive aspects

Concern: for patient in religious healing, 51, 56, 63; for penitent in revivalism, 77, 95; for prisoner in thought reform, 83, 95; for patient in psychotherapy, 115, 130, 217, 249n29

Conditioned reflex theory, 5

Confession: in healing rituals, 51-52, 63, 239n21; in thought reform, 88-91, 92; in group therapy, 180; as affirming assumptive world, 241-42n16

Conflict: in assumptive world, 21, 27; in therapy groups, 180-81, 187

Conflicts, inner: and illness, 21, 27-29, 35, 38, 216. *See also* Guilt

Conformity: and incentive, 100-01

Confusion: and influencibility, 159, 244n33. *See also* Ambiguity

Convalescence delayed, 27-30

Conversion. *See* Religious conversion

Corrective emotional experience, 158, 168

Criminals, 6, 10